The Who's Who of Heaven

Saints for All Seasons

DATE DUE

The Who's Who of Heaven

Saints for All Seasons

by

John P. Kleinz

Christian Classics
Westminster, Maryland
1987

Copyright © 1987 by John P. Kleinz

ISBN 87061-136-4

Library of Congress Catalogue Card Number: 87-071420

Typography by Publications Technologies
Printed in the United States of America

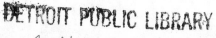

Contents

Preface

The selection of saints in this book — some with a capital "S," some with a small "s" — is a revision of some columns I have written since 1978 for *The Catholic Times,* the diocesan newspaper of the diocese of Columbus in Ohio.

The weekly columns cover a multitude of different topics, including the stories of "Holy Men and Women," which is the term used for two Mass prefaces in the revised Sacramentary.

In order to impose some kind of unity on the book, I have treated the saints in various categories. The introduction answers the question, "What is a saint?" and tells the reason why we should venerate them. It gives a brief history of devotion to the saints, a tradition of the Catholic Church since the remembrances of the martyrs of the Early Church. The first and longest chapter is about Mary, Mother of God and Mother of the Faithful. It treats the myriad ways in which Catholics honor Mary, of her role in the Church as seen by the Second Vatican Council, some of the favorite Marian prayers, and a history of some popular Marian shrines.

The choice of saintly role models for priests follows the list of the saints suggested to priests by Pope John Paul II on various occasions. In his preface to the new Calendar of the Saints, Pope Paul VI suggested the missionary martyrs on various continents; the pope wanted to stress the universality of the Church. There is a chapter on the missionaries from Europe who brought the Good News to North and South America. The nine foundresses of the orders of religious women, except for three American women, enriched the Church of the United States by sending their Sisters from Europe to an immigrant Church in this country. The Jesuits have enriched the whole Church and I have written about eight Jesuits who illustrate a rich variety of contributions; they are missionaries, scientists, poets, martyrs and theologians. I have gone back to the saints of the Early and Medieval Church to tell the stories of eight saints, including the saint who gave his name to America and the two preeminent theologians of the Church — Augustine and Aquinas.

In the Introduction to this book I hope to show that devotion to the saints, when pruned of excesses of the past, has been revived and deepened in the years after the Second Vatican Council of the Sixties. Several paragraphs in its documents describe the benefits of that devotion and root it in our relation to Christ and his Church. I quote Chapter Seven of the Dogmatic Constitution on the Church at length. Entitled "The Pilgrim Church" because it undergirds this book, it bases devotion to the saints on the doctrines of the Mystical Body of Christ and the Communion of Saints:

When the Lord will come in glory, and all his angels with him (cf. Mt. 25:31), death will be no more and all things will be subject to him (cf. I Cor. 15:26-27). But at the present time some of his disciples are pilgrims on earth. Others have died and are being purified, while still others are in glory, contemplating "in full light, God himself triune and one, exactly as he is." All of us, however, in varying degrees and in different ways share in the same charity toward God and our neighbors, and we all sing the one hymn of glory to our God. All, indeed, who are of Christ and who have his Spirit form one Church and in Christ cleave together (Eph. 4:16). So it is that the union of the wayfarers with the brothers and sisters who sleep in the peace of Christ is in no way interrupted, but on the contrary, according to the constant faith of the Church, this union is reinforced by an exchange of spiritual goods. Being more closely united to Christ, those who dwell in heaven fix the whole Church more firmly in holiness, add to the nobility of the worship that the Church offers to God here on earth, and in many ways help in a broader building up of the Church (cf. I Cor. 12:12-27) (on the Mystical Body of Christ). Once received into their heavenly home and being present to the Lord (cf. II Cor. 58), through him and with him and in him they do not cease to intercede with the Father for us, as they proffer the merits which they acquired on earth through the one mediator between God and us, Christ Jesus (cf. I Tim. 2:5) serving God in all things and completing in their flesh what is lacking in Christ's afflictions for the sake of his Body, that is, the Church (cf. Col. 1:24). So by their concern for us as their brothers and sisters is our weakness greatly helped (49).[1]

Acknowledgments

For their help and encouragement I thank the staff of the Augustine T. Wehrle Memorial Library of the Pontifical College Josephinum in Columbus, Ohio — Joan Oelgoetz, Carolyn Saffen, Eleanor Byerly, the reference librarian, Peter Veracka, the director of the library, and Monsignor Anthony A. Kleinschmidt, the former director.

The Who's Who
of Heaven

Introduction

On May 20, 1521, the French stormed the fortress at Pamplona in Spain. A stray cannon shot wounded the leg of a soldier named Iñigo of the noble Basque family of Loyola. Other soldiers in the service of the Viceroy of Navarre, under whom Iñigo served, brought him back to his ancestral castle of Loyola. (We know him well as Ignatius of Loyola.) At first the wound in his leg refused to heal and the physician told him to get ready for death. On June 29 he unexpectedly felt better. For days he lay in bed and suffered more from boredom than pain. The former handsome courtier asked for his favorite books of chivalry and romance, but there were none in the castle. They brought him the only books in his home at Loyola, a *Life of Christ* and a collection of "Lives of the Saints." One biographer tells what happened: he "set about reading them, and as it happened, this was the most important reading he would ever do."[1]

St. Ignatius of Loyola, who was born in 1491 in that family castle, began a new era in the history of the Catholic Church when he read those lives of the saints and asked himself why he should not imitate them and live a life like theirs instead of a life in quest of military glory. He asked himself, "Why can I not walk the same glorious paths as did the saints?" Ignatius went on to found "the Company of Jesus," the Jesuits, and died as their General in 1556.

This is a book about saints. Some are canonized, some are beatified, some are "venerable" on their way to beatification, and some are people who will never be canonized but led saintly lives and could or should be canonized.

St. Ignatius of Loyola is only one of the thousands of canonized saints — and innumerable millions of holy people — of whom it may be said, in the words of one of the two new

Prefaces of "Holy Men and Women" in the new Sacramentary suggested by the Second Vatican Council:

> You renew the Church in every age
> by raising up men and women
> outstanding in holiness,
> living witnesses of your
> unchanging love.
> They inspire us by their heroic
> lives, and help us by their constant prayers to be the
> living signs of your saving power.

One purpose of venerating the saints, the prayer says, is the inspiration they give us by their heroic lives. One could make that more specific by citing the opening prayer of the feast of St. Alphonsus Liguori on August 1:

> Father,
> you constantly build up your Church
> by the lives of your saints.

What Is a Saint?

The *American Heritage Dictionary of the English Language* defines a saint as "a person officially recognized by the Roman Catholic Church and certain other Christian churches as being entitled to public veneration and as being capable of interceding for men on earth; one who has been canonized." The word derives from the Latin word *sanctus*, which means "sacred" and comes ultimately from the Latin *sancire*, to sanctify, consecrate. This would, I think, be its first meaning in the minds of a Catholic — the Saints with a capital "S."

What is a saint? It is a question often asked. I have read and heard dozens of answers to it.

It helps to begin with a distinction. We could start with the way St. Paul used the word. Monsignor Romano Guardini, a powerful German preacher and theologian (1865-1968), writes about Paul as the great witness to the Christian life in its beginnings in his introduction to an inspiring little book, *The Saints in Daily Life:* "St. Paul will always remain a great watershed of truth about any religious question that concerns us. But if we inquire into his writings for an explanation of the meaning of sanctity, his ideas seem at first quite strange."[2] Guardini then suggests that we read Paul's greeting at the opening of Second Corinthians: "Paul, an Apostle of Jesus Christ by the will of God ... to the Church of God that is at Corinth, with all the saints that are in the whole of Achaia" (II Cor. 1-2.) At the end of the letter, Paul wrote, "All the saints send you greetings" (II Cor. 12.) The reference is to the people of the country from which the Apostle is writing, Macedonia.

When he used the word "saint," St. Paul meant all the Christians who had received the Good News, who confessed the Christian faith, and were reborn in baptism to a new life. It was a dangerous way to live in those times, in a pagan world around them that worshipped idols of Greece and Rome. The "new life" to which, Paul often reminds them, they had been called meant misunderstanding, persecution, and even martyrdom.

In the liturgical calendar of the Church, the name "saint" is given to those who are canonized, either by official declaration of the popes over the past thousand years, or by acclamation of the people of God in the first millenium. These are the men and women acclaimed by the liturgy in another preface for "Holy Men and Holy Women":

> Father, you are glorified in your saints,
> for their glory is the crowning of all your gifts.
> In their lives on earth you give us an example.
> In our communion with them
> you give us their friendship.
> In their prayer for the Church
> you give us strength and protection.

One way to discover the meaning of "saint" is to leaf through the Eucharistic Prayers of the revised Sacramentary and read the words the Church uses in the "memento for the dead." In the first Prayer — the ancient Roman Canon — the priest prays, "Remember, Lord, those who have gone before us marked with the sign of faith ... May all who sleep in Chirst find light, happiness, and peace." The second Prayer asks God "to remember our brothers and sisters who have gone to their rest in the hope of rising again." The fourth Prayer wants the Lord to "remember those who have died in the peace of Christ and all the dead whose faith is known to you alone."

Monsignor Guardini says that Jesus enjoined upon all his followers without exception what he called the "first and greatest commandment": "You shall love the Lord, your God, with all your heart and with all your soul and with all your strength ..." The second is like it: "You shall love your neighbor as yourself." Guardini builds his definition of a saint on that: "Viewed in this perspective, a saint is simply a man or woman to whom God has given the strength to take this primal commandment with utter seriousness, to understand it profoundly, and to bend every effort to carry it out."[3] Another way to say it is, to use a consecrated phrase, that the saints lived lives of heroic virtue.

The Veneration of Saints

At the end of one of his "University Sermons," Monsignor Ronald Knox of England spoke of the reaction of people who listened to Jesus in his lifetime on earth — to his simple, direct methods of preaching with the feeling that "never man spoke like this man." Knox comments, "What wonder, then, if the saints in every age have caught and handed on in their measure, the kindling enthusiasm of his appeal? The saints, after all, are the best advertisement the Christian religion ever had. And we know that the saints are the characteristic products of Christendom, its natural fruit, when we have looked back at the life of Jesus of Nazareth, to find all their inspiration centered, and all their light focused, in his."[4]

In the Seventh Chapter of the *Dogmatic Constitution on the Church,* it is stated that "the church has always believed that the apostles, and Christ's martyrs who had given the supreme witness of faith and charity by the shedding of their blood, are quite closely joined with us in Christ. She has always venerated them with special devotion, together with the Blessed Virgin Mary and the holy angels. The church too has devoutly implored the aid of their intercession. To these were soon added those who had imitated Christ's virginity and poverty more exactly, and finally others whom the outstanding practice of the Christian virtues and the divine charisms recommended to the pious devotion and imitation of the faithful" (50.)

This brief history of the development of the veneration of the saints in a key document of Vatican Council II could be traced back to certain promises by Jesus to his apostles which would seem to indicate a gift of special privileges for certain persons in the next world: "I give you my solemn word, in the new age when the Son of Man takes his seat upon a throne befitting his glory, you who have followed me shall likewise take your places on twelve thrones to judge the twelve tribes of Israel" (Matt. 19:28).

There is a Jewish anticipation of the idea of the power of prayer for the dead in Second Maccabees, where Judas Maccabeus sees Onias and Jeremiah in a dream "with outstretched hands invoking blessings on the whole body of the Jews" (II Macc. 15:12). In the New Testament there is support for the idea that the dead may intercede for us in Jesus' parable of Dives and Lazarus (Luke 16:19-31). In the Letter to the Hebrews there is a description of the saints of the Hebrew Scriptures as a "cloud of witnesses" whom Christians should imitate.

The principal theological basis for devotion to the saints is in the eloquent passages in Paul's letters where he develops his doctrine of the church as the Mystical Body of Christ in which all the members have their particular office as "fellow citizens with the saints, and of the household of God." In an excellent and concise article on "Saints, devotion to" in the *Oxford Dictionary of the Christian Church,* it is stated that it is the implications of the doctrine of the Mystical Body rather than specific passages in the Bible which theologians commonly hold to be the biblical foundation of devotion to the saints."[5] This article, likewise, is the source for the following sketch of the development of the veneration of saints.

In the first three centuries of the early church people honored the martyrs who died for the faith. An account of the martyrdom of St. Polycarp (circa 156 A.D.) says that his followers express their intention of "celebrating the birthday of his martyrdom" in days to come. Besides those martyrs who died for the faith, others who survived their sufferings were termed "confessors" and given special honor. St. Cyprian of Carthage in the third century asserted their power of intercession after death.

Origen, an early writer, gave to the cult of the martyrs a theological foundation in the doctrine of the Communion of Saints and taught that the prayer of the saints is efficacious insofar as the faithful follow in their footsteps. After the fourth century devotion to the saints spread rapidly; the great Fathers of the church defended it vigorously. St. John Chrysostom exhorted the people to have confidence in the intercession of the martyrs. Soon the honors were paid not only to the martyrs, but extended to include "confessors" and "virgins"; it was argued that a life of renunciation and holiness might equal the devotion of those who actually died for Christ.

Some abuses crept in, and the charge of idolatry made by some was answered by a distinction between the worship of God and the cult of honor and imitation due to the saints. In the fifth century Pope St. Leo the Great wrote that the saints obtain the mercy of God for us by their prayer. Pope St. Gregory the Great (d. 610) did much to further the cult of the saints; he urged the faithful to place themselves under the protection of the saints. The names of martyrs and saints were included in the liturgical celebrations at an early stage. Liturgy followed the teaching of the Fathers and popular devotion.

"Lives of the Saints" became popular. One scholar comments that, just as many people today find their entertainment in reading novels, so the people of the Middle Ages took great pleasure in reading biographies of saints and hearing edifying and enthusiastic sermons about them. Much of this material was based on meager thin historical evidence embellished with legends. One of the most popular books of the Middle Ages was the *Golden Legend* by a Dominican bishop named Jacobus de Voragine. Modern scholars treat this collection of lives and legends of the saints with a great deal of skepticism about many of its details.

Several church councils wrote laws to curb the excesses of devotions which, by the end of the Middle Ages, included a great deal of superstition. Some of the Protestant Reformers denounced devotion to the saints and claimed it was not explicitly recommended in the Bible. In the "Thirty-Nine Articles" of the Church of England, written in the second half of the sixteenth century, "the Romish doctrine" on the matter was called "a fond thing vainly invented." Today, however, in the Church of England the practice of devotion to saints has been widely revived. The Council of Trent in the middle of the sixteenth century showed a healthy moderation and later theologians developed the more prudent approach of great thirteenth-century theologians like St. Thomas Aquinas.

Aquinas treats devotion to the saints as part of the Holy Spirit's Gift of Piety, which is reverence paid to parents and others. Thomas explains: "Through piety the virtue a person offers service and respect not only to his actual parents but also to all blood relatives by reason of their kinship with parents. Similarly, the Gift of Piety offers honor and service not only to God but also to all men and women on the basis of their relationship to God. Thus it is its concern to honor the saints..."[6]   In another place under "devotion" he writes, "Devotion to holy people, whether living or dead, does not terminate in the people themselves. Rather, it passes on to God, and thus while honoring his servants we are actually honoring God."

The Eve of All Hallows

The great majority of people in the United States, I think it is safe to say, will know what Halloween is and will know, too, some of the customs clustered around it. Comparatively few, I think, will know that its origin is from a lovely Middle English word, a shortened version of All Hallow E'en — The Eve of All Saints' Day. It is fun for children to go out on Beggars Night and ask for trick or treat and to perpetrate the pranks of Halloween, but it would be more profitable to contemplate the celebrated sentence Leon Bloy wrote as the last line of his powerful novel, *The Woman Who Was Poor*: "The only tragedy in life is not to have become a saint."

The Solemnity of All Saints honors ("hallows") the holy men and women who have not made tragedies of their lives and whose glory, as the Preface of the Solemnity puts it, fills us with joy and "whose communion with us in your Church gives us inspiration and strength as we hasten on our pilgrimage of faith, eager to meet them." As a previous preface of a Mass says, we seek from the saints "example in their way of life, fellowship in their communion, and aid by their intercession."

In the Creed of the Council of Nicaea in which Catholics profess their faith on Sunday, we proclaim our belief that "we look for the resurrection of the dead and the life of the world to come." In the Apostles' Creed we also profess our faith in the "Communion of Saints," a consoling facet of that faith and the theological basis of the Catholic conviction that we can pray to God through the intercession of the saints.

By that hallowed term, the "Communion of Saints," we mean the unity under Christ and in him, of the faithful on earth, a pilgrim people, the Church Militant (an outdated term), the souls in Purgatory (the Church Suffering), and the saints in heaven (the Church Triumphant.) All three can pray for each other. In *A Catholic Dictionary*, Donald Attwater spells it out: "The living pray to God on behalf of the suffering, and to God in honor of the blessed saints; the blessed intercede with God for the suffering and the living; the holy souls pray to God and the blessed for others; by virtue of his merits Christ intercedes continually for the living and the dead."[7]

Saints are persons who know God more intimately, love God more intensely, serve God more heroically. For the love of God, they serve their fellow humans more selflessly. In the deep democracy of God's creation, where every person is equal to every other person in human dignity, the crown of sanctity, that greatest award of all, can come to any man or woman.

The saints are poor people, beggars, even thieves. Some, no doubt, were butchers and bakers and candlestick makers. Among the poor are the apostles, Bernadette Soubirous, Francis of Assisi, Peter Claver, Elizabeth of the Visitation, Vincent de Paul, the patron of those who work for the poor, and John Bosco, the helper of homeless boys. And then there is Mary, the Mother of God, poorest of the poor, yet greatest of mortals, who sang in the *Magnificat* of God "who has looked upon his servant in her lowliness... He has deposed the mighty from their thrones and raised the lowly to high places." Sociologists sometimes make wealth and heredity the standard for a person's social class. It is almost true to say that in heaven the standard is reversed. It is not necessary to be poor, but it helps. In Matthew's summation of Jesus' blueprint for salvation, which we call the Eight Beatitudes, there is what one German philosopher called "a transvaluation of values." Jesus says, "How blest are the poor in spirit; the reign of God is theirs. Blest are the lowly; they shall inherit the land."

There are rich saints — kings like Louis of France, Edward of England, Queen Margaret of Scotland. Thomas Aquinas was a nobleman. Francis de Sales was born into a wealthy family. And so it goes through all degrees of social class and caste. There were beggar saints; the Franciscan and Dominican saints were beggars by profession. There were even thieves: who has not heard of St. Dismas, the Good Thief, who stole heaven on the cross?

To judge that someone is a saint is a complex business, I

suppose, but the degree of love of God and neighbor in a person's life comes to mind as the first criterion. St. Augustine put it simply, "We go to God not with talking, but with loving."

Another sign of sanctity is the joy with which some saints fill their lives and the lives of others. Albino Luciani, who ruled the Church as Pope John Paul I for only a month, was a newspaper columnist who captured the hearts of millions with his warm smile and the joy he radiated in everything he did. His columns were imaginary letters to all kinds of people, real and fictional. They were collected after his death in a book called *Illustrissimi* because the letters were addressed to illustrious people; they were simple, witty, and profound. In writing to his favorite saints, he says that the essence of holiness is the joy which the saints evoke in the people around them. "A sad saint," he cites from Teresa of Avila, "is a bad saint." He writes to St. Therese of Lisieux, "Joy can become exquisite charity, if communicated to others, as you used to do at Mount Carmel during recreation." Frank Sheed, in his book *Saints Are Not Sad,* quotes St. Francis de Sales on its first page: "A sad saint would be a sorry saint." Gilbert Keith Chesterton once wrote, "Joy is the gigantic secret of the Christian."

The man whom the media named *The Smiling Pope* told the story of an Irishman who came to the gates of Paradise for judgment. As he waited in line he heard Christ welcome those who gave him food and drink and visited him in prison. The Irishman trembled; he hadn't done such things. But Christ said to him: "There's not much in your ledger, but you also did something; I was sad, dejected, humiliated; you came, you told me jokes, made me laugh, and restored my courage. Paradise!"[8]

The story of the Irishman is something of a joke, too, the pope admits, but it is not a bad subject for meditation on the Eve of All Hallows.

The Day of All Souls

On November 1 the Church in its liturgy celebrates the Church Triumphant — All Saints' Day. The next day it celebrates the Church Suffering — All Souls' Day, on which we pray for all who have gone before us and stand in judgment before God. We do not judge them; we simply love them, and God also loves them.

There is a rather touching description of All Souls' Day in the entry for November 2 in an official book of the Church called the *Roman Martyrology,* which lists all the saints for each day. The moving entry for All Souls is:

The solemn celebration of all the faithful departed in which the Church, their common Mother, after being careful to celebrate with due praise her children already rejoicing in heaven on All Saints' Day, strives to help all those who still long in Purgatory by supplication to Christ, her Lord and Bridegroom, that they may quickly attain to the fellowship of the heavenly citizens.[9]

The term *Purgatory* has been used since the Middle Ages to describe the defined doctrine of the Catholic Church, according to Karl Rahner's *Theological Dictionary,* "that purifying growth in all dimensions of man which according to the Church's teaching exists, to which a person who dies in justifying grace is subject insofar as the debt of 'punishment' he has incurred has not necessarily been cancelled when his sins were forgiven in justification, and this debt can be paid by 'expiatory suffering.' "[10]

In 1969, Pope Paul VI promulgated a complete revision of the Rite of Christian Burial. Its first paragraph noted that it has been the Church's custom in the funeral rites not only to commend the dead to God but also to support the Christian hope of the people and give witness to its faith in the future resurrection of the baptized with Christ. The introduction to the document stresses the consoling hope infused into the new rite:

"In the funeral rites the Church celebrates the paschal mystery of Christ. Those who in baptism have become one with the dead and risen Christ will pass with him from death to life to be purified in soul and welcomed into the fellowship of the saints in heaven. They look forward to his second coming and the bodily resurrection of the dead. The Church therefore celebrates the eucharistic sacrifice of Christ's passover for the dead, and offers prayers and petitions for them...."[11]

Canon 1126 of the revised Code of Canon Law (1983) gives other reasons for the new Catholic rites: "Through ecclesiastical funeral rites the Church asks spiritual assistance for the departed, honors their bodies, and at the same time brings the solace of hope to the living."[12]

The special thrust of the liturgy of All Souls' Day takes all this for granted, and, more specifically, emphasizes the Church's prayers for the dead. It presupposes that those who die worthily may not have sufficiently repented of certain sins and that the prayers of the living can help them.

The practice of praying for the dead is commended in the Scriptures. Second Maccabees tells us that it is holy and wholesome to pray for the dead (II Macc. 12:46). Protestants, in general, do not pray for the dead. One can prove that the first Christians prayed for their dead by studying the walls of the catacombs where the underground Church worshiped in the first centuries. Praying for the dead is recommended by the Fathers of the Church and has been the constant custom of Catholics since then. In the great decree of the Second Vatican Council, the *Dogmatic Constitution on the Church* describes the "pilgrim Church and its union with the heavenly Church" and asserts that "this Synod accepts with great devotion the venerable faith of our ancestors regarding this vital fellowship with our brothers and sisters who are in heavenly glory or who, having died, are still being purified."[13]

The conviction that "it is a holy and wholesome thought to pray for the dead" has been part of the Church's faith from the beginning, but she was slow in introducing a special liturgical day for the purpose. It was not until the Middle Ages that All Souls' Day was extended to the whole Church. The reason may have been the stubborn persistence of pre-Christian superstitious practices in the rites of burial.

With its focus on Christ, the Resurrection and the Life, the revised burial liturgy removes much of the fear of what *The Constitution* calls the "abuses, excesses, or defects" and the morbid overemphasis on grief and mourning which may have been part of the past. The central symbols now are the joyful white, not the mournful black of the pall draped over the coffin and the vestments of the priests. The bright flame of the paschal candle at the head of the funeral procession leads to the hope and optimism of the opening prayer of one of the Masses on All Souls' Day: "Merciful Father, hear our prayers and console us. As we renew our faith in your son, whom you have raised from the dead, strengthen our hope that all our departed brothers and sisters will share in the resurrection."

Saint Francis de Sales once said: "The name of death is terrible, as it is usually proposed to us, for someone says, 'Your dear father is dead.' ...This is not well-spoken among Christians. We should say, 'Your father is gone to his country and to yours; and because necessity required it, he passed by way of death, in which he lingered not.' "

The Saints as Patrons

In the revised *Code of Canon Law* promulgated by Pope John Paul II on January 25, 1983, Canon 1186 speaks of the veneration of saints:

> *To foster the sanctification of the people of God the Church recommends to the particular and filial veneration of the Christian faithful the Blessed Mary ever Virgin, the Mother of God, whom Christ established as the Mother of the human race; it also promotes true and authentic devotion to the other saints by whose example the Christian faithful are edified and through whose intercession they are sustained.*

In the Catholic tradition it was customary to assign a patron saint as a name to a person during the rite of baptism and again at confirmation. This practice still prevails and certainly is highly recommended by the Church and by many religious educators.

Besides patron saints as names for individuals, the saints are also adopted and appointed by the popes as patrons of four groups: parishes and other Church institutions; for dioceses; countries; and a wide variety of trades and professions. Pope Pius XII particularly fostered the practice. In his pontificate (1938 to 1958) 151 Apostolic Briefs named heavenly patrons for nations, dioceses, cities, professions, sports, and many states of life. The Blessed Virgin Mary was given as patroness to eighty-three groups, including skiers, cyclists, motorcyclists, and the Association of Speleologists, who study caves. Another sixty-eight Briefs proclaimed saints for various activities.[14]

Patron saints, especially designated by the Church as intercessors for occupations, are very numerous; custom has elevated some to that honor, others have been adopted by a popular response. The Church encourages such paraliturgical devotions to bring greater spiritual depth to the association of veneration of saints with one's occupation.

I once watched on television as the nation, with solemn ceremony, honored an unknown soldier who died in Vietnam as a symbol of all the men and women who died in that war. With prayer and pomp they laid him to rest alongside the unknown soldiers of the wars the United States fought earlier in the century.

Speaking of the unknown soldiers at Arlington National Cemetery, Monsignor Leonard J. Fick wrote a tribute for All Saints' Day, entitled "The Who's Who of Heaven," in *The Josephinum Review*:

> *The U.S.A. was paying its most splendid tribute, not to a man or to an individual, but to an ideal, to a symbol. For that unknown hero represented a virtue, the virtue of loyalty in the face of the greatest obstacles... So, too, does the Church officially honor her unknown and unsung heroes — men and women whose moral courage achieved for them life's only true victory, eternal salvation.*[15]

For a more light-hearted treatment of the subject of patron saints, I turn to an article by Marine Lieutenant Gene F. Diamond which I found, undated, in my files. Lieutenant Diamond, a Navy doctor serving with the Leathernecks at Camp Lejeune, long ago wrote, with tongue in cheek, an article called "A Marine Tells it to the Marines — about Saints, that is." In the Preface to his catechism he wrote:

> *There were no canonized saints who were Marines. There were many saints, who had to put up with many things the Marines have to put up with. They used these unpleasant things to build up merit for their heavenly bank account. Let's take a look at some of the saints who parlayed a bad situation into a high place in heaven.*

Lieutenant Diamond gave fellow Marines some examples:

> *Does your platoon leader think you are stupid? St. Thomas Aquinas, one of the great philosophical minds, was known to some of his associates as the Dumb Ox. He had to put up with people who got the wrong impression.*
>
> *Have you been sick? St. Aloysius had malaria, an occupational disease of the Leathernecks in the South Pacific. His lasted eighteen months; quinine had not yet gotten into the medical journals.*

Are you handsome? St. Andrew Avellino was so good looking that he had to become a cleric to keep them out of his hair. If you have the same trouble, pray.

Do your feet hurt? St. Ignatius was a military man who had a great deal of trouble with his legs, and had several operations on them. He never complained about them, however, and made very few visits to sick bay even for legitimate reasons.

Do you have a rough assignment? St. Anselm was kicked around much of his youth by his father. He finally got some "good duty" as archbishop of Canterbury, and they exiled him. Do you think you have it so tough?

Do your horses run out of the money? St. Camillus was a gambling man and bet on everything that moved. He had sense enough to re-form and be converted before he ran out of cash. Most Marines don't, but should.

Are you broke most of the time? St. Cosmas was known as the "moneyless one" and this was a permanent assignment. We at least have cash two days a month.[16]

In an article entitled "Why Catholics Keep Bugging the Saints," in the *U.S. Catholic* magazine of May, 1986, Mary O'Connell quotes historian Richard Kieckhefer's opinion: "In the West, at least, many Roman Catholics find the veneration and legends of saints to be vestiges of a tradition they no longer share." The author comments, "Some attribute such changes to the Second Vatican Council, which stressed the centrality of Christ and re-emphasized the Eucharist over other ... observances, such as novenas. Many blame the 1969 directive that wiped a whole list of popular saints right off the calendar. That move left the liturgical year 'less cluttered,' says Kieckhefer, 'but also more impersonal.' "[17]

Mary O'Connell then quotes Martin Marty, the well-known Lutheran historian who has written much about Roman Catholicism, when he explained: "Once you hear that there wasn't a Saint Nicholas or a Saint Christopher, it's hard for the church to go back and inculcate a firm devotion to other saints. One set of ideas is gradually supplanted by another. If you're held hostage today, you would probably pray directly to God; your grandparents would be more likely to take it up with St. Jude."

The same article includes an analysis of letters to the National Shrine of Saint Jude League in Chicago. Flowing from faith in the intercession of the saints, these letters constitute a long litany of troubles — sickness, alcoholism, a brain-damaged daughter, health and family problems of all kinds. One letter sums up the conviction of many who write to St. Jude, the patron for desperate cases, when the writer speaks of the traditional belief: "I pray to God directly, too; but I believe the saints have special power. They've accomplished their mission on earth, they're in heaven with God, and their intercession is powerful."

Robert E. Burns, longtime editor of *U.S. Catholic* and former manager of the Saint Jude League, believes that devotion and prayer to saints:

> *... will be part of Catholicism until the end of time ... the time-honored belief in the "communion of saints" has just as much meaning today as it ever did... It's a family, a community. We all hope to be part of it. We ask the saints to pray* with *us,* not *for* us *— while we pray for ourselves, too. We're not asking them to run interference, or take our message to the Lord for us. We're asking them to pray with us, the way we pray together in a prayer group.*[18]

I do not think that the practice of prayer to God through patron saints will ever be eradicated from the Catholic soul.

The Human Side of Saints

One of the high points in the musical, *Fiddler on the Roof*, has Tevye, the musical milkman, bellowing a song about "Tradition! Tradition!" Tevye seems to sense that his cherished way of life was about to become the victim of wholesale changes.

The way of life which many millions of men and women cherish as "Catholicism" has a two-thousand-year-old cluster of traditions, many of which remain with us today. These are not "Tradition" as Catholic theologians used the word when they contrasted it with "Scripture" as a source of faith. These are pious traditions, such as Benediction of the Blessed Sacrament, the Holy Hour, the Rosary, and many others. These include the more important sacred traditions such as the way we celebrate the Eucharist and other Sacraments, and the way we progress through the liturgical year. Many Catholics have been shaken and confused to see some of the traditions they loved in their younger days seemingly abandoned in the wake of the Second Vatican Council.

An important tradition about which I write here is the veneration of the saints. Hagiography or writing about the saints nourished it. Reading about the saints and writing about them both seem to have fallen into disfavor in our time. My purpose here is threefold: to explain why former "Lives of the Saints" turned so many people off; to describe the significant improvement in hagiography born of the Catholic Literary Revival earlier in this century; and to maintain that reading more recent lives of the saints can be a highly satisfying experience.

Too often in the past the biographers, in writing about the saints, were equipped with nothing more than an ardent devotion to their subjects; consequently they suppressed the human side of the saints. The result was the common objection:

"The saints are too remote, too far above me for me to have any hope of imitating them." In his stimulating book, *The Catholic Heritage*, Lawrence Cunningham wrote that "our experience of saints — save on those rare grace-filled moments when we might actually meet one — tends to be in the rather hieratic and artificial context of stained glass windows, edifying stories of doubtful credibility, or those austere marble figures in churches displaying their instruments of torture or emblems of holiness."[19]

Ordinary Catholics in this country cannot relate to such saints when they are described as existing on a plane far above the nitty-gritty details of their lives in the world. Most of the saints are European or members of religious orders. Most Catholics are layfolk who work and raise families and pursue vocations and live lives untouched by professional connection with the church. The main task in vast areas of the Catholic world, Cunningham notes, "is to acquire food and secure shelter for one's family. Who could imitate those people in the stained glass windows or in the marble statues in their niches in the cathedrals?"

St. Thomas and St. Augustine, whom many consider the two greatest minds of Christendom, have no qualms about urging the faithful to venerate those who have gone before us and now sleep in peace. In his section on "The Reverence due to Christ," St. Thomas asks himself: "Should any form of veneration be paid to the relics of the saints?" He answers the objection that paying honor to the relics of the dead appears to favor the pagan practice of honoring the dead and, consequently, the relics of the saints should not be venerated. In response Aquinas quotes Augustine, who wrote, "The greater the love of children for their parents, the more precious to them are such souvenirs as their father's clothing, or his ring. If this is so, the bodies of the dead ought not be treated with dishonor, for they are much more intimately associated with persons than any clothing, forming, as they do, part of their being." Thomas concludes: "It follows clearly from this that a person who holds others in affection will venerate whatever remains of them after their death, not only their bodies and their parts, but also their material possesions such as clothing and the like." Now it is evident that we are bound to hold in veneration the saints of God as being members of Christ, children and friends of God and our advocates with him. We are equally bound, therefore, in memory of them, to accord due honor to any of their relics; and this is primarily true of their bodies, which were the temples and instruments of the Holy Spirit, dwelling and acting within them, and which are to be made the body of Christ by glorious resurrection. It is for this reason that God himself grants honor to their relics by performing miracles when they are present.[20]

Before Vatican Council II collections of "Lives of the Saints" and biographies of individual saints were prominent on Catholic publishers' lists. There are not so many of these items now, but books about the saints published in recent years are of better quality from an historian's point of view. This improvement owes much to what has been called a "Catholic Literary Revival" in the earlier years of this century.

Some authors of this "Revival" contributed to what is called the "New Hagiography." They wrote books attractive in style and nourishing to the spirit of the reader. They put the saints into their proper historical perspective and showed that many of the saints were not always the perfect persons they strove to be. In the more modern biographies saints no longer occupy an icy and aloof pinnacle of perfection. They are brought down to earth and walk the human ways of people on the earth. But through it all you sense a great difference. They are still holy, saintly, and strong-willed people who were utterly logical; they went the full way with Christ and concentrated on making the best possible use of the short life God gave them.

The saints, described by the new hagiographers, are far above "ordinary people," but not too far, not utterly remote from us. They are so grasped by a religious vision that their lives were radically changed; these changed lives serve as a model for us all. Karl Rahner said that people can look at a saint's life and see there a particular means of being Christian and that they create a new style; they prove that a certain form of life and activity is a really genuine possibility; they show experientially that one can be a Christian even in 'this' way; they make a certain type of person believable as a Christian type.

One example of the New Hagiography is *The Vocation of Aloysius Gonzaga,* by Cyril Martindale, an English Jesuit who wrote extensively on the saints. Early biographies of St. Aloysius made him a sweet, angelic youth who would not look up to see a woman, even his own mother! Martindale stresses the human character and heroism of this youth in whom the lascivious blood of the Gonzagas, a powerful Italian family, ran strong; but he could turn that turbulent tide into strong channels and become a saint whom one can admire and imitate.

Aloysius is shorn of the lilies and skull which framed his almost effeminate features in the "holy cards" the Sisters of an earlier day used to distribute to children. He became, Father Martindale writes, that "monstrosity of a Gonzaga ... a man who had taken all the hereditary forces of that family and turned them full against what they had always been used for — self-aggrandizement, self-enrichment, self-worship."[21] Martindale paints the ugly background from which Aloysius Gonzaga emerged in the sixteenth-century Italian history in which he walked his arduous way to heaven; he does not hesitate to say the young Aloysius, a patron saint of youth, far from being too pusillanimous a character, could have been the strongest statesman of that strong country if he had set his mind to it.

In an issue of *The Tablet* of London, David Hugh Farmer wrote a review of a book by David Sox called *Relics and Shrines*. He begins thus: " 'The saints are out,' I was told in a northern abbey in 1976. In 1986, however, there are three dictionaries of saints in print in English and plenty of recent books on saints' lives and writings on sale."[22] (Modestly, Farmer does not say that his own excellent *The Oxford Dictionary of Saints* (1978) was one of the three.) He continues, "According to travel agents, pilgrimages increased by 20 per cent in 1985. This renewed interest in saints and shrines is entirely appropriate to the pilgrim Church of today." Farmer also praises Herbert Thurston, S.J., who revised Alban Butler's massive four-volume eighteenth-century *Lives of the Saints,* for his critical acumen in pointing out the exaggerations and legends. Father Thurston sometimes shocked the devout, but won the admiration of sceptics. Farmer remarks, "The Church cannot afford to be without such men."

It seems that veneration of the saints is alive and well — and more balanced.

Chapter One:

Mother of God — Mother of the Faithful

Introduction

On January 25, 1979, Pope John Paul II stopped at the island of Santo Domingo on his first trip to Latin America. During this first stop on American soil, he reminded the people that it was on Santo Domingo, where Columbus first landed, that the first "Hail Mary" was prayed on the American continent.

Later in that year John Paul, the passionate Polish mountain climber, rode by cable car 10,709 feet to the peak of Marmolada to dedicate a statue of the Madonna on the highest mountain of the Dolomite Alps in northern Italy. In a freezing snowstorm, wearing a fur ski cap, he proclaimed Mary, the Mother of God, the "Queen of the Dolomites." On August 26, her feast day, he told the people with him of Our Lady of Czestochowa, who had inspired in him a profound devotion to Mary — a devotion so deep that it led him to express in the motto on his papal coat of arms *"Totus Tuus,"* which translates into "Totally Yours."

On October 7, 1979, the pope went to the Shrine of the Immaculate Conception in Washington. He began his talk by saying that his first desire in that American shrine to its patroness was "to turn my heart to the woman of salvation history." He said:

"In the eternal design of God, this woman was chosen to enter into the work of the Incarnation and Redemption. And this design of God was to be actuated through her free decision given in obedience to the divine will. Through her *yes* — a *yes* that pervades and is reflected in all history — she consented to be the Virgin Mother of our saving God, the Handmaid of the Lord and, at the same time, the Mother of all the faithful who in the course of centuries would become brothers and sisters of her Son."[1]

After a high point in the Fifties in what was called the

"Marian Age" there are many who say that devotion to the Mother of God has all but disappeared in the Church after Vatican II. There are many who mourn the passing of some beautiful ways of devotion to her in the past.

There was one quite unknowing American reporter who wrote Pope John Paul II off as a "conservative theologian" after he heard him twice refer to the Virgin Mary in his speech from the balcony of St. Peter's just after his election. The reporter remarked that "liberal" Catholic theologians have "lately avoided references to the cult of the mother of Jesus to spare Protestant feelings." The truth is that some of those "liberal theologians," named Karl Rahner, Edward Schillebeeckx, and Bernard Häring, have written beautiful books about Mary. And some of the best Protestant theologians of our day show an increasing interest in her and are re-examining her place in the Communion of Saints. In the book, *Where We Are: American Catholics In the 1980s,* Robert McAfee Brown, a prominent American theologian, contributes a chapter on *"American Catholicism Now: a Protestant View."* About the role of Mary in ecumenical discussions he writes:

"There are probably many reasons for feminist initiatives within Roman Catholicism of which I am necessarily unaware, but I believe that in the church a large part of the prophetic upsurge is due to a rediscovery, or at least a redefinition, of the role of Mary, once almost anathema to Protestants; there is now emerging as an important rallying point in social justice struggles — the Mary of the Magnificat rather than the Mary of the holy pictures, and it is my perception that this is happening in Catholicism as well. Rather than the demure passive maiden dressed in blue, we now see the powerful leader whose home is with the oppressed of the world, and who enlists our support to see that the hungry are fed and the poor are lifted up."[2]

I do not think we should speak of a decline in devotion to Mary, but rather say that the devotion is becoming more profound as we "get a better knowledge of her presence among us." The words are those of Marianist Father Theodore Koehler, a prominent Mariologist and director of the Marian Library at the University of Dayton, who thinks that Marian devotion is not declining, but that "a process of interiorization" is taking place so that devotion is becoming less superficial. De-emphasis on statues of Mary is not a sign of lessening interest in Mary, but of "roots" replacing "routine."

Devotion to the Mother of God has waxed and waned over the years. It reached a high point in our century when Pope Pius XII proclaimed 1954 a "Marian Year" to be celebrated worldwide to commemorate the hundredth anniversary of the solemn definition of the Immaculate Conception by Pope Pius IX. Pope Pius XII had himself solemnly defined the Assumption of Mary four years before, and as the Marian Year of 1954 drew to a close, he instituted the feast of the Queenship of Mary. In 1958, the year he died, Pius XII invited the whole world to come to Lourdes to celebrate the hundredth anniversary of Mary's appearance there to the teenage Bernadette Soubirous.

Devotion to Mary began at the birth of the Church in that Upper Room as the apostles made a "novena" to await the Holy Spirit which Jesus had promised. Luke reports that Mary the Mother was with them. A few days before, in his dying agony on the cross, Jesus turned to John the Apostle and told him, "Behold your mother"; he had made her Mother of the Church. Today Pope John Paul II is fond of taking us back to the Upper Room to pray with Mary and the apostles to gain inspiration for our work as witnesses to Jesus in the world.

Devotion to Mary developed over the early centuries with a healthy enrichment by liturgy and scripture, the evolving Christology of the first Church councils, and the instinctive approval of the laity in a process theologians call "the sense of the faithful" as they learned to appreciate Mary's demonstrably unique role in the Redemption. In the Middle Ages and after the Council of Trent in the sixteenth century, however, extra-liturgical devotions and reliance on questionable "private revelations" drew attention away from the Church's authentic mode of teaching through Word and Sacrament.

In this chapter about the woman whom Pope John Paul II called the "The Mother of the Faithful" I look at her from various viewponts. I shall discuss modern Marian doctrine after Vatican Council II, some of the titles under which she has been revered, some of the most popular Marian prayers, several of the best known shrines which have brought millions of pilgrims to pray to her, and her role in the history of America.

I shall begin with short articles on St. Joseph, her husband, the patron saint of workers, and on St. Anne, the mother of the Blessed Virgin Mary.

Saint Joseph:
Husband of Mary

The Saint in the Background

There are times when publicity is a powerful science and art — the art of pushing oneself forward. Once a man in history named Joseph was asked by God to take upon himself the greatest responsibility ever given to a man by God — the protection of God's son, Jesus, and his mother, Mary. It was said of Joseph that he was the very model of holy men, more an angel than a man in conduct, the protector of the Church of God. He never pushed himself forward; he was happy to fade into the background.

There is a charming passage in the autobiography of Saint Teresa of Avila describing a vision she had. She saw our Lady clothed in shining garments. St. Joseph was there, too. "I did not see St. Joseph so distinctly," Teresa wrote, "though I saw clearly that he was there." It was always so; Joseph would have wanted it that way. Always he was the man in the background, but it was in the background of the earthly life of God and his mother.

The new Preface of St. Joseph sums up the reasons why the Church honors Joseph the Husband of Mary:

He is that just man,
that wise and loyal servant,
whom you placed at the head of your family.
With a husband's love he cherished Mary,
the Virgin Mother of God.
With fatherly care he watched over Jesus Christ your
son,
conceived by the power of the Holy Spirit.

In 1521 a writer named Isidore de Isolanis wrote a prophecy: "Before the day of judgment it must happen that all people know, honor, and adore the name of the Lord and the great gifts which he himself placed in St. Joseph and which he has left in obscurity for a long period ... his name will be listed on the calendar of the saints, no longer at the end, but at the beginning." The prophecy has been fulfilled, but it was a long time before it was. When Isidore wrote those words, Joseph was not honored by a special feast day nor even mentioned in the Litany of All Saints.

He whom we now honor as the principal patron of the Church remained in the background of Catholic consciousness for eighteen centuries. For the early centuries, this is not hard to understand. There were bitter theological battles then about the Trinity, the Incarnation, and the perpetual virginity of Mary. The theological status of Joseph was not as important as those doctrines. It would have been imprudent to stress the foster-father of Christ at the time; it would have confused the issue. Besides, Joseph had probably died before John the Baptist appeared to proclaim the public life of Christ.

It was in the nineteenth century that pleas for greater recognition of St. Joseph became insistent. Catholics of all walks of life wanted him proclaimed official patron of the Church. Pope Pius IX responded by establishing the feast of the Solemnity of St. Joseph in 1847; and on December 8, 1870, he solemnly proclaimed Joseph the Patron of the Universal Church. In 1937 in an encyclical on Communism, Pope Pius XI appointed Saint Joseph the patron of the "vast campaign of the Church against world Communism." In 1955 Pius XII introduced the feast of St. Joseph the Worker, to be celebrated on May 1. (American Catholics use the mass of this feast for their Labor Day celebrations.) Pope John XXIII named St. Joseph, together with St. John the Baptist, as the official patrons of Vatican Council II. There is now a special branch of theology called "Josephology," and a professional theological journal has been established to discuss the place of Joseph in the history of salvation.

But something was lacking. A strong movement developed to put the name of Joseph into the Eucharistic Prayer next to that of Mary, his wife. Rome did not respond. Then in a touch of drama, on November 10, 1962, a month after the Vatican Council began, the aged Bishop Peter Cule of Yugoslavia meandered through a hesitant, repetitious plea for the inclusion of Joseph in the Mass. Cardinal Ruffini, director of that day's session, cut him short with a sarcastic remark. There was laughter in St. Peter's basilica when he loudly invoked the name of St. Joseph at the end of the session. Pope John XXIII, watching on closed television, was not amused. He knew Bishop Cule personally and knew that the hesitant speech pattern was caused by years of imprisonment by the Communists in his country. Bishop Cule had suffered two broken hips after an attempt to murder him; he struggled to get to Rome and put in his plea for St. Joseph.

Three days later, Pope John put the name of Joseph, Husband of Mary, into the Mass without waiting for any approbation by the Council.[3]

The Worker

In 1955 Pope Pius XII introduced the new feast of St. Joseph the Worker into the Church's calendar of saints. He ordered it to be celebrated on May 1 — May Day. He chose that date to counteract the May Day celebrations of the Communist world, when television pictures show parades of soldiers and tanks and guns and machines of war in capitals like Moscow and Ho Chi Minh City in Vietnam. The pope wished to emphasize the dignity of each person to foster Christian ideals in labor relations, and to stress the example of Joseph the Carpenter as a model for working people.

Joseph was the husband of Mary the Virgin and the foster father of Jesus Christ by right of marriage and spiritual and legal ties. It was not until the year 1479 that the name of Joseph was placed in the Roman calendar of saints, but in recent centuries the Church has honored him in many ways. He is patron of the Universal Church. To recognize his example as a worker, Pope Benedict XV named him protector of working people. Pope Pius XI named him patron of social justice, and in 1937 in his encyclical *Divini Redemptoris*, which proposed the Catholic tradition of social teachings as an antidote to Communism, Pius XI named Joseph as patron of the Church's campaign against Marxism.

On August 15, 1889, Pope Leo XIII devoted one of his many encyclicals, *Quamquam pluries*, to St. Joseph in which he declared that he is Patron of the Universal Church because "this is his numberless family scattered throughout all lands, over which he rules with a kind of paternal authority, because he is the husband of Mary and father of Jesus Christ." The encyclical declared Joseph a model for fathers of families and confirmed that his pre-eminent sanctity places him next to the Blessed Virgin among the saints. Pope Leo asserted in his letter on Joseph that from his position as husband and father, there "arise all his dignity, grace, holiness, and glory ... Since the bond of marriage existed between Joseph and the Blessed Virgin, there can be no doubt that more than any other person he approached the supereminent dignity by which the Mother of God is raised far above all created natures."[4]

In the Litany of St. Joseph he is invoked as patron of families, virgins, the sick, the dying, and working men and women. In papal documents and by popular acclaim he has been hailed also as patron of prayer and the interior life, of the poor, of those in authority, fathers, priests and religious travelers, and, because of his closeness to Mary, as patron of devotion to Mary.

When Pope Pius XII declared Joseph the Worker the patron of working people in 1955, a new Mass was written for the new feast on May 1. It was revised after Vatican Council II. The liturgical texts on the feast (in the United States they are also used on Labor Day), together with some passages from the Council's *Pastoral Constitution on the Church and the Modern World* can serve as meditation text for the role of St. Joseph in helping us to realize the beautiful truth written by Teilhard de Chardin when he said that "we make our way to heaven by doing the work of the world."

The opening prayer of the Mass of St. Joseph the Worker on May Day is:

> God our Father,
> creator and ruler of the universe,
> in every age you call people
> to develop and use their gifts for the good of others.
> With St. Joseph as our example and guide,
> help us to do the work you have asked
> and come to the rewards you have promised.

In the first reading of the Mass, Paul urges Christians to work energetically, with their whole being, but to work for the Lord and in the spirit of love. Such is the Christian view of work:

"Over all the virtues put on love, which binds the rest together and makes them perfect ... Whatever you do, whether in speech or action, do it in the name of the Lord Jesus. Give thanks to the Father through him ... Whatever you do, work at it with your whole being. Do it for the Lord rather than for men, since you know you will receive an inheritance from him as your reward. Be a slave of Christ the Lord" (Col. 3:14,17,23-24.)

The opening prayer in the new "Mass for the Laity" in the modern missal makes the same point:

> Fill with the spirit of Christ
> those whom you call to live in the midst of this world
> and its concerns.
> Help them by their work on earth
> to build up your eternal kingdom.

On September 15, 1981, Pope John Paul II issued his encyclical *On Human Work*, in which he states that work is for human beings, not human beings for work.

In this tribute to human workers John Paul goes beyond an older tradition of spirituality which looked fearfully on anything "worldly" to elaborate a stimulating vision of the values of daily work. From the Vatican Council's *Church and the Modern World*, he clarifies the Christian vocation of "Building the Earth," a favorite phrase of Teilhard de Chardin, whose works had a deep, though mostly unacknowledged, influence on the Council. Here is what the fathers of the Council had to say about the spiritual meaning of one's daily work:

"Those who believe in God take it for granted that, taken by itself, man and woman's activity, both individual and collective — that great struggle in which men and women have sought to improve the conditions of human living — is in keeping with God's purpose.

"Men and women, created in God's image, have been commissioned to master the earth and all it contains, and so rule the world in justice and holiness. They are to acknowledge God as the creator of all, and to see themselves and the whole universe in relation to God, in order that all things may be subject to them, and God's name be an object of wonder and praise over all the earth.

"This commission extends to even the most ordinary

activities of daily life, where men and women, in the course of gaining a livelihood for themselves and their families, offer appropriate service to society; they can be confident that their personal efforts promote the work of the Creator, confer benefit on their fellows, and help to realize God's plan in history."[5]

Ten years after Pius XII established the feast of St. Joseph the Worker, the bishops of Vatican II in their document on the modern world and John Paul in 1981 have provided beautiful commentaries on what Joseph the Carpenter of Nazareth can teach us about making our way to heaven by doing the work of the world.

Saint Anne: Grandmother of Jesus

Jesus Had a Grandmother, Too

In 1956 Frances Parkinson Keyes, a convert and a best-selling Catholic author, whose numerous novels and biographies of the saints had endeared her to millions of readers, published a life of St. Anne. She tells how the book began when a friend of hers told her of a dialogue she had with her granddaughter. "I was trying to tell my little granddaughter the story of the Nativity. And the child kept saying, 'But I don't understand why Mary and Joseph had to go a stable.' 'Don't you see,' I repeated, 'there was no room for them in the inn. I said that before, Darling. And they needed shelter. That's why they went to the stable.' " The child looked more and more bewildered and she began to look troubled, too. " 'I still don't understand,' she said again, and this time her voice trembled a little. 'Why didn't they go to Grandma's?' "6

Inspired by this incident, Mrs. Keyes sent out a Christmas story to her friends entitled *Our Lord Had a Grandmother, Too*. This Christmas letter was a warm, folksy meditation on the life of St. Anne, the mother of Mary, the mother of Jesus. Later reprinted in magazines, it brought an avalanche of correspondence from Grandmother Anne's admirers.

In her letter Mrs. Keyes wrote that the little girl's question about "Grandma" made her visualize St. Anne primarily in her role as a grandmother of Jesus:

If she stayed at home in Nazareth when Mary, who was "with child," went to Bethlehem, wasn't she very anxious about her daughter and very eager to learn about the new baby? Did she hear the "good tidings of great joy," if not directly from the angels, then from some kindly neighbor who came back to Nazareth before Mary and Joseph? Did the Star in the East shed its light far enough for her to see? Did her first anxiety mount to anguish when she learned about the Slaughter of the Innocents? Was she very lonely while her daughter was in Egypt? Did Jesus spend much time with her in the little house where the angel had announced His coming? Did she invite John to stay there, too, so that the small cousins would be company for each other? Was it she who taught Jesus to read? Did she live long enough to see Him advanced in wisdom and age and grace with God and men?"[7]

The author set out in search of answers. She visited the shrines, great and small, of the mother of Mary around the world, studied the art and legends enshrined in early Christian writings, especially the so-called *apochrypha*. From the Greek word, meaning "hidden," these writings are considered by the Church to be of spurious or at least doubtful value to Christian thought. Though spurious, and not recognized by the Church as part of the Bible, these forty New Testament apochrypha may be of great value in the historical knowledge they give; from a theological standpoint, they are of slight value.

There is nothing known with certainty about the parents of the Blessed Virgin Mary — not even their names. Their names are found in the *Protoevangelium of James*, a book written about 150 A.D. by an unknown author. It is claimed (falsely) to have been written by St. James the Less, the first bishop of Jerusalem, killed by Jews in the earliest days of the Church. This book, which gives the names of Mary's parents as Anne and Joachim, is also called *The Birth of Mary, The Revelation of James, and the Gospel of Pseudo-Matthew*. It begins:

> *The Blessed and Ever Glorious Mary, sprung from the royal race and family of David, was born in the city of Nazareth, educated at Jerusalem, in the Temple of the Lord.*
>
> *Her father's name was Joachim and her mother's Anna. The family of her father was of Galilee and the city of Nazareth. The family of her mother was of Bethlehem.*
>
> *Their lives were plain and right in the sight of the Lord, pious and faultless before men.*

These, too, are the opening lines of the book which Frances Parkinson Keyes was asked to write to expand on her acclaimed Christmas letter on the Grandmother of the Lord which she published in 1955 under the title, St. *Anne, Grandmother of Our Saviour*. At the beginning she quotes that ubiquitous author "Anon" as saying "I do not know it, but I believe it because I feel it" and dedicates the book to her own ten grandchildren "with their grandmother's love and the hope that the blessing of St. Anne, Grandmother of Our Saviour, will always rest upon them."

In the Middle Ages a collection of stories known as *The Golden Legend* of Jacobus de Voragine spread the early apocryphal account of Anna and Joachim. St. Anne's birth, it was said, was miraculously foretold to her mother and father, called by some Mathan and Maria; upon their couch appeared the word *Anna* (grace) in gold letters. Anna grew up and married a young man known as Joachim, whose name means, propitiously, "Preparation for the Savior." A legend states that Joachim was rebuked by the high priest for his childlessness after many years of marriage; he then was visited by an angel who foretold the birth of Mary who was to be the Mother of the Lord.

Some time between Mary's and Christ's childhood, Joachim died; the grandfather of Jesus is rarely mentioned. (In the present calendar of the Church the feastday of both Anne and Joachim is celebrated on July 26.)

Keyes asks "How did St. Anne feel when the Angel Gabriel announced that her daughter was with child?" "Exalted," Keyes says, though she suspects husband Joachim may have received the news "with feelings of more tempered happiness … a human father's natural concern for his daughter." As to when St. Anne died, the legends are silent. Where she is buried is a subject of pious argument. In *Time* magazine (Dec. 26, 1955) a generous review of Keyes' book concludes by quoting the author's feeling that Anne's tomb is in the French city of Apt. In a hidden crypt under the cathedral's high altar, the great Emperor Charlemagne himself is said to have discovered her stone-sealed coffin in 801 A.D. Above this tomb is carved a tree branch, interlaced with a grapevine — a perfect illustration, Mrs. Keyes observes, for the Church's Litany to Saint Anne: St. *Anne, Fruitful Vine … pray for us.*

Keyes includes an account of many of the shrines to St. Anne which were popular in the Middle Ages. In the West the cult of St. Anne was introduced in Rome in the eighth century; it became widespread in the fourteenth century. In 1584 Pope Gregory XIII extended her feast to the whole Church.

Keyes thinks that St. Anne "seems closer to Christ than any

other saint and closer to us even than the Blessed Mother."
"However this may be," says the *Time* review, "Anne is widely
and warmly venerated." She is the patron saint of Brittany,
with hundreds of Catholic churches dedicated to her there.
She is patron of the world's second most famous healing
shrine (after Lourdes) at St. Anne de Beaupré in Canada. In
1955 there were nearly four hundred churches dedicated to her
in the United States, plus many Episcopal churches.

There are many reasons for the great popularity of St. Anne
and St. Joachim. One of them is their close connection with
the cult of the Blessed Virgin Mary. Another is the fact that the
family, especially in former days, could not be thought of
without the grandparents. Mary's mother and father belong,
in a certain sense, to the "Holy Family." Finally, Joachim and
Anne are becoming symbols of the Messianic expectations of
the Hebrew Scriptures, while they introduce the New Testament. With Mary, they form the point in history where divini-
ty entered into humanity.[8]

As the grandparents of Jesus, Saints Anne and Joachim are
also the grandparents of the faithful as parents of Mary, Mother of the Faithful.

Mary's Role
in the Church Today

Mary at Vatican II

On November 21, 1964, during the last meeting of the third session of Vatican II, Pope Paul VI concelebrated with twenty-four prelates who had major Marian shrines in their territories. Then the bishops at the Council, by a vote of 2,151 to 5, passed the *Dogmatic Constitution on the Church*. The pope approved and promulgated it that day. In his talk to the bishops, he also proclaimed Mary, the Mother of God, the "Mother of the Church."

The eighth and final chapter of the Constitution is titled, "The Blessed Virgin Mary, Mother of God, in the mystery of Christ and of the Church." This chapter, containing seventeen of the sixty-nine paragraphs in the document, had been the subject of fierce debate in the fall of 1963, on whether it should be included at all. On October 29, the bishops voted to include their declaration on Our Lady in the Constitution on the Church, but the vote was close — 1,114 to 1,074. By the end of the Council, however, it was agreed that the final version of the Marian chapter was a beautiful and concise summary of the role of Mary in her Son's redeeming work and in the Church.[9]

The eighth chapter is a skillful and prudent compromise between two tendencies in modern Catholic theology in 1964: one would emphasize Mary's unique connection with Christ; the other stressed her close connection with the Church and all the Redeemed. The chapter exhorts preachers and theologians, in treating the unique dignity of Mary, to avoid carefully and equally the falsity of exaggeration on the one hand, and the excess of narrow-mindedness on the other.

There have been two important documents published later which, it could be said, were developments of the Mariology of Vatican II. One, an apostolic exhortation by Pope Paul VI on devotion to Mary, was published on February 2, 1974, under the title *Marialis Cultus*, treating the right ordering of and development of devotion to the Blessed Virgin Mary.[10] The other, a pastoral letter of the American Catholic bishops, was published on November 21, 1973, and called *Behold Your Mother, Woman of Faith*.[11]

In a sermon he preached at the University of Oxford, Cardinal John Henry Newman praised Mary's faith when she said *Yes* at the Annunciation, when Elizabeth at the Visitation called her "blessed" because "she believed," when Jesus at twelve was missing in the Temple. Then Newman continued: "Accordingly, at the marriage-feast of Cana, her faith anticipated his first miracle, and she said to the servants, 'Whatsoever he saith unto you, do it.' Thus, Mary is our pattern of faith, both in the reception and in the study of Divine Truth. She does not think it enough to accept, she dwells upon it; not enough to possess, she uses it; not enough to assent, she develops it; not enough to submit the reason, she reasons upon it, not indeed reasoning first, and believing afterward, with Zacharias, yet first believing without reasoning, next from love and reverence, reasoning after believing."[12]

The eighth chapter of the Constitution on the Church begins with a survey of Mary in God's plan of human salvation through which we achieve the adoption of sons. This divine mystery of Incarnation is revealed to us through the Virgin Mary and continued in the Church. Therefore, the faithful must reverence her memory because she is the Mother of our God and Lord Jesus Christ, the Son of God. She is also the daughter of the Father and the temple of the Holy Spirit and because of this gift of sublime grace she surpasses all creatures. As a pre-eminent member of the Church, she is the model for all the redeemed in that she said *Yes* to God, who through the archangel Gabriel asked her to be the mother of his son. When she said, "Behold, I am the handmaid of the Lord; let it be done to me according to your word" to the archangel, she said *Yes* to God from the Incarnation of Jesus in her womb to his death on the cross.

The title of chapter eight of the Constitution also implies that Mary plays a unique role not only in the mystery of Christ, but also in the mystery of the Church, which is the Mystical

Body of Christ. The chapter develops other titles of our Lady;
she is Virgin Mother and exalted Queen of heaven and earth.

The Second Vatican Council, the bishops say, intends to
describe Mary's role in the mystery of the Incarnate Word and
the Mystical Body. It does not intend to give a complete doctrine on Mary, nor decide all theological questions. "Those
opinions, therefore," they warn, "may be lawfully retained
which are freely propounded by schools of Catholic thought
concerning her who occupies a place in the Church which is
highest after Christ and very close to us."[13]

The chapter on Mary goes on to discuss, on the basis of
scripture and tradition, especially in the Fathers of the
Church, how Mary is prefigured in the preparation of Christ's
coming in the Hebrew Scriptures (55.) I quote from the article,
"Vatican II and Mary," in the *Dictionary of Mary*, published
in 1985:[14] "She begins the New Testament at the Annunciation, where her faith, her Immaculate Conception, her Divine
Motherhood move into focus (56.) Mary is a close associate in
the work of salvation throughout the life of the Savior, her son:
Mother at Nazareth, Disciple from Cana to the Cross itself,
where Jesus dying gives her as *Mother* to John (57-59.)"

In the close vote of October 16, 1963, which included the
chapter on Mary as part of the Church document, some bishops who opposed the move did not want Mary to be treated at
all, primarily for ecumenical reasons. The section on Mary,
therefore, stressed that there is only one mediator of redemption, the man Christ Jesus:

> *The maternal duty of Mary toward men and women in no wise ob-
> scures this unique mediation of Christ, but rather shows his power.
> For all the salvific influence of the Blessed Virgin on men and women
> originates, not from some inner necessity, but from the superabun-
> dance of the merits of Christ, rests on his mediation, depends entire-
> ly on it, and draws all its powers from it.[15]*

Because Mary is the Model of the Church, her prayer, especially her *Yes* to the Lord, is an example of her own prayer. In
heaven she constantly intercedes for us to bring us the gifts of
eternal salvation; she cares for the brothers and sisters of her
son who are the Pilgrim Church on earth. St. Ambrose of Milan taught that the Mother of God is our model in the matter of

faith, charity, and perfect union with Christ (63.) The followers of Christ, striving to increase in holiness, turn to Mary as a living example and model of all the virtues (65.) She calls the faithful to her Son and we look to her, in her apostolic work, as a living example.

The last part of the chapter on Mary treats "The Cult of the Blessed Virgin in the Church," and notes that it differs essentially from the cult of adoration offered to the Incarnate Word, the Father, and the Holy Spirit. The document closes with a section on "Mary, a Sign of Sure Hope and of Solace to God's People in Pilgrimage." It ends with these words: "Now still, exalted above all the Angels and Saints, the Mother of God continues to intercede before her Son, in communion with all the Saints, until all families ... may be happily together in peace and harmony into the people of God for the glory of the Most Holy and Undivided Trinity."[16]

The eighth chapter of the *Dogmatic Constitution on the Church* at Vatican II struck the right balance at the Council between those "maximalists" who would overstress the role of Mary in the Redemption and those "minimalists" who would play down her role.

Theotokos: The "God-Bearer"

At the invitation of Pope John Paul II, many bishops from around the world met in Rome at Pentecost in 1981 to commemorate the 1,600th anniversary of the First Ecumenical Council of Constantinople in 381 A.D. and the 1,550th anniversary of the Council of Ephesus in 431 A.D. It was defined at Ephesus that Mary was truly the Mother of God. The Greek word used in this definition was *Theotokos* (God-Bearer.)

One name for the intellectual history of the Catholic Church in the fourth and fifth centuries of the Christian era might be "The Church in Council."

The birth and initial developments of the Church must be understood against the background of the kind of world into which Christ was born. It was ruled by Rome but dominated by Greek thought. In this same world the early Church grew from seeds sown by Peter, Paul, and the other Apostles. It preached the Good News and gave witness to Jesus, the Son of God, in a pagan world which soon began to persecute it.

After an underground existence through the first three centuries, the Church was set free by converted emperor Constantine, who called the first Ecumenical (a Greek term for "worldwide") Council at Nicaea, a city near his capital of Constantinople, in 325 A.D. This Council dealt with the belief preached by the priest Arius that Christ was only the adopted son of God and not equal to the Father. The Nicene Council condemned Arianism, which had almost split the Church, and solemnly defined in the Creed (still recited on Sundays) that Jesus was "the only begotten Son from the substance of the Father, God from God, light from light, true God from true God, begotten not made, *of one substance with the Father.*" (The Greek word for "of one substance" was *homoousios;* Arius had said *homoiousios,* which means "similar to God.")

Nicaea was the first of eight councils, which were all held in the eastern part of the Church within the confines of what is now Turkey in Asia Minor. All were concerned with understanding the most staggering fact to confront the human mind — the Incarnation: God become man.

The definition at Nicaea did not stop the bitter controversies in which the key dogmas of Christianity were debated and defined in the councils which followed Nicaea. The great Church fathers of the East — St. Athanasius, St. Basil, St. Gregory of Nazianzen, St. Gregory of Nyssa, Cyril of Jerusalem, and others — used Greek philosophy to define more clearly key terms such as *person* and *nature*, as they theologized about the Incarnation and the Trinity and the place of Mary the Mother in the Creed. The Fathers saw the distinction between the three divine persons as existing solely in their inner divine relations, one Godhead in three persons. They explored the mystery of the Incarnation: Christ was one person with two natures, human and divine.

At the first council of Constantinople in 381 an addition was made to the Nicene Creed which defined the role of the Holy Spirit:

> We believe in the Holy Spirit, the Lord, the giver of
> life,
> who proceeds from the Father and the Son.
> With the Father and the Son he is worshipped and
> glorified.
> He has spoken through the prophets.
> ...and in the Holy Spirit, the Lord and life-giver, who
> proceeds from
> the Father, who with the Father and the Son, is to-
> gether worshipped
> and glorified.

Later in the Western Church, after a long development which included the approval of several popes and two medieval Councils, the Creed was changed to assert that the Holy Spirit proceeds from the Father *and* the Son (in Latin, *filioque*) not, as the Eastern Church insisted, "*from* the Father *through* the Son." The word *filioque* was one significant cause of the split between the Eastern and Western Churches. The separation continues today, but there have been some significant signs of reconciliation between the two churches. When Pope Paul VI journeyed to the Holy Land in 1964, he embraced the Orthodox Patriarch Athenagoras. The Pope and the Patriarch mutually removed the excommunications which the two Churches had imposed upon each other nine hundred years before. The controversy over *filioque*, however, continues.

In the fifth century Nestorius, the Patriarch of Constantinople, considered the role of Mary in these christological and trinitarian developments and concluded that Mary was not truly the Mother of God. She could not be called *theotokos,* "God-bearer," but merely "Christ-bearer," since she had given birth to only a human being, Jesus. St. Cyril, the Patriarch of Jerusalem, strongly protested that statement, and the stage was set for the confrontation at the Council of Ephesus in 431 A.D.

Twenty-five years ago I visited the excavated ruins of Ephesus in Turkey after a dusty bus ride from the port of Izmir forty miles to the north.

It was a thrill to wander through the ruins of Ephesus, where, some people believe, the Apostle John brought the Virgin Mary after Jesus had told him from the cross, "Son, behold your mother." It was a thrill to walk in the path of St. Paul where he first preached the Good News and the joy of the Resurrection to the Ephesians.

The temple of Diana at Ephesus was one of the seven Wonders of the Ancient World. It was a thrill to visit the stadium where Paul confronted the rioting silversmiths whose statues of the goddess Diana did not sell very well after Paul had organized the Christian community in the city.

My greatest thrill in Ephesus, however, came when I stood amid the weeds and brambles around the roofless ruins of the Church of the Blessed Virgin Mary. In that church in 431 the bishops at the Council of Ephesus listened to the debates between Cyril and Nestorius. In front of that church of the Virgin a jubilant throng of Christians with flaming torches met the bishops in the twilight of a day in June as the bishops emerged from the church to announce their decision that Mary is truly *Theotokos,* the Mother of God.

St. Cyril of Alexandria preached a homily in that church to

the bishops of the Council to express his joy at their decision. He told them:

> *I see here a joyful company of Christians, met together in ready response to the call of Mary ... Holy and incomprehensible Trinity, we salute you at whose summons we have come together in this church of Mary, the Mother of God ... Mother of God, we salute you, precious vessel, worthy of the world's reverence ... the symbol of orthodoxy, an indestructible temple, the place that held him whom no place could contain ... We salute you, for in your womb he, who is beyond all limitation, was confined ... Because of you, the angels and archangels make merry ... What more is there to say? Because of you the light of the only-begotten Son has shone upon those who sit in darkness and in the shadow of death.*[17]

That day in Ephesus was the beginning of that devotion to Mary which has brought blessing and beauty to Catholics across the centuries. The People of God found it good to honor the *Theotokos*. She is the only mother God ever had.

The Church's
"Foremost Member"

In the August 5, 1983, issue of the prominent Protestant periodical, *Christianity Today*, a rather enthusiastic news item called "Homecoming for Poland's Favorite Native Son," ended with a short paragraph: "Perhaps the most troublesome aspect of the pope's message in Poland was his sharply increased veneration of Mary, an emphasis that runs counter to the aspirations of Poland's evangelicals."

That paragraph is a heritage of the bitter debate about devotion to the Mother of God which has marked the history of Catholic and Protestant polemics since the Reformation. This debate has eased considerably since the Second Vatican Council brought Catholics into the Age of Ecumenism, but it continues on some fronts, especially in the Fundamentalist approach of a good percentage of Protestants. One may still find references to Catholic "adoration" of the Virgin.

Throughout twenty centuries Catholics have indeed given special love and devotion to the Mother of God. They have fulfilled the prophecy which Luke the Evangelist puts into her mouth as she prayed the *Magnificat* in her encounter with Elizabeth at the Visitation:

My soul proclaims the greatness of the Lord …
for he has looked with favor on his lowly servant.
From this day all generations will call me blessed;
The Almighty has done great things for me (Luke 1:46-49.)

The special role of Mary in Catholic spiritual life, a role entirely subordinate to that of Jesus in the Redemption, as the Vatican Council stressed, is something non-Catholic Christians have found difficult to understand. Many Catholics, too, do not seem to have a clear comprehension of her role. This could be a remnant of what the Council called "false exaggerations" and "vain credulity" of previous generations of writers and preachers about what the Council called "the subordinate role of Mary." In the chapter on Mary in the Constitution on the Church, it is written that Mary occupies "a place in the Church which is highest after Christ and also closest to us." The Constitution quotes St. Augustine: "Mary is clearly the mother of the members of Christ ... since she has by her charity joined in bringing about the birth of believers in the Church, who are members of its head." The document continues: "Wherefore she is hailed as pre-eminent as a wholly unique member of the Church, and as its type and outstanding model in faith and charity."[18]

The new Preface of the feast of the Assumption of Mary reflects what the Council said:

> ... the mother of Jesus, in the glory which she possesses body and soul in heaven, is the image of the Church as it is to be perfected in the world to come. Likewise she shines forth on earth, until the day of the Lord shall come, a sign of sure hope and comfort for your people on their pilgrim way.

In a homily written by Father John Jay Hughes in *The Priest* magazine, there is an explanation:

> *In calling Mary "the image and beginning of the Church," the Council meant that Mary is perfectly what the Church has yet to become fully: Christ's immaculate bride. We owe this image to St. Paul, who wrote in* Ephesians *that Christ wants "to present the Church to himself all glorious, with no stain or wrinkle, or anything of that sort, but holy and without blemish." This work of purification has already been completed in Mary, the Church's foremost member.[19]*

After Vatican II and the eighth chapter of the Constitution on the Church, it is clear that the Church's doctrine about Mary is now seen to occupy a secondary position in relation to the great primary truths about the Trinity, Incarnation, Justification, and Atonement, the Holy Spirit, and the Church. A prominent Episcopalian theologian, Reginald Fuller, a participant in dialogues between Roman Catholics and Episcopalians, has written that "Post-Second Vatican II presentation of Marian doctrine by Roman Catholic theologians in a more moderate form (for example, Mary as first of the redeemed rather that co-redemptrix) has done something to allay the anxieties of Protestants that Mary was on the way to being subsumed into the Trinity."[20]

One of the hymns which the Liturgy of the Hours suggests for the Morning Prayer of the "Common of the Blessed Virgin Mary" was written by an anonymous poet and "altered by the Dominican Sisters of Summit" in 1972.[21] It speaks rather beautifully of the relationship between Jesus and his mother:

Mary the dawn, Christ the Perfect Day;
Mary the gate, Christ the Heavenly Way!
Mary the root, Christ the Mystic Vine;
Mary the grape, Christ the Sacred Wine!
Mary the wheat, Christ the Living Bread;
Mary the stem, Christ the Rose blood-red!
Mary the font, Christ the Cleansing Flood;
Mary the cup, Christ the Saving Blood!
Mary the temple, Christ the temple's Lord;
Mary the shrine, Christ the God adored!
Mary the beacon, Christ the Haven's Rest;
Mary the mirror, Christ the Vision Blest!
Mary the mother, Christ the mother's Son
By all things blest while endless ages run. Amen.

Queen of Heaven and Earth

Somewhere I read an article which began, "Christian piety knows few titles for the Virgin Mary older than Queen, and such equivalents as Empress, Lady, and *Notre Dame*." That brought my memory back to a summer day when I stood with 1,600 priests on what is now the playing field of the Chicago Bears at Soldier Field in Chicago, surrounded by 125,000 Catholics in the stands during a spectacular salute to Mary, Queen of the Universe, which was part of the celebration of the "Marian Year" of 1954. Pope Pius XII had proclaimed the Marian Year to commemorate the hundredth anniversary of the definition of the dogma of the Immaculate Conception of Mary by Pope Pius IX in 1854.

That salute to the Mother of God in Soldier Field came at the height of what has been called the "Age of Mary" in the modern Church. It was Pius XII who insistently urged the faithful to a heightened devotion to the Virgin. In 1942 he consecrated the world to the Immaculate Heart of Mary and introduced a new feast under that title into the calendar of saints. The consecration formula read: "As the Church and the entire human race were consecrated to the Sacred Heart of Jesus ... so we in like manner consecrate ourselves forever also to you and your Immaculate Heart, the mother and queen of the world, that your love and patronage may hasten the triumph of the Kingdom of God."

One of the splendid events in that Marian Year came at its close when, on November 1, 1954, Pope Pius XII crowned an ancient icon which the legend had it, was painted with a tiara of diamonds, topazes, sapphires, and aquamarines by Luke the Evangelist. Then the pope proclaimed the feast of the Queenship of Mary to be celebrated each year on May 31 and he requested all Catholics in the world to consecrate themselves to the Immaculate Heart of Mary on that date each year. He wrote: "At the present hour, when world unity and peace, nay more, the very source of life, are endangered, what can Christians do except turn their eyes to her whom they see vested with royal power." Then — impressively — 400 banners from Marian shrines around the Catholic world dipped in salute to the Queen of Heaven and Earth.

There was a mutter of protest in some sources, and even the old words like "worship of the Virgin" and "Mariolatry." But the vast majority of Catholics who celebrated the Marian Year knew that the Pope was not calling for prayer *to* Mary; he was asking for prayers *through* Mary. He spelled it out again in the encyclical he wrote about the new feast of Mary the Queen: "It is certain that only Jesus Christ, God and Man, is King, but Mary as Mother of the King and associated with him in the work of divine redemption participates in his royal dignity."[22] He was careful to point out in the encyclical that this was no new dogma being proclaimed; it was a new liturgical feast.

Christian piety knows few titles for the Virgin Mary older than queen. When Gabriel, the messenger of God, spoke to the Virgin in that small town of Nazareth, he told her that the Son she would bear would be "great ... and his kingdom shall never have an end." A few months later, when Mary walked across the hills of Galilee to visit Elizabeth, the mother of John the Baptist greeted her as "mother of my Lord" — an Old Testament phrase for the queen-mother. As used in the Gospel of Luke, it reflects the faith of the early Church that Jesus is the royal Messiah.

Even though Mariologists after Vatican II have toned down the exaggerated acclamation of the Queen of Heaven and Earth that were part of the past, there was something to the pageantry of the past — something like the shouts of homage with which people once greeted their queen, something like a ceremonial lifting of swords amid the knightly splendor of the Middle Ages. There should be poetry, too, perhaps these lines from Hilaire Belloc's *Ballade to Our Lady of Czestochowa:*

> *Lady and Queen and Mystery manifold*
> *And very regent of the untroubled sky,*
> *Whom in a dream St. Hilda did behold*

And heard a woodland music passing by:
You shall receive me when the clouds are high
With evening and the sheep attain the fold.
This is the faith that I have held and hold,
And this is that in which I mean to die.[23]

Mary the Mother of God is Queen of Heaven and Earth by divine decree and the acclamations of the People of God, but there is none of the earthly pride and panoply of kings and queens about her. She will listen as attentively to the prayers of a child lisping her name as she will to the clanking of a thousand swords in salute.

Star of the Sea

The crucifix is everywhere in the Catholic world. It forces us to reflect on what was achieved for us on Calvary, which was called the Hill of the Skull. The darkness in the afternoon of that first Good Friday surely is symbolic of the darkness which has crept over the world as we move toward the end of the twentieth century. Who can blame the average watcher of the evening TV news for his or her deep emotions of fear and dread, or even despair, as we hear statistics of the homeless, the poor, the victims of violence, wars and rumors of wars, racism, and religious intolerance? The list seems endless.

Yet, there is an answer to this timeless but now aggravated problem of world pain. We remember what Jesus told his mother and the Apostle John, as he was wracked with the agony and pain of the crucifixion. John reported the scene at the end of his Passion Story: "Seeing his mother there with the disciple whom he loved, Jesus said to his mother, 'Woman, there is your son.' In turn he said to the disciple, 'There is your mother' " (John 19:26-27.) Then he died. But he had made his mother our mother, too.

Since the third century or early fourth century, Catholics have prayed the oldest prayer to Mary. Known from its first in Latin as the *Sub tuum praesidium*, it reads like this in a modern translation: "Under your protection, we take refuge, O holy Mother of God; accept our petitions in our hour of need and deliver us from all dangers, O ever-glorious and blessed Virgin." Since the sixteenth century Catholics have recited another prayer to Mary in their time of troubles, the *Memorare,* which derives its key elements from the *Sub tuum praesidium* prayer. In it Mary's people express their confidence to Mary, "Never was it known that anyone who fled to your protection or sought your intercession, was left unaided."

It seems to many in the modern world that we have lost our moorings and are tossed on seas of doubt and dread. Many fear that there is no one to help plot our future course, no one to steer us straight. But in the twelfth century St. Bernard of Clairvaux, in a beautiful flight of rhetoric, reminded the monks of his abbey — and us today — that there is a pilot after all; her name is *Stella Maris* — Star of the Sea:

> *Let us speak a few words about that name, Star of the Sea, which fits the Virgin Mother so well. O you, whoever you are, who think that you are tossed in the tempest of this century, fix your eyes on the shining of this Star ... If the winds of temptation blow up, if you are dashed toward the rocks of tribulation, look at the Star, call on Mary! If you are washed in the waves of pride, or ambition or detraction or envy ... if anger or avarice or the allurements of the flesh break up the ship of your mind, look up to Mary! If you are terrified at the enormity of your crimes, confused by the shame of your conscience, or terrified at the thought of judgment, if the depths of your sorrow begin to pull you down in the abyss where no hope is, think of Mary, look to the Star![24]*

A look back in history at the Moslem Turks in their efforts over several centuries to conquer the Christian West has convinced many of the devotees of Mary that the light of the Star of the Sea shone though many of the darkest centuries of the Church's history when the Catholic cause seemed hopeless. It was St. Cyril of Alexandria who called her "the torch whose light is never extinguished."

There was the threat of the Turk for several centuries, for instance. In 626 two pagan armies converged on Constantinople whose Christian defenders were outnumbered ten to one. The Emperor and his citizens carried a picture of the Mother of God in a Rogation procession around the walls. After the attack, there were not enough survivors among the attackers to bury their own dead. For centuries the Turks hammered at the gates of western Christendom. In 1365 Louis I turned them back after he had prayed at the shrine of Mariazell. At Vienna in 1683, on the feast day of Mary's Assumption, the people prayed against a Turkish army swooping down upon them, and on her birthday, September 8, John Sobieski of Poland came to lift the siege. Four days later, he routed the Turk in three brilliant charges. On October 7, 1571, the Grand Sultan of Byzantium launched the most powerful fleet known until that time against the navies of the Christian West at the port of Lepanto in western Greece. The holds of his galleys were crowded with Christian slaves at the oars. Months before Pope St. Pius V had asked some Christian powers to face the Turkish menace. Gilbert Keith Chesterton put it into a stirring ballad he called *Lepanto*:

> *The Pope has cast his arms abroad for agony and loss,*
> *And called the king of Christendom for swords about the Cross.*[25]

The pope also called on a higher power than the kings of Christendom. He asked the faithful of Catholic Europe to recite the Rosary for the success of the Christian navy. After the battle was won and the Turks defeated, the Christian slaves came up from the oars, "white for bliss and blind for sun, and stunned for liberty," as Chesterton wrote it. The feast of Our Lady of the Rosary on October 7 still commemorates what some think as an intervention of Mary into the affairs of men and women, when the threat of the Turks was broken for the last time.

St. Bernard of Clairvaux ended his homily on Mary, the Star of the Sea, with an exhortation: "Do not let her name be away from your lips and heart ... following her, you will not go astray; beseeching her, you will not despair ... Holding fast to her, you will not fall; under her guidance you will not falter ... and you will experience in yourself how justly it was said, 'And the Virgin's name was Mary.' "

Marian Prayers

The Oldest Prayer to Mary

After *Hail Mary,* the favorite prayer of most Catholics to the Mother of God is, I suspect, the *Memorare.* After the invocation, "Remember, O most gracious Virgin Mary," this prayer implores her help and protection with a confidence that no one "who fled to your protection or sought your intercession was left unaided...we fly unto you...despise not our petitions."

The *Memorare* is of unknown authorship. Although it has been popularly attributed to St. Bernard of Clairvaux in the twelfth century, it is probably more recent. It first appeared in the twelfth edition of the *Raccolta,* an official Church book of prayers, in 1849.

A far more ancient Marian prayer from which the *Memorare* has drawn some key elements, is called *Sub tuum praesidium* from its opening words, meaning "Under your protection."[26] This prayer can be traced back to the third or early fourth century. It appears in many different ways in the prayers and liturgies of the Eastern and Western Churches and is a favorite form of intercession in many religious orders.

On October 29, 1963, the bishops at the Second Vatican Council included, by a small majority, an eighth chapter to the *Dogmatic Constitution on the Church* entitled "The Role of the Blessed Virgin Mary, Mother of God, in the Mystery of Christ and the Church." The last major division of that chapter concerns "Devotion to the Blessed Virgin in the Church." It begins with the statement that "Mary was involved in the mysteries of Christ. As the most holy Mother of God she was, after her Son, exalted by divine grace above all angels and men and women. Hence the Church appropriately honors her with special reverence." The next sentence begins a short history of the Church's devotion to Mary: "Indeed, from most ancient times the Blessed Virgin Mary has been venerated under the title of 'God-Bearer.' In all perils and needs, the faithful have fled prayerfully to her protection." A foot-note to that last sentence was rather cryptic; it read simply: *Sub tuum Praesidium.* These three words recall the rich history of that prayer to the Mother of God.

A modern translation of the prayer would read:

> Under your protection we take refuge, O holy
> Mother of God;
> accept our petitions in our hour of need
> and deliver us from all dangers,
> O ever-glorious and blessed Virgin.

The *Sub tuum praesidium* is the oldest known prayer to Mary. In 1917 a papyrus fragment was discovered in Egypt. It contained ten incomplete lines of clearly legible Greek script on one side. The fragment was brought to the John Rylands Library in Manchester, England. It was published in 1938 by C. H. Roberts, who dated it from the fourth century. Another scholar dated it from the third century. The debate turned on the use of the Greek word, *Theotokos*, meaning "God-Bearer" or "Mother of God." The fragment contained that word, which figured prominently in the debate at the Council of Ephesus in 431 A.D. as to whether Mary was mother of the man Jesus or whether she was the mother of the Godman. The climactic end of the debate came when the Council proclaimed in its definition that Mary was truly the Mother of God — *Theotokos!*

In 1939 Dom F. Mercenier, a French Benedictine monk, identified the papyrus fragment as an early Greek version of the *Sub tuum praesidium,* which up to that time had been considered a prayer from the Middle Ages. Dom Mercenier attempted a reconstruction of the fragmentary prayer, basing his judgment on a comparison with the prayer as it was used in various ancient liturgies. This is his reconstruction:

> *Under the protection of thy tender-mercy, we flee for mercy,*
> *O Mother of God our entreaties do not despise in evil time(s);*
> *but from danger deliver us, thou only chaste (or:glorious) and*
> *blessed one.*

Many theologians and scholars have written about this prayer to the Mother of God. They find that its most significant word is Theotokos ("Mother of God".) It anchors the whole text. Other adjectives in the fragment emphasize the dignity of Mary. The Greek "only chaste" ("virgin" in the Latin text) stresses not merely chastity, but also the unique privilege of Mary's virginity in her divine motherhood. In the Latin form, Mary is said to be the "glorious and blessed one." The *Theotokos*, the prayer says, is the "highly exalted of God." This special dignity of Mary is the reason why we can flee to her for refuge when we are in trouble and entreat her to help us. We can ask her to "deliver" us and "ransom" us when we are in the grip of evil and difficulties.

Another important theological point about the prayer has been quite controversial, namely, that the prayer is addressed to Mary, asking her directly to intervene on our behalf, and not merely to intercede for us, which is what we mean when we ask Mary to "pray for us."

Most prayer to Mary is "intercessory prayer," in which we ask Mary to "pray for us," but not to perform saving acts such as "to deliver us" or to "have mercy" on us. A third type of prayer to Mary is the prayer of remembrance in which we remember her faith or love or other qualities and want to be in communion with her as a model for our prayer and spirituality. The "remembrance" prayer is scattered through the "collect" (opening) prayers and the Eucharistic Prayers of the Mass. It is found, for example, in the first Eucharistic Prayer, the Roman Canon, which dates back to the sixth century. There we pray: "In union with the whole Church we honor Mary, the ever virgin mother of Jesus Christ our Lord and God. We honor Joseph, her husband (Pope John XXIII inserted that) ... and all the saints. May their merits and prayers gain us your constant help and protection."

In all the centuries, Catholics have prayed to or through the Mother of Jesus for protection in time of troubles. *Sub Tuum Praesidium* was the favorite prayer of many of them for most of those centuries.

The History of the "Hail Mary"

Overwhelmingly, the *Hail Mary* is the most popular prayer for Catholics. It is also known as the "Angelic Salutation" because the Archangel Gabriel saluted her as "full of grace" in that home in Nazareth when he appeared to her. This prayer is also called the *Ave Maria* from the first two words in the Latin version.

The angel did not say, "Hail Mary," but "Hail, full of grace." The name of Mary was added later; it appeared on a fragment of pottery excavated in Egypt and dated about the year 600 A.D.

The prayer is divided into three parts: *1) Hail (Mary), full of grace, the Lord is with thee; blessed art thou among women.* These, of course, are the words with which Gabriel greeted Mary when, as a messenger of God, he reported to the young woman of Nazareth the request of God the Father that she should become the mother of his Son. (In the Bible text Catholics use in this country for the liturgy, the full "angelic salutation" is "Rejoice, O highly favored daughter! The Lord is with you. Blessed are you among women.") When Mary, after some hesitation, said *Yes* to God's request, "The Word was made flesh and made his dwelling among us." Then that tremendous moment in the history of our salvation occurred: the Incarnation of Jesus Christ.

2) And blessed is the fruit of thy womb (Jesus.) Three months after the Incarnation, as Luke writes in his Gospel (1:42), Mary "set out, proceeding in haste into the hill country to a town of Judah." (It is identified now as Ain Karim) where she greeted her cousin Elizabeth. Elizabeth, inspired by the Holy Spirit, cried out: "Blest are you among women, and blest is the fruit of your womb ... Blest is she who trusted that the Lord's words to her would be fulfilled."

The name of Jesus was added to Elizabeth's "blest is the fruit of your womb" in the Middle Ages. Herbert Thurston, S.J., who wrote an impressive treatment of the origins of the Angelic Salutation at the beginning of this century, says this in the old *Catholic Encyclopedia:*

> *As to the addition of the word "Jesus," or as it usually ran in the fifteenth century, "Jesus Christ, Amen," it is usually said that this was due to the initiative of Pope Urban IV in 1261 ... A popular German religious manual of the fifteenth century (1474) even divides the Hail Mary into four portions, and declares that the first part was composed by the Angel Gabriel, the second by St. Elizabeth, the third, consisting only of the Sacred Name, by the pope, and the last, i.e., the word Amen by the Church.[27]*

3) The formula of the petition in the second section, "Holy Mary, Mother of God, pray for us sinners now and at the hour of our death. Amen" was added in the sixteenth century and was framed by the Church itself.

The Catechism of the Council of Trent (1545-1563) taught:

> *Most rightly has the Holy Church of God added to this thanksgiving, petition also and the invocation of the Most Holy Mother of God, thereby implying that we should piously and suppliantly have recourse to her in order that by her intercession she may reconcile God with us sinners and obtain for us the blessings we need for this present life and for the life which has no end.[28]*

The prayer as we pray it today is the result of a gradual development from the sixth to the sixteenth century, when the present wording was adopted as general liturgical usage. In its present form the *Hail Mary* received official recognition from the Church with its inclusion by Pope St. Pius V in the Roman Breviary of 1568. It was dropped from the Divine Office (now called "The Liturgy of the Hours") in 1955.

From the theological point of view the key word in the *Hail Mary* is a Greek word which is translated as "full of grace" in the usual formula. It is the word which Gabriel first spoke to Mary at the Annunciation. The Jerusalem Bible translates Gabriel's greeting as "Rejoice, so highly favored"; the New American Bible translates it as "Rejoice, O highly favored daughter"; the New English Bible translates it as "Greetings, most favored one"; the Revised Standard Version has "Hail, full of grace."

During the Lent of 1273 St. Thomas Aquinas, who died in 1274, preached to the students and townsfolk of Naples in Italy. In the local dialect he gave conferences on the Our Father, the Hail Mary, and the Apostles' Creed. They were published in Latin by Reginald of Piperno, one of his secretaries.

St. Thomas began his short "Commentary on the Angelic Salutation, namely, the Hail Mary," by dividing it into three parts: first the words of the angel Gabriel; second, the words of Elizabeth, and the third was added by the Church, namely, "Mary." He first discusses angels in relation to humans and states that Mary, because of the graces God gave her, is above the angels in dignity:

Accordingly, the Blessed Virgin surpassed the angels in these three points. Firstly, in the fulness of grace, which is greater in her than in any angel; and to indicate this the Angel paid reverence to her by saying: Full of grace, *as if to say: "I bow to thee because thou dost surpass me in fulness of grace."*[29]

In commenting on Gabriel's greeting, "full of grace," Aquinas continued:

The Blessed Virgin is said to be full of grace in three respects. Firstly as regards her soul, wherein there dwelt all the plentitude of grace. For God's grace is given for two purposes, namely, the performance of good deeds and the avoidance of evil. As regards both, the Blessed Virgin received grace in the most perfect degree, inasmuch as after Christ she was free from sin more than any other saint.

Thomas then notes that, while other saints were conspicuous in certain particular virtues, Mary practiced the works of all the virtues. Other saints are an example to us in one special virtue, one for humility, another for chastity, another for mercy (St. Nicholas of Bari is his example for that), but, Thomas says: "The Blessed Virgin is a model for all virtues: thus thou findest in her a model of humility; 'Behold the handmaid of the Lord,' and further on 'He hath regarded the humility of his handmaid,' of chastity, 'because I know not man,' and of all other virtues, as can easily be shown."

The most popular prayer of Christians is *Our Father. Hail Mary* is often prayed with it. It seemed to become a natural appendix, so often are they prayed together. It may be said that children *recite* these two prayers. Adults should *pray* them.

The Prayer We Call the Angelus

A rather beautiful thing happens at noon on the playground of the Catholic school a few miles from where I write this. During their noon recess children shriek across their playgrounds but when the bells in the belfry of the church ring out at noonday, there is a sudden silence as the children pause to pray that ancient prayer we call the *Angelus*.

Like other popular Catholic devotions which have been an important part of the tradition, the Angelus had its beginning in the obscure mists of history. We know that the morning, midday, and evening recital of the *Angelus* did not develop simultaneously. Perhaps it began with a connection to the evening curfew bell, for the word *curfew* comes from two French words meaning "to cover the fires" in preparation for bed.

In the thirteenth century, Pope Gregory IX is said to have prescribed the daily ringing of the evening bell to remind the people to pray for the Crusaders in the East. St. Bonaventure of Bagnorea, the Franciscan Minister General, suggested in 1269 that the friars should exhort the faithful to revive the Franciscan custom of reciting three Hail Marys when the bell rang at eventide. In the early fourteenth century Pope John XXII attached an indulgence to the practice of praying three Hail Marys at the evening bell. The morning *Angelus* seems to have begun in monasteries in the fourteenth century when the bell struck during Prime, the first of the "hours" of daily prayer in the Divine Office. The *New Catholic Encyclopedia*, from which I excerpt these historical details,[30] says that the noon Angelus originated in a devotion to the Passion of Christ that caused the ringing of a bell at noon on Friday; it also grew into a daily prayer for peace. In 1456 Pope Callistus II invited the whole world to pray for victory over the Moslem Turks, who were threatening to overrun Catholic Europe.

In the sixteenth century, the three customs of prayer at morning, noon, and eventide were unified, and the Angelus as we prayed it for centuries became commonplace in the Catholic world. Popes Benedict XIV, Leo XIII, and Pius XI granted indulgences to those who prayed the Angelus, even if there were no bell to remind the people of it.

To recite the Angelus means to pause three times — morning, noon, and evening — in the day's work or play to commemorate the mystery of the Incarnation of Jesus, to reflect on a few versicles from Luke's beautiful account of the Annunciation by the archangel Gabriel in which God asked Mary to be the mother of his Son; to pray three Hail Marys which repeat the salute by Gabriel in that little town of Nazareth to the young Mary when he called her "full of grace"; and to conclude with a prayer which sums up the Mystery which is at the heart of the Christian religion:

> The Angel of the Lord declared unto Mary,
> And she conceived of the Holy Spirit.

The Angelus celebrates the Lord Jesus' coming as man. A prayer has been added to the verses from St. Luke which evokes the Paschal Mystery: "Pour forth, we beseech you, O Lord, your grace into our hearts, that as we have known the incarnation of Christ, your Son, by the message of an angel, so by his passion and cross we may be brought to the glory of his resurrection ... "

The prayer we call the Angelus allows us to contemplate the long centuries of waiting for the Messiah. It is the beginning of the New Covenant in which God sends his Son to liberate us from the ancient curse of sin and death and gives us that new life in Christ which is the foundation of all our faith and hope and love of God and all people. It is the revelation of the Mystery which God had concealed over all the long years of expectation. It is the central moment in the history of humankind.

The Angelus is God condescending to ask one of his creatures for her *Yes* to his request. The young girl at Nazareth did say *Yes* to God's messenger, Gabriel. It was the response of perfect faith to that all-important initiative of the Father. "Behold the handmaid of the Lord; be it done unto me according to your word." When Mary said *Yes* to God, it happened. The Word was made Flesh.

Mary and Her Rosary Today

Since the Second Vatican Council, our appreciation of the liturgy, especially of the Mass as that act "in which the work of our redemption is exercised," has been deepened. We realize more clearly now that liturgy is our public worship of God through the Church and that it takes precedence over all private devotions.

This does not mean, however, that cherished private devotions of Catholics over the centuries have been abolished or forbidden, although many of those devotions have declined in popularity since the Council.

In the Council document on the liturgy, the Church speaks about private devotions: "Popular devotions of the Christian people are warmly recommended, provided they accord with the laws and norms of the Church. Such is especially the case with devotions called for by the Apostolic See."[31] We might add that such is especially the case with the age-old devotion to the Mother of God. At the end of the seminal *Dogmatic Constitution on the Church* we are told that "the cult of the Blessed Virgin Mary should be generously fostered and that practices and exercises of devotion toward her should be treasured as recommended by the teaching office of the Church in the course of centuries."[32]

This recommendation comes at the end of the eighth chapter of the Constitution, which deals with the role of Blessed Virgin Mary, Mother of God, in the Mystery of Christ and of the Church.

In the opinion of Father Avery Dulles, S.J., America's foremost expert on the Theology of the Church, that chapter represents a skillful and prudent compromise between two tendencies in modern Catholic theology, one of which would emphasize Mary's unique connection with Christ; the other,

her close connection with the Church and all the redeemed. Father Dulles writes,

> *To all who are troubled by what they see as an abandonment of tra-ditional practices of devotion to Mary, I warmly recommend this chapter, in which the Council fathers earnestly exhort theologians and preachers of the divine word that in treating the unique dignity of the Mother of God, they carefully avoid the falsity of exaggeration on the one hand, and the excess of narrow-mindedness on the other.33*

In an excellent article which is part of a series on "Prayer Beads in the World Religions," Father Frederick M. Jelly, O.P., wrote on "The Rosary" in an issue of *Worldmission*, a scholarly journal published by the Society for the Propagation of the Faith. He begins by showing that the rosary has indeed been emphatically approved by the Church. In his apostolic exhortation on devotion to Mary in 1974, Pope Paul VI called for a renewal of this pious practice. He quoted Pope Pius XII, who called the rosary "the compendium of the entire Gospel." He referred to previous popes who "recognized its suitability for fostering contemplative prayer ... and recalled its intrinsic effectiveness for promoting Christian life and apostolic commitment."34

It is enlightening to follow Father Jelly as he traces the historical background of the modern form of the rosary to its rich beginnings in the liturgy and its biblical sources in the Psalms and shows how the rosary beads were developed for the praying of the Hail Marys and Our Fathers through fifteen decades of ten beads each (or five decades in the shorter version) during which the person praying the rosary meditates on the five Joyful, the five Sorrowful, and the five Glorious "Mysteries" in the life of Mary and her Son. The modern form of the rosary was established by the Dominican pope, St. Pius V, in 1569.

The rosary is much more than a meaningless repetition of prayers, because the prayers are accompanied by contemplation of the fifteen (or five) "Mysteries." It is a summary of the principal events of salvation in the life of Mary and Jesus as well as a compendium of the Church's liturgical year of Advent, Christmas, Lent, Easter, and Pentecost.

In reciting the rosary "with a quiet rhythm and lingering pace," as Paul VI advised, Father Jelly suggests that the continuous recitation of the vocal prayers may be "likened to good background music, which, far from distracting us from our mental prayers, only deepens our gaze of loving faith and hope upon our redeemer."[35]

The Rosary as Remedy

Praying the rosary, I think, has been the most popular Marian devotion across the years. The beloved practice has been renewed at a deeper level in our time.

On October 7, 1571, a Christian fleet of two hundrd six galleys with eighty thousand men aboard, organized by Pope St. Pius V and commanded by Don John of Austria, decisively defeated a Turkish Moslem fleet of three hundred twenty galleys with one hundred twenty thousand soldiers and rowers, Christian captives of the Turks, in the Gulf of Lepanto in Greece. Once more the threat of Turkish Moslem control on Christian Europe was turned aside.

Gilbert Keith Chesterton began his superb ballad, *Lepanto*, with the Soldan of Byzantium smiling because

> *... the inmost sea of all the earth is shaken with his ships.*
> *They have dared the white republics up the capes of Italy ...*
> *And the Pope has cast his arms abroad for agony and loss,*
> *And called the kings of Christendom for swords about the Cross.*[36]

During the naval battle of Lepanto, the Rosary Confraternity of Rome was reciting the rosary for the victory of the Christian fleet at Rome's Dominican headquarters in the Church of Santa Maria Sopra Minerva. When news of the great victory came, they attributed it to the intercession of the Virgin. Pope Pius V, a Dominican devotee of the prayer, established the feast of Our Lady of Victory to commemorate the victory; later it was changed to the feast of Our Lady of the Rosary, which the Church still celebrates on October 7 each year.

When the rosary is prayed in funeral homes the night before the Rite of Christian Burial, the leader takes the occasion to complete the recitation of the "Mysteries" with the opening prayer of the feast of Our Lady of the Rosary. It is an apt summary of the role of Mary and Jesus in our lives:

Lord,
fill our hearts with your love,
and as you revealed to us by an angel
the coming of your Son as man,
so lead us through his suffering and death
to the glory of his resurrection ...

The popes of the twentieth century continued the custom of calling on Catholics to recite the rosary during October of each year for protection against evils threatening the world and the Church. None was more fervent in this than Pope Leo XIII, who was called "the Pope of the Rosary." In almost every year of his long reign (1878-1903) he wrote an encyclical (a letter to the Catholic world) describing the power of this popular Marian devotion.

In his best-known encyclical, *Rerum Novarum*, "On the Condition of the Working Man" in 1891, he suggested some remedies for problems for what he called the "social question" of that time — the relation of Capital and Labor.[37] His letter helped in the solution of some of the problems. He advocated labor and social legislation, but he also stressed an element which his commentators tend to overlook. This is the truth that "if human society is to be cured, only a return to Christian life and institutions will cure it." Again he wrote: "There are ills for which it is useless to seek a remedy in legislation, in threats of penalties to be incurred, or in any device of human prudence." He urged the people of God to see in the Eucharist the great remedy for social evils; it was instituted by Christ so that "by awakening charity toward God, it would promote mutual charity among men and women." For Pope Leo, it was as simple as that.

One of the most remarkable documents I have read about the work of the Mother of God in this world is Pope Leo's encyclical of 1892, *The Rosary and the Social Question*.[38] "We are convinced," he wrote, "that the rosary, devoutly used, is bound to benefit not only the individual but society at large." He noted three influences which seemed to him at the time to be the chief reasons for the downgrade movement of society: first, the distaste for a simple and laborious life; secondly,

repugnance to suffering of any kind; thirdly, forgetfulness of
the future life. As a remedy, Pope Leo suggested that meditation on the Joyful Mysteries would cure the first evil because
the Holy Family would provide "an all-perfect model of do-
mestic society." Who could fail to realize the value of suffering, he asked, after praying the Sorrowful Mysteries? And the
vision of heaven in the Glorious Mysteries can make us aware
"that this life is not our destination, but a stage in a journey."

Each in his own way, the popes of the twentieth century have
continued to call on Catholics to seek a remedy for their troubles in the Mother of God, who, as St. Augustine put it, "by
her love cooperated in the birth of the faithful in the Church."
Each in his own way, in reading the "signs of the times," recommended Our Lady of the Rosary as a remedy to restore the
tranquillity of peace to unquiet hearts and as a reminder that
we should pray to her to hasten the day when the world would
return to Jesus Christ, who, as the *Letter to the Hebrews*
phrases it, "is able at all times to save those who come to God
through him" (Heb. 7:25.)

"Mary Save Us" —
A Prayer Book From Prison

One of the most gripping of books I have read was not intended for publication. It is called *Mary Save Us*.

In early 1953, somewhere in a prison camp in northern Siberia, four young Lithuanian girls produced it. They wrote it by hand, bound it by hand, dedicated it to someone named Frances, and in a preface signed by someone named Adele explained how it came to be:

We send this prayer book to you in order that you may be able better to feel, think, and worship the Lord together with us. Lione made it, Vale drew it, Levute glued it together, and I wrote it.

Nobody knows anything more of the authors than that. Somehow the booklet was rescued from its hiding place under a straw mat and was smuggled back to Lithuania, from which the four girls had been torn away. It turned up later in West Germany and was given to the world. The Paulist Press published it in the early Sixties in English with a subtitle: "Prayers written by prisoners in northern Siberia."

It must have been one of the smallest books published in this century, for it measured only two by three inches, but it can teach a Catholic the most profound truths about the Faith.

Of the eventual fate of the four girls who put their prayers on scraps of paper we know nothing. Their young lives were swallowed up in the grim oblivion of the Soviet slave camp. Of their unquenchable spirit we know much — through the love and faith and hope that shines through their prayers, through the resignation and Christian fortitude with which they lived through the dragging prison days and nights, through their love of their motherland and of the Mother of Mercy at Girkalnis, their patroness, and for their love of all people, including the Russian prison guards, and this last is the chief mark of the Christian who really loves God.

On Ascension Thursday, 1961, Cardinal Frings of Cologne wrote a few lines of introduction for the German edition of the booklet. He took a line from the liturgy of the day: "Christ ascending on high has taken captivity captive," and went on to comment: "Those whom raw power held prisoner Christ made prisoners of his love. He drew them on their ascent into heaven, led them to heroic virtue, to eternal reward. By their example they will shake us; they renew our trust in heaven."

There are prayers for all occasions in the book. As they rose to another day of slavery, the four girls prayed a morning prayer:

A day of hard toil is dawning. I wish to glorify you by patience and respect for my fellow workers. Give us wisdom and strength to endure calmly all misunderstanding, contempt, and hatred.

In a place where no chalice could be lifted openly in the Mass, these girls united themselves with the entrance prayers of all the Masses celebrated in the world in prayers they composed for the Mass they could not attend:

Together with this tremendous sacrifice, accept my fatigue and suffering, my humiliations, tears of longing, hunger and cold, all my soul's infirmities, all my efforts for the freedom of my motherland.

They composed a Way of the Cross. This is how they prayed at the twelfth station in their meditation on the death of Christ:

"I have nothing in this world," says Christ. The spirit of the world is pride and self-love, vainglory, greed, and jealousy ... Savior, help me to die to the spirit of this world and feel joy in loving humbly and generously, purely and prayerfully.

New books on prayer are published every year for the many who want to pray more meaningfully. The Prayer Book from Prison which Adele, Lione, Vale, and Levute called *Mary Save Us* is, I think, among the most powerful of them all. It gives us a solution to the persistent problem of pain and suffering. It proves again the Pauline principle that if we have died with Christ, we shall also live with Christ.

Marian Shrines

Our Lady of Lourdes

I suspect that few people could give the answer to the question: "What is the second largest Catholic church in the world after St. Peter's basilica in Rome?" I ran across the answer in the 1982 *Catholic Almanac.* The answer is "the underground Church of St. Pius X at Lourdes," which was consecrated on March 25, 1958, during the hundredth anniversary of the apparitions of the Blessed Virgin Mary to 14-year-old Bernadette Soubirous. Eighteen times between February and July in the grotto of Massabielle near the small town of Lourdes in southern France Mary appeared and told her at the end that "I am the Immaculate Conception." Lourdes is now one of the most popular Marian shrines in the world.

A hundred years after Mary revealed herself to Bernadette in the grotto on the Gave de Pau river in the village at the foot of the Pyrenees, Pope Pius XII wrote an encyclical called *The Lourdes Pilgrimage* to invite people all over the world to come to Lourdes to celebrate the centennial of the appearances of Mary to Bernadette in 1858.[39] He wrote a special invitation to the sick and the poor:

> *Go to her, you who are crushed by material misery, defenseless against the hardships of life and the indifference of others ... Go to her, beloved invalids and infirm, you who are truly welcomed and honored at Lourdes as the suffering members of our Lord. Go to her and receive peace of heart and strength for your daily duty, the joy of sacrifice offered.*

I was one of six million pilgrims who went to Lourdes in 1958 in response to the pope's invitation. I saw thousands of the sick in wheelchairs in the daily procession of the sick get blessed by the host in a golden monstrance. I read some of the authenticated reports of miraculous cures of the Medical Bureau. I marched through the dusk with thousands of pilgrims with

lighted candles who sang the Lourdes Hymn in a dozen different languages. I felt the overwhelming presence of the Lady
who asked the people of the world through Bernadette to do
penance and offer their sufferings in union with the sufferings
of her Son. I saw — and believed that God had indeed intervened directly to give a message through the Lady who called
herself the Immaculate Conception and spoke to a fourteen-
year-old girl in that grotto along the River Gave.

On May 15, 1981, another pope spoke on tape in a weak and
shaky voice from his hospital bed in Rome to the more than
one hundred fifty thousand people in the piazza of St. Peter's
where he had been shot four days before. The suffering Pope
John Paul II expressed himself especially, he said, to all who
were sick:

> *I, now sick as they are, come with a word of comfort and hope. I
> am happy in the suffering I am going through for you and complete in
> my own flesh the suffering of that which may be lacking in the suffer-
> ing of Christ toward his Body, the Church. Suffering accepted in un-
> ion with the suffering Christ has an unequaled usefulness in bringing
> about God's design for salvation.*[40]

St. Bernadette Soubirous, who was canonized in 1933, would
have understood completely what John Paul was saying that afternoon. She was born on January 7, 1844, at Lourdes, of a
very Christian family. Her parents were millers. The family
had fallen on hard times but maintained its dignity and an atmosphere of love and understanding. In 1858 they moved into
the "Jail," an abandoned municipal prison put at their disposal by a kindly cousin. Bernadette was sickly; she had had
cholera and was asthmatic. She was often wracked with pain
because of the asthma she endured in the cold and dank prison in which the family Soubirous was forced to live during her
childhood. In her life as a nun away from Lourdes in her later
years she was filled with the excruciating pain of tuberculosis of
the bone. Mary at Lourdes had asked her for penitence for the
sins of the world. When she lay sick in bed one day, she told
another Sister that she was working at her "calling." "And what
is that?" the Sister asked. "Being ill," replied Bernadette.

To the physical pain and suffering was added the psycho-
logical torment caused by publicity hounds who wanted to see

the famed visionary of Lourdes. Church authorities were reserved at first in their opinions of the young girl. Although she herself never showed any emotional extravagances, there was an epidemic of false visionaries in the district. She refused the many offers of the money visitors offered to her and always displayed a heroic patience in her sufferings.

Two years after the apparitions of 1858, she left her beloved Lourdes and the grotto on the Massabielle to enter the convent of the Sisters of Notre Dame at Nevers and was separated from her family. She never left the convent and had no part in the dedication of the new basilica at Lourdes in 1876. It was by her own choice that she did not return, but the deprivation cost her much. From her convent cell she spoke a poignant lament, "Oh! If only I could be there without being seen." And there was the stuffy nun at the convent who sneered at her as "a peasant who knows nothing" and wondered haughtily why the Blessed Mother did not choose to appear to some woman of the upper classes. She could take consolation from the words of the Blessed Virgin when she gave her a personal message during the first apparition, "Do me the favor of coming here for fifteen days; I do not promise to make you happy in this life but in the next."

Bernadette was thirty-five years old when she died in 1879. She was canonized by Pope Pius XI in 1933, not because of the visions of the Lady, but because of the sheer saintliness of her acceptance of the Cross.

Surely, this self-effacing young woman was the most unassuming celebrity of the nineteenth century, but she can teach us how to live in Christ. In 1923, as he published a "decree on the heroism of her virtues," Pius XI summed up her life: "Bernadette was faithful to her mission; she was humble in her glory; she was strong when she was put to the test."

I can think of no better formula for a successful life.

The Real Miracle of Lourdes

A legless girl named Nancy took a plane to Lourdes in the mid-fifties. Her mother wrote Nancy's story in a 1955 book, *Red Shoes for Nancy*. As the cameras clicked at the airport in New York, the reporters asked Nancy, "Are you hoping for a miracle at Lourdes?" "No," she said with a smile, "I'm not even going to pray for a cure," she replied. "Our Lady will do what is best for everybody, not just what is best for me."[41] I am reminded of the conclusion of an article in an encyclopedia. After an account of the rigorous medical examination of alleged cures at the Grotto of the Massabielle at the famous Marian shrine, the conclusion was that "the most widely attested phenomenon, however, is the increase of faith, love, and patience experienced by the pilgrims to Lourdes."

The mention of miracles at Lourdes has been enough to set some people fuming. In the past, some scientists have ridiculed the claim that God has intervened in history in 1858 or even that he can so intervene. That attitude, frankly, is quite old-fashioned today. To refuse to consider any evidence for the miracles claimed at Lourdes is a relic of the nineteenth century, when an outmoded philosophy called positivism insisted that no knowledge is possible unless it comes through the "scientific method."

Scientists today are not so sure that they can give the final answers to all questions about the universe. Benedictine Father Stanley Jaki, who received a Ph.D. in physics from Fordham in 1957 under the guidance of Nobel-laureate Victor Hess, the discoverer of cosmic rays, is one such scientist. He was awarded the prestigious Templeton Prize for Progress in Religion in 1987, as the citation read, to honor "the original pioneering ways" Jaki has "advanced the knowledge and love of God." In his first book, *The Relevance of Physics,* published by the University of Chicago Press in 1966, one interviewer wrote, "he showed in exact detail the limitations of the method of exact science within physics and within the interaction of physics with biology, philosophy, ethics, theology, and with culture in general ... the book won high praise and is considered by many critics to be 'must reading' for all scientists and science students."[42]

The doctors who study the miracles of Lourdes (and all doctors, no matter what their attitude toward religion, are welcome to study them) are not superstitious fools who are quick to call every remarkable recovery a miracle. After rigorous examination of alleged cures, they have judged that thousands of them are unexplainable on natural grounds, but their slightest doubts have been sufficient to rule out thousands more.

The Church itself is harder to convince than doctors. Somewhere I read that between 1882, when the Bureau of Medical Verification was founded at Lourdes (the International Medical Commission of Lourdes, located in Paris, re-examines the Bureau's findings), and 1956, the Church has recognized only forty-nine cures as completely proved miracles.

One might say that the trouble with those scientists who laugh at Lourdes is that they are not real scientists. The scientific method demands first of all that an investigation should begin without any pre-conceived notions about the final results of the investigation; it requires an open mind. Those who dogmatize about the "folly" of dogma do so because they have made up their minds beforehand never to accept any explanation which does not fit into their narrow scientific categories. They will not admit that the supernatural, on occasion and at the will of nature's God, can touch the world of nature because the implicit premise of all their arguments is the pre-conceived idea that there can be no supernatural. Such scientists would refuse to look at the evidence which has piled up in the Lourdes Medical Bureau. Their fallacy of the unproved assumption is one of the oldest errors in logic.

Two well-known novels have been written about Lourdes. One was Emile Zola's *Lourdes*,[43] which the head of the Medical Bureau at Lourdes proclaimed a "complete fabrication." Zola had said that he did not believe in miracles and that if he saw all the sick at Lourdes get well in a moment, he would still

not believe. The other Lourdes novel was Franz Werfel's rever-
ent and moving *The Song of Bernadette,* which Hollywood
made into a popular movie.

Franz Werfel was a Jew. In late June, 1940, he and his wife
were in southern France fleeing for their lives from the Nazis,
who had singled him out because of Franz Werfel's opposition
to them. They took refuge in Lourdes, where he learned the
story of Bernadette. One day, he wrote in the preface to his
novel, "if I escaped from this desperate situation and reached
the saving shores of America, I would sing, if I could, the Song
of Bernadette."[44]

At the start of the movie based on Werfel's novel, there
were a few lines on the screen: "To those who do not believe,
no explanation is possible; to those who believe, no explanation is necessary."

Our Lady of Guadalupe

Somewhere, I recall, Gilbert Keith Chesterton wrote a beautiful paragraph about the Virgin Mary as "The Lady of a Thousand Names." He was thinking of the hundreds of titles given her in shrines, litanies, and churches around the Catholic world.

There is one American shrine dear to the hearts of the people of Mexico especially, and to those of Latin America in general, the Shrine of Our Lady of Guadalupe. Her feast is celebrated in the United States as well, on December 12, and not only by the rapidly increasing Hispanic population in this country. We remember the day she came to Mexico through a humble peasant named Juan Diego and through him to Archbishop Zumarraga of Mexico City. In 1754 the pope named Our Lady of Guadalupe patroness of Mexico; another pope crowned her image and declared her Our Lady of America, the Queen and Patroness of all of Latin America. Pope Pius XI extended her reign to all the Americas. The Virgin of Guadalupe is, quite simply, Our Lady of America.

It all began on a hill named Tepeyac, twelve miles from the center of Mexico City, in 1531.

Mexico became a colony of Spain when Hernando Cortez started the march from Vera Cruz on the eastern coast to the Aztec capital in 1519. An image of Mary was blazoned on his standard. (When the revolution of 1810 freed Mexico from the control of Spain, the banner under which Father Manuel Hidalgo rallied the revolutionaries was an image of Our Lady of Guadalupe.)

The priests who came with Cortez had already baptized many converts, among them a 57-year-old Indian named Juan Diego. One Saturday morning — December 12, 1531 — Juan was trudging to the Mass in honor of the Mother of God which the Franciscan priests celebrated each Saturday. At dawn he came to the little hill called Tepeyac. Suddenly, as he described it later, the morning was full of music, celestial, "like a choir of birds," he said. Juan looked up and saw a bright white cloud with a rainbow around it. Instead of fear, he felt a strange happiness steal over him. He heard a woman call his name; the voice was soft and low. She called him *pequeñito* — "my little one" — and asked him to have a church built on the spot of the apparition. She told him she was the Virgin Mary, the Mother of God; she wanted to help the poor Indians so that they could have a place to come to her. She told him to go to the Archbishop, Juan de Zumarraga, and tell him about her request.

Juan Diego hurried to the archbishop's house. He had to wait a while to get in, and the archbishop did not give him much consolation when he told his story; he did not seem to believe it. It was a sad Juan Diego who plodded the long way home that evening. He came again to the place where he had seen the Lady, the hill called Tepeyac, now called Guadalupe. Once more Mary appeared. Juan apologized. Mary spoke a second message, "Go to the archbishop again," she said in his own language. "Tell him to build a church to me since the one who sends you is the Mother of God."

Once more Juan Diego went to the archbishop, who was more impressed this time. He told Juan to bring a sign from the Lady to prove the truth of his statement. Again the Lady appeared at Tepeyac; Juan said that the archbishop wanted proof. She asked him to come back the next day, when she would give him the sign.

The next day, however, Juan's uncle was sick, and he stayed home to care for him. The next time he went to church, he took a different road; he was ashamed he had missed the meeting he had promised. The Lady appeared on the other road; she told him to go to Tepeyac and gather the roses he would find there in his rough woven cloak and take them to the archbishop. Juan found the roses and went once more to Archbishop Zumarraga. He unfolded his cloak — and the archbishop fell to his knees. Again Juan was puzzled. He did not know that instead of the miraculous roses there was an image of the Lady on his cloak.

That image on the *tilma*, the cloak, holds the place of honor today in the new basilica of Guadalupe, and it is reproduced by the millions in pictures around the world. The Mexicans call the Lady *La Moreñita* — the "little brown one." Mary had appeared and left her image as a peasant Indian woman.

Almost anywhere you go in the Americas today, you will find it. I have seen it in a taxicab in Mexico City; the driver said he did not go to church but that he was certainly a *guadalupano*. I have seen the peasants of Mexico come by the thousands, some perched perilously on the top of overcrowded busses; I have seen many of them crawling on their knees a half mile over rough pavement at the old basilica of Guadalupe to reach the Lady's image. Of the thousand names of Mary, Americans should put Our Lady of Guadalupe toward the head of the list. She is the patroness of all America.

Our Lady of Chartres

Long ago I read a classic study of medieval Catholic culture which Henry Adams wrote under the title of two of its great shrines, *Mont St. Michel and Chartres.*[45] A fascinating book, it described the art and culture of two shrines so vividly that there was born in me the desire to visit them some day. My dreams came true in 1982, when I climbed the many steps to the abbey on top of Mont St. Michel, and in 1983 when on Holy Saturday I saw the two great towers of the Cathedral of Notre-Dame de Chartres as I rode in a car with some friends toward the town of Chartres on a cold and rainy day.

Notre-Dame de Chartres is one of the supreme monuments of Gothic architecture and embodies in its different sections a history of this style from the twelfth through the sixteenth century.

Chartres, a town of some thirty thousand people on the Eure River, is forty-eight miles southwest of Paris. Its Cathedral of Notre-Dame is an immense edifice that has been called "the apogee of Gothic architecture in Ile-de-France." Two crypts of the ninth and twelfth centuries testify to the existence of earlier structures. Its facade was begun about 1135; its north tower has a high flamboyant spire of the early sixteenth century. The *Encyclopedia of Art* from which I take these details has a sentence baldly stating that "Reconstruction of the entire nave began in 1194 and was completed in 1220."[46]

Behind that sentence is one of the most compelling reasons why the Middle Ages are called "The Age of Faith."

On June 20 and 21, 1194, a huge conflagration consumed much of Chartres, including the Episcopal Palace and the eleventh-century Cathedral. The destruction excited a whole series of dramatic reactions culminating in the construction of the most famous medieval edifice in Europe. A master builder, whose name is unknown, designed and supervised the erection of a new type of Gothic cathedral within the short span of 26 years.

In his book, *Monastery and Cathedral in France,* Whitney Stoddard describes what happened after the fire of 1194 and the reconstruction of the Cathedral within 26 years:

> *By 1220 the vaults, which soar 116 feet above the pavement through the 422-foot length of the cathedral, were completed. This prodigious achievement was the result of an extraordinary outburst of enthusiasm and energy difficult to explain in twentieth-century terms, since by habit we distinguish between religious fervor, economic interest, community pride, and political enterprise. The late twelfth-century man made no such distinction between religious and worldly concerns, and the creative explosion that built Chartres Cathedral took its energies from all aspects of Medieval life.*[47]

One reason for this amazing rebuilding of the Cathedral in such a short time was that Chartres was a center of the cult of the Virgin Mary; it was thought to have in its cathedral the Sacred Tunic worn by Mary at the time of the birth of Christ. This holy relic was considered a protector of the people of the town and for them the tunic was a symbol of the Virgin's palace on earth. Another reason was that the Chapter of Notre-Dame voted to commit most of its enormous revenues to the construction. Contributions and generous donations flowed in from wealthy townspeople and elsewhere, even from outside France because of the fame of the Sacred Tunic. Stoddard explains, "The religious and economic sides of medieval life are interlocked. Without the cathedral as its center of focus, not only the religious but also the economic life of Chartres was threatened with meaninglessness."[48]

There was another enormous contribution to the rebuilding of Chartres which Henry Adams beautifully describes as "The Cult of the Carts," an act of devotion to the Virgin that is difficult to equal in history. People of noble birth and humble peasants flocked to Chartres from as far away as Normandy, according to the old chronicles, to give their Virgin Queen a place of refuge; the cathedral had to be rebuilt!

Rich and poor came to pull the carts with stone from quarries some distance from Chartres. It was a spontaneous and continuing migration. Pilgrims crowded the roads, both men

and women, dragging huge tree trunks and great beams behind them. They brought the cripples and the sick with them;
their role was to pray while the others worked. A city of tents
sprang up around Chartres. The huge crowds of builders of all
social conditions — knights, ladies, peasants, clerics, trades-
men — set aside their rank and calling to submit to the rigorous self-discipline for the honor of working on the Palace of
the Virgin. One chronicler reported that the enterprise was so
sacred that no one dared touch the tools unless he or she had
first gone to confession and reconciled themselves with their
enemies.

Chartres is no less famous for its sculpture and stained glass
than for its architecture. Once the builders finished the framework and the walls of the soaring body of the cathedral, the
glass-makers and the sculptors took over. Father Alfred
McBride, in *The Story of the Church* summarized their work:

> *The glass-makers used colored glass in order to soften the light,*
> *present a jeweled effect, and offer to the people who came to view*
> *them Bible stories in living color. They were wildly successful, so*
> *much so that we are unable to match the extraordinary coloring they*
> *achieved ... The sculptors brought life to stone, creating an army of*
> *saints, kings, guildsmen, angels, demons, witches, and animals.*
> *Even the rainspouts on the roof shared in the world of beauty formed*
> *by the sculptors.*[49]

When the Cathedral was built, there was no printing press.
Both rich and poor had to learn the fundamentals of their
Faith in the rich symbols which the sculptors put into the por-
tals and the artists and painters put into their stained glass windows and walls. They made the cathedral of Chartres into a
"Bible in stone" which every one, both rich and poor, could
read.

The "Palace of Our Lady," as the people called it, is a
triumph of art — and of faith.

Our Lady of Czestochowa

On October 7, 1979, Pope John Paul II prayed to Mary, the patroness of the United States, in a crowded National Shrine of the Immaculate Conception at Washington. "This shrine," he said,

> *speaks with the voice of all the sons and daughters of America who have come here from the various countries of the Old World. When they came, they brought with them in their hearts the same love for the Mother of God that was a characteristic of their ancestors and of themselves in their native lands ... They came together from different backgrounds of history and tradition around the heart of a Mother they all have in common.*[50]

In the national shrine at Washington there are different chapels sponsored by different ethnic groups; these are adorned with the images of the Madonna who is the national patroness of their own homelands. I am sure John Paul was thinking especially of the "Black Madonna," Our Lady of Czestochowa, which Polish-Americans have enshrined in a chapel in the Marian shrine at the nation's capital. She has been a powerful unifying force in the pope's homeland.

In 1982 Poland celebrated the six-hundredth anniversary of the arrival in that country of the venerated image of the Black Madonna, which is enshrined in the basilica at Jasna Gora ("hill of light") above Czestochowa. This most renowned shrine of Mary in central Europe is a famous place of pilgrimage. Its famed icon of the "Black Virgin" (blackened by centuries of smoky candles and restored to its original colors in 1925) is the central symbol of Polish spirituality and patriotism. It was brought to Czestochowa in 1382 by Prince Ladislaus Opolszyk from his home in the Ukraine; he built a chapel and monastery for it on the hill called Jasna Gora.

Legend has it the icon was painted by St. Luke on a wooden tablet made for the Holy Family by St. Joseph. (Several icons of the Virgin have been attributed to Luke!) This tradition holds it was brought to Constantinople from Jerusalem and given to a Princess Anna; it was later brought to the Ukraine, from which it came to Jasna Gora. The icon is probably of ninth-century Greek or Greek-Italian origin. There are three cuts on the Virgin's right cheek which are said to come from an attack by robbers in 1430. After the monastery on Jasna Gora withstood a siege by anti-papal Swedes, Our Lady of Czestochowa was proclaimed Queen of Poland and has been a rallying point for Polish nationalism and Catholicism ever since.

At the beginning of the twentieth century, Henryk Sienkiewicz, author of *Quo Vadis* and Nobel prize winner for literature in 1905, wrote a fascinating trilogy of historical novels emphasizing the religious character of the wars between Poles and Russian Cossacks and Swedes to dramatize the miraculous defeat of the Swedes at the shrine of Our Lady of Czestochowa. It was in them that I learned of the power of the Black Madonna in the history of Poland, so often torn by war and rapine. She is on the banners of Polish Catholics today as they protest the Communist occupation of their country. It is Our Lady of Czestochowa who helps sustain the Polish people today in their battle against an atheism which tries to crush that sustaining devotion which they have to the Mother of God.

In 1977, three million pilgrims flocked to her shrine. In 1978, thirty thousand Poles walked 130 miles from Warsaw to Czestochowa for the feast day of the Assumption; Cardinal Karol Woytila of Cracow was asked about the significance of this rather incredible pilgrimage. He answered, "It is a pilgrimage which does not expect miracles...The significance goes beyond faith and religion. Here the people find, confirm, and celebrate their national unity, which gives them strength and hope." A few months later Cardinal Karol Woytila became Pope John Paul II. He brought with him his coat of arms with its motto that is a pledge of devotion to Mary the Mother: *Totus tuus*—"Totally yours." The coat of arms is dominated by an unusual cross and under its vertical area is a large and majestic M-M for Mary. John Paul never fails to pray a special prayer to Mary in the countries he visits.

The Virgin of the Pillar

In 1932 a London newspaper sent Gilbert Keith Chesterton, a superb journalist, to report on the thirty-first international Eucharistic Congress in Dublin. The result was a short book called *Christendom in Dublin*. I remember one stirring passage which that tribute to the Eucharist evoked in him:

> *Dublin is full of flags, and London is full of stories about flags. And it will be very difficult to explain to the Londoners that Dublin, which is full of flags, is not thinking about flags at all.*
>
> *Englishmen understand men rallying around a flag. They will not understand so easily that these Irishmen, during these seven days, were not rallying around a flag. It was the flags that did the rallying; they were rallying around something else.*[51]

This is not about Christ in the Eucharist. It is about the mother of Christ, the Lady of a Thousand Names, as Chesterton called her, and the flags also flutter around a thousand shrines to which pilgrims come to do her homage — and pray to her. At journey's end they find her image painted or sculpted in a thousand different images. At the center of the shrines, whether simple or grandiose, the pilgrims become suppliants to the Refuge of Sinners and the Hope of the Sick and the Lady of Perpetual Help.

There is one shrine at Saragossa in northeastern Spain where her statue stands on a pillar and is loved and revered as The Virgin of the Pillar. The people celebrated her nineteen hundredth anniversary in 1940, just after the Civil War had torn the country apart.

At another famous shrine in northwestern Spain Mary plays an indirect role. It is the grand basilica of Santiago de Compostela, where, according to the pious legend, St. James the Apostle is buried. Spanish piety alleges that James disembarked in a port on the eastern coast of Spain to bring the good news of the Resurrection to that province of the Roman empire. Then, the story goes, when he was discouraged at his lack of success, Mary the Mother appeared to him at the river Ebro to encourage him. At the place where Mary appeared stands the statue of the Virgin of the Pillar in the cathedral of that city. The legend also claims that she left a small statue with him. The angels who accompanied the Lady placed it on the same pillar where the Spaniards revere her today as the official patroness of Spain.

What happened during the Holy Year of 1940 at Saragossa makes for fascinating reading. Pilgrims kept coming to the Pillar all through the year. Priests would tell of other priests and seminarians, now known as martyrs for the Faith, who were killed by the Communists in the Civil War of the late Thirties, along with religious sisters and brothers and lay people — thousands of martyrs who died for their religious beliefs. Toward the end of the year the Virgin of the Pillar was enthroned in the Bank of Spain in Madrid; the governor of the Bank spoke of the need "for moral values to be placed above material interests."

In the last days of August in that centennial year, the Catholic youth of Spain clogged the roads to Saragossa. Twenty thousand of them prayed before the Pillar and touched the feet of Our Lady; then they swore a solemn oath to defend the dogmas of the Immaculate Conception and the Assumption of Mary. On August 30, a surging army of young men and women marched into the cathedral to offer the Virgin a precious new mantle inscribed with the names of martyred Catholic youths.

Then there was a touch of poetry. The young pilgrims brought their own statues of Our Lady with them from the many cities in which the Lady of a Thousand Names had other shrines to honor her. The visiting Madonnas were paraded to the pillar and the crowds cheered at each of her appearances.

Barcelona brought the famed Black Virgin from Montserrat, where St. Ignatius had dreamed the dream which became his Company of Jesus. Calahorra carried its beloved Virgin of Valvanera. Thousands from Madrid accompanied their Virgin of the Dove and the standards of Our Lady of Sorrows. Toledo unfurled its flags for the Lady and shouted in the streets for Spain's own Lady of Guadalupe. With the young people of

Valencia came *la Virgen de los Desamparados,* the Virgin of the Forsaken.

They were all there — the *Virgen del Coro* from San Sebastian, the *Virgen del Transito* with the pilgrimage from Zamora. Every great city and some of the tiny hamlets sang in sacred symbolism around the Virgin standing on the Pillar.

Eight years before that day the flags of the world had rallied around an altar in Dublin, statues came in procession to greet their sister on the Pillar. And always in the background I hear the thunder of the Church as it shouts its Credo that Jesus was born of the Virgin Mary and died for all in the Paschal Mystery — the Good News which Spaniards first preached in the New World.

Our Land and Our Lady

In 1846, nine years before the definition of the dogma of the Immaculate Conception of Mary by Pope Pius IX, the Sixth Provincial Council of the American bishops at Baltimore asked the pope for permission to choose the Mother of God as the patroness of our country under that title. It was a courageous thing to do. Not many years before, there had been rioting against Catholics along the eastern coast and "Native Americans" were claiming that only Protestants could be good Americans. They charged, among other things, that Catholics were "Marialoters" who worshipped the Blessed Virgin Mary.

To choose Mary as the patroness of the United States was a very appropriate thing to do. She has been part of American history from its beginnings. Long before the Pilgrims spread the first Thanksgiving feast, the Spanish missions of Mexico and the Southwest were named Santa Maria and "Concepcion" along all the mission trails of Latin America and New Mexico.

Daniel Sargent once wrote a beautiful book about the Mother of God and called it *Our Land and Our Lady*. It begins this way: "In our beginning it was the *Santa Maria* that sailed toward our shores — Columbus's *Santa Maria,* Queen Isabella's *Santa Maria*, Castile's *Santa Maria*, Christendom's *Santa Maria* — She has left a furrow in the ocean that pointed to our country as an arrow points to its mark. The furrow never closed."[52]

In the Grande Galeria of Madrid once hung a tapestry showing the Virgin's mantle protecting Spain's seafarers. Christopher Columbus kneels below Mary's left hand. The caravel, the *Santa Maria*, in which he began the Age of Discovery and Exploration of the Americas (1492-1602) is in the center foreground. There is a Latin inscription which reads: "With the most ardent Queen of the Sea, the vigorous sailors of Spain have endured the dangers of winds and waves," and a prayer, "Our Lady, in perils of the sea, be a protection to us."

It was in the spirit of the prayer that Christopher Columbus called his sailors in the three small caravels on that perilous voyage of 1492 around his flagship, the *Santa Maria*, each evening and led them in the *Salve Regina*, the "Hail, Holy Queen."

The Spanish explorers who followed the furrows first plowed through the seas by Columbus invoked in prayer "Stella Maris" — Star of the Sea, pleading for Mary's protection in their times of confusion and doubt and fear of the unknown. Mingled with the wash of the waves and the creaking of the sails one could hear sailors singing:

> Hail, thou Star of ocean,
>> Portal of the sky!
> Ever-Virgin
>> Of the Lord Most High!

In her beautiful book, *Mary U.S.A.*, Anna Wirtz Domas summed up the devotion of the Spanish and French captains and conquistadors:

Explorers coming to the shores of the vast continent of America named landfalls, ports, and rivers with Marian titles and feast days. Their gratitude for safe voyage was expressed in many ways. Columbus returned in triumph to Spain, then, barefooted and in penitential garb, brought his offerings to the Church of Our Lady of Guadalupe; DeSoto made provision in his will for a Marian chapel; Jacques Cartier vowed a pilgrimage to her shrine; Cortez tumbled heathen idols to the ground, replacing them with images of Mary; Champlain's last will and testament began, I nominate the Virgin Mary my heir.[53]

In his masterful geographical and nautical history, *The European Discovery of America*, Samuel Eliot Morrison wrote "that from the decks of ships traveling the two great oceans and exploring the distant verges of the earth, prayers arose like clouds of incense to the Holy Trinity and to Mary, the Queen of the Sea.[54]

We know the Spanish story of conquest. Spain occupied much of the United States before the English drove them back, and everywhere *La Conquistadora*, the "Lady Who Conquers," went with them. We still can recite the Marian litany along the California coast from San Diego to Carmel to Mission Dolores in San Francisco and back again to the city they called the Queen of All Angels. In 1531 Our Lady spoke to Juan Diego at Guadalupe in Mexico City, long before the Puritans struggled for a foothold on that rocky New England shore.

The French soon followed with Our Lady — *Notre Dame*. In 1638 King Louis XIII consecrated his person and his empire to Our Lady. Part of his empire was New France, across the Atlantic. From Quebec and Montreal the "blackrobes" fanned out across the North and upper Midwest, and everywhere *Notre Dame* went with them to be the patroness of their missions. Father Marquette and Joliet discovered the Mississippi, the "Great River," and named it for the Immaculate Conception.

Even the English brought Mary to America. After George Calvert, first baron of Baltimore, decided to establish a Catholic colony in America, Father Andrew White, S. J., joined the expedition sent in 1633 on the ships the *Ark* and the *Dove*. They landed at St. Clement's Island on May 25, 1634, where Father White celebrated Mass for the first time in Maryland. This state, named by Lord Calvert to honor the British queen, was the first state to grant religious freedom. But within fifty years the Protestants had driven the Catholics back, and the lights of religious freedom were darkened in Maryland. When Baltimore's — and America's first — Catholic bishop, John Carroll, died in 1815, Our Lady's patronage had ceased to be acknowledged save by a humble few. Catholic Marylanders had no sooner founded their colony than they were declared outlaws in it.

Then came the hundred-year flood of Catholic immigrants. The Virgin reasserted her claims to her country and soon her name was everywhere. Germans brought Our Lady of Altötting; Irish brought Our Lady of Knock; Poles, Our Lady of Czestochowa; Italians, Our Lady of Loretto; and in 1531 the Lady came herself to Mexico to a man named Juan Diego. The name of Mary was given to the first churches in many cities; her image looked down from thousands of classrooms in Catholic schools. In 1846 Rome made her patroness of the United States under her title of the Immaculate Conception.

Giovanni da Verrazano gave the name of *La Nunciata* — the Annuntiation — to a place on the Outer Banks of North Carolina in 1524. The Kennebec River in Maine was first called *Rio de Buena Madre* — River of the Good Mother. Point Concepcion in California still recalls the Immaculate Conception. In Hawikuh, New Mexico, there was a Church of the Most Pure Conception.

And so it went as the Spanish, French, Italian, and other explorers dotted the landscape of the United States with the thousand names of Mary from the River of the Good Mother in Maine to the second largest city of the country in California, which was first called "Our Lady of the Angels, the City of our Queen Mother Mary" — now reduced to Los Angeles.

Our Lady of Santa Fe

If we ask, "Who is the favorite Madonna among the Hispanic people of the United States?" the answer is, of course, Our Lady of Guadalupe. Yet another Marian shrine in the Southwest, much less known, is also part of the history of Spanish exploration and settlement of this country. The pilgrims come to it, too, for it enshrines a small statue of Mary which the people of New Mexico call *La Conquistadora* — the Spanish word for "She who Conquers." This statue usually stands near the altar of the Cathedral of St. Francis in Santa Fe, the capital of New Mexico. The cathedral itself is a place of pilgrimage and is well known to the readers of Willa Cather's novel, *Death Comes for the Archbishop*, about which a critic wrote, "Of all the distinguished novels written by Willa Cather, none has brought her greater prestige or a wider circle of readers than *Death Comes for the Archbishop*."

The tomb of Archbishop Jean Baptiste Lamy, the first Archbishop of Santa Fe, is in the cathedral. The inspiration for the fictional Father Latour in the story of the cathedral in Willa Cather's novel has its roots in the life of Archbishop Lamy. The novel begins this way: "One summer evening in the year 1848, three Cardinals and a missionary Bishop from America were dining together in a villa in the Sabine hills, overlooking Rome." It ends with the death of Archbishop Lamy: "When the Cathedral bell tolled just after dark, the Mexican population fell upon their knees, and all American Catholics as well. Many others who did not kneel prayed in their hearts. Eusebius and the Tesuque boys went quietly away to tell their people, and the next morning the old Archbishop lay before the high altar in the church he had built."[55]

Willa Cather's gripping novel is, in part, the story of Father Latour's — and Archbishop Lamy's — dream of building the

Cathedral against the steep carnelian hills of Santa Fe, the "Royal City of the Holy Faith," as the Spanish settlers called it, and the story of how the Archbishop brought his dream into reality. The tomb of the Archbishop is in the Cathedral. *La Conquistadora* is also there nearby. I want to tell the story of "She Who Conquers" who stands next to his tomb.

La Conquistadora is a small statue of the Virgin. She is robed richly now, but she started her reign as a simple wooden image in Spain. She came to New Mexico more than three hundred years ago with the first Spanish settlers of New Mexico. Fray Alonso da Benavides, a Franciscan missionary, brought to the parish church of Our Lady of the Assumption a statue of the Assumption which gained lasting fame as *La Conquistadora*, the Queen of the Kingdom of New Mexico and the Villa of Santa Fe. This parish Church of the Assumption, later named the Cathedral of St. Francis, was the first Marian shrine in the United States.

The ruling medicine men of the Indians opposed the Spanish colonists and in 1680 the great Indian Pueblo revolt produced twenty-one Franciscan martyrs in a single day. Santa Fe was sacked. The Church of Our Lady's Assumption was destroyed completely. The Spanish colonists fought their way out and fled south to El Paso, then called Guadalupe del Paso. They remained exiled for thirteen years until late in December, 1693, when they returned under Diego DeVargas to Santa Fe. They had saved *La Conquistadora* from the destruction and ruins; in the DeVargas reconquest they brought the statue back with them in a wagon that jolted across the arroyos. As DeVargas approached Santa Fe, he vowed that if he would retake the city, he would carry the statue once a year around the plaza in Santa Fe in a procession. The Spanish won the victory without bloodshed. The Lady of the Conquest still ruled over Santa Fe.

In his biography, *Lamy of Santa Fe,* Paul Horgan tells a charming story about the tiny statue in painted gesso and wood, which was the most venerable sacred object in the city. She was carried every year in the May procession and the men who carried her often stopped at small shrines set up before houses or shops whose owners wanted to have the statue pause and bless them. One year in the Corpus Christi procession the

marchers paused before the house of Willi Spiegelberg to rest
for a moment. They set the decorated litter on the ground.
The youngest Spiegelberg child saw the tiny Madonna and,
unobserved, took the statue and raced home with her new
"doll." Not till they came to the cathedral did the bearers find
that Our Lady was not with them; there was a mixture of aston-
ishment and fear. The mystery was solved that night when Flo-
ra Spiegelberg, the Jewish mother, found it tucked in her
daughter's bed. She raced to the Archbishop Lamy's house,
full of apologies. He laughed and asked her to have some wine
with him (she was an old friend). The little girl felt robbed of
her doll. Many months later, "a beautifully dressed wax doll"
came from Paris, with a note from the Archbishop to the girl
to explain that it was "to replace the little Madonna."[56]

I spent the summer of 1954 as an assistant priest in the old
Guadalupe parish in Santa Fe not far from the cathedral and
experienced at first hand the simple but deep piety of the Hispanic people of the city. One striking aspect of their religious
lives was their simple familiarity with the saints, their easy acceptance of the doctrine of the Communion of Saints. Their
statues in the old sanctuaries mean something. Every year on
the patronal feasts of the parishes there is *fiesta*; it is the big-
gest celebration of the year.

For the first time in hundreds of years *La Conquistadora* was
taken from Santa Fe to make a triumphant tour of all the
churches in the archdiocese in 1954, the Marian Year declared by Pope Pius XII to celebrate the centennial of the definition of the dogma of the Immaculate Conception. Some of
the older folk did not like to see her leave the city at first, but
they felt better when they heard of the love and devotion that
their "Lady of Conquest" inspired throughout New Mexico.

Mary and the Ballad
of the White Horse

For the Christian believer, the central event in history is the passage of Jesus from death to life in the Paschal Mystery. The Church celebrates the Resurrection of Jesus, together with his blessed Passion, in a sacred triduum during Holy Week which culminates in "the mother of all vigils," as St. Augustine called it, the Vigil of Easter. Within the Paschal Mystery is locked the meaning of life for every man and woman. The "Passage of Jesus" we celebrate at Easter is the origin and meaning of all liturgical celebration. Every Mass is offered in its memory.

On one of the "sacred three days" there is no Mass. On Good Friday, at the Celebration of the Lord's Passion, the altars are stripped bare, without cross or candle or cloth; after the reading of the Passion according to John, the cross is carried to the altar to be unveiled in three stages for the veneration of the faithful. At each stage the celebrant sings the theme song of Good Friday, "This is the wood of the cross, on which hung the Savior of the world." The people will respond, "Come, let us worship." The crucifix they kiss in veneration is the tree of life, the standard of the King, the symbol of salvation that adorns every altar and dominates the spires of many of our churches.

The cross is our source of hope in what to so many is a hopeless world. In one of the most powerful epic poems I have ever read, *The Ballad of the White Horse,* [57] Gilbert Keith Chesterton, states its thesis: that a human race which produced the mother of the man who hung upon the cross at Calvary has no grounds for ultimate despair. The ballad tells how King Alfred of early Britain gathered the Christian chiefs against the heathen Danes who had invaded his country. Mary, the Mother of God, appears to him to symbolize the Faith and what it has to offer to those who are in despair at the

coming of Christless darkness over the world. She speaks to
the twentieth century, too:

> The men of the East may spell their stars,
> And times and triumphs mark,
> But the men signed of the cross of Christ
> Go gaily in the dark.

Chesterton's Ballad sings beautifully of the joy and strength
of Christian hope. The poem opens with King Alfred hiding in
a forest. This Saxon King in the Dark Ages symbolizes the
Christian leader. The invading Danes have taken his land, but
there is hope left in him. This hope is reinforced by a vision of
the Virgin Mary, who gives him a strange message to rally the
Christian chiefs against the enemy:

> I tell you naught for your comfort,
> Yea, naught for your desire
> Save that the sky grows darker yet
> And the sea rises higher...
> Do you have joy without a cause,
> Yea, faith without a hope?

This was the message of the Lady — to have inner joy which
springs from no human cause and to have hope even when
there is no human hope. The King relays the message of the
Lady to the Christian chiefs:

> To die in a battle, God knows when,
> By God, but I know why!

The words of Mary electrify the chiefs — Mark the Roman
and Colan the Celt, Eldred the German and Mark of Italy.
They march out under the banner of Mary to crush the Danes
in the Valley of the White Horse.

Joy without a cause and faith without a hope are the only
Christian call to battle. One commentator of *The Ballad of the
White Horse* explains,

> *Others may demand the promise of certain victory and profitable
> peace. What the Christian wants to know first and finally is whether he
> is fighting God's battle. If he knows this, he is willing to fight and be
> defeated ... rise from defeat to more fight and more defeat, laughing-
> ly and with enthusiasm. For he knows his fighting is perseverance and
> his defeat, victory.*[58]

This recalls a passage by Paul in *Romans*: "We know glory

also in tribulation, knowing that tribulation worketh patience, and patience, trial, and trial, hope; and hope confoundeth not."

This is the Christian paradox of Jesus — and us, too, with him and because of him — passing through death to life. It is the Folly of the Cross.

This is the Christian idealism of those who believe that good can come from evil, that "God writes straight with crooked lines," as the Portuguese proverb says. We can dare to go gaily in the dark of today's world because we can catch gleams from the radiant crown of Mary, Help of Christians. The little old woman kneeling in church with a rosary entwined in her fingers may not know much about military strategy and international diplomacy, but she knows of powers stronger than these. In his ballad Chesterton has Mary tell King Alfred:

> And any little maid that walks,
>> In good things apart,
> May break the guard of the Three
>> Kings
> And see the dear and dreadful things
>> I hid within my heart.

Chapter 2

Eight Role Models for Priests

Introduction

On June 15, 1984, Pope John Paul II met with representatives of the priests of Switzerland at the famed abbey of Einsiedeln. He told them that the Church counts on priests to challenge the secularization and indifference of the modern world:

It is Christ who will convert and save the secularized world. And he will do it through acts of our ministry, but on condition that we will not be content to perform those acts ritually and formally: Imitamini quod tractatis — *Practice what you preach. They have to be located in a whole atmosphere of prayer and sacrifice whereby our whole person is intimately united with the action of Christ the mediator.*[1]

Among those acts of priestly ministry listed by the Pope is "the Eucharist which we celebrate every day. It is obviously the summit of our sacerdotal lives." He mentions daily prayer, the Liturgy of the Hours, the "grace of reconciliation which we offer to others and which we ask for ourselves, of all the other sacraments and preparation for them with the faithful."

John Paul continues:

Manifold pastoral contacts are again an occasion for incarnating Christ's patient and confiding solicitude for all, to reach men and women in the midst of their cares, to put the appeal of faith before them.

"Yes, it is through our behavior, the care and conviction with which we carry out our priestly duties, that persons, families, and groups — even those far from religious practice — will discover the faith dwelling in us and mystery whose bearers we are, even though the 'vessel of clay' which we are, is constantly called to humility (cf. 2 Cor. 4:7)."

To the priests of Switzerland — and to all priests — John Paul said that it is above all through the truthfulness of his life that the priest announces the Gospel and suggested six priest-saints as role models for Catholic priests of today:

It is salutary for us as well to fix our gaze on model priests who went before us. Each of them exemplified the grace of the priesthood in his own fashion: St. Francis de Sales, St. Vincent de Paul, St. John Bosco, St. Jean-Marie Vianney — the patron of parish priests — Father Charles de Foucauld, St. Maximilian Kolbe.

In this section I describe the lives and works of the six priest-models suggested for our meditation and imitation by Pope John Paul. I have added St. Philip Neri and St. Charles Borromeo to the six suggested by Pope John Paul II to priests as models for imitation.

(I have adapted these brief biographies from columns I wrote in *The Catholic Times,* of the diocese of Columbus, with which the Pontifical College Josephinum has been associated in many ways for more than a hundred years, beginning with the ordination for the diocese of Father Joseph Jessing, the founder, in 1870. Hence the references in some of the lives to the Columbus diocese.)

Saint Francis de Sales

(1567-1622)

St. Francis de Sales, who died as bishop of Geneva in 1622, is a powerful presence in the Church. Editors and publishers honor him as the patron saint of journalists. His name has been given to many institutions as patron saint.

Saint Francis de Sales was an inspiration for the religious congregation known as the Salesians of St. John Bosco. The work of the Salesians is their prime inheritance from their charismatic founder — the education and spiritual formation and the care of young and poor boys in the Inner City.

In the old Latin breviaries from which priests prayed their Divine Office before Vatican II, the second nocturn included a life of the saint of the day. It was easy to get the impression that practically every saint was born of "poor but honest" parents, a phrase which crept into many of the "lives." St. Francis de Sales proves wrong the theory that one has to be forged in the school of want or desperation or poverty to become a person of heroic virtue.

Francis was born into an aristocratic family on August 21, 1567, in a castle called the Chateau de Sales in Thorens, Savoy. It was the era of the Counter-Reformation, when the battle between Protestants and Catholics was waged with ferocity. Francis went to the Jesuit College in Paris; he then studied law and theology at Padua, receiving his doctorate in law at the age of 24. His father wanted a secular career for his brilliant first-born son, but Francis persisted against the opposition of the family and was ordained a priest in 1592 for the diocese of Geneva, the center of Calvinism. Through the influence of a cousin, he had been named to the prestigious position of Provost of Geneva by the Pope a short time before.

Within the diocese was a Calvinist stronghold on the south shore of the Lake of Geneva called the Chablais. Francis soon volunteered to go there as a missionary, despite the dangers of assassination by the Calvinists or attacks from wolves. Through his preaching and his writings he succeeded, but mostly because of the practice of his own principle: "Whoever preaches with love, preaches effectively." Within four years, most of the Chablais had returned to the Catholic Faith.

After a severe examination in theology at Rome by the Pope and by scholars such as St. Robert Bellarmine, Francis de Sales was appointed Bishop of Geneva. He threw himself with zeal and expertise into the reform and reorganization of that very difficult diocese. He became an outstanding leader of the Counter-Reformation and was famous for his wisdom as a preacher and confessor. He wrote two classics of the spiritual life: the *Introduction to the Devout Life* and the *Treatise on the Love of God*.

With St. Jane Chantal, Francis founded the Order of the Visitation nuns. He died in 1622. Canonized in 1655, he was declared a Doctor of the Church in 1877, and named patron of journalists and writers by Pius XI in 1923.

What can Francis de Sales teach the priests and people of today? One answer is found in the opening prayer of his feast on January 24, which highlights his chief characteristic: "Father, you gave Francis de Sales the spirit of compassion to befriend all people on the way to salvation. By his example, lead us to show your gentle love in the service of all." Long ago, I heard a retreat master quote one of his favorite sayings, "You can attract more flies with a spoonful of honey than by a whole barrel of vinegar." St. Francis also wrote, "The measure of love is to love without measure."

One of his basic principles was that spirituality is for everyone, not just for monks and nuns.

The first point he makes in *Introduction to the Devout Life* is that the way of perfection is meant for all people: "Religious devotion does not destroy; it perfects ... It is a mistake, a heresy, to want to exclude devoutness of life from among soldiers, from shops and offices, from royal couples, from the homes of the married."[2] He believed that sanctity is compatible with any legitimate occupation and is spurious if it conflicts with one's earthly duties. The everyday practice of humble virtues, he wrote, is the most direct road to sanctity, for by it the habit of virtue is more solidly established than by occasional heroic sacrifices.

Until a few decades ago few writers followed the lead of St. Francis in writing a spirituality for married people. Over the past four centuries hundreds of spiritual books for priests and nuns have been published for every one meant for the laity, and that one book, *Introduction to the Devout Life,* is still being printed and still worth reading today.

Saint Vincent de Paul

(c. 1580-1660)

In his monumental eighteenth century volumes on the *Lives of the Saints* Alban Butler wrote:

Even in the most degenerate ages, when the truths of the Gospel seem almost obliterated among the generality of those who possess it, God fails not to raise to himself faithful ministers to revive charity in the hearts of the many. One of those instruments of the divine mercy was St. Vincent de Paul.[3]

There may still be some Catholics in this country who may ask, "Who is Vincent de Paul?," even though every fourth parish in the United States has a St. Vincent de Paul Society. The answer to that question could begin almost four hundred years ago when a young tramp asked a shepherd boy for some money. The young shepherd gave him all he had — twelve cents. The boy grew up to become Vincent de Paul, the great apostle of charity in France.

Vincent de Paul (more correctly, Vincent Depaul) was born in 1581 and died in 1660. His parents were Gascon peasants at Ranquine (now Saint-Vincent-de-Paul, Landes). His parents provided a living for their four sons and two daughters and themselves on the produce their farm gave them. Vincent was the third child. His father noted the strong inclinations of the boy and the quickness of his intelligence and so he determined to give him a school education. He sent Vincent to the Franciscans at Dax, then on to Toulouse. The peasant's son was ordained a priest at the very young age of 19. (There is a story, no longer believed by scholars today, that Vincent was enslaved at Marseilles and after two years in Tunisia escaped to Avignon in his home country.)

By his own account, Vincent's ambition as a young priest was to be comfortably well off. He became one of the chaplains of Queen Margaret of Valois and, according to the evil custom of the age, received the income of a small abbey. He went to lodge with a friend in Paris. There, after a false charge of theft by the friend, he bore the slanderous accusations with great patience and humble silence for six months. This accusation brought a conversion in his life. He became associated with Pierre (later Cardinal) de Berulle, who admired the young priest and arranged for him to be the tutor of the children of Count Philip de Gondi; he was also Mme. de Gondi's confessor.

In 1617 Vincent became the parish priest of Chatillon-les-Tombes. Called to hear the confession of a poor peasant he found that some of the masters of the poor did not think that they owed any care or provision for their dependents. This led him to turn to care for the poor.

From the beginning he involved the laity in his work. The first confraternity he established in the ravaged countryside of Chatillon was of peasant women.

In the years that followed, his sermons and work with the poor attracted attention — and imitation. He became ecclesiastical superior of the Visitation nuns after he met St. Francis de Sales in 1618. His service to God and the People of God touched — and inspired — all kinds of men and women, rich and poor, galley slaves, princes and peasants.

Vincent de Paul's whole life was inflamed with love, devoted to the alleviation of human misery. He ransomed Christian slaves in North Africa; he helped form better priests by founding new seminaries; he organized the Sisters of Charity, who attended the sick and poor. Vincent told them that "their convent was the rooms of the sick, their chapels the parish church, their cloister the streets of the city." He founded that other of the "twin Vincentian orders" — the Congregation of the Mission, better known simply as the Vincentians. First serving as missionary to the neglected peasants of France, this Congregation soon spread to all parts of France, America, and many other countries. With St. Louise de Marillac in 1623 he also founded the Sisters of Charity, who still serve the poor.

Vincent de Paul died at age eighty in Paris, where his tomb and the motherhouse of the Sisters of Charity are still places of pilgrimage for huge numbers of Catholics today. Monsieur

Vincent, as they called him, was canonized in 1736 and declared patron of all charitable works by Pope Leo XIII in 1885. In 1948 his life was made into a magnificent film, Monsieur Vincent, by Bernard Luc and Jean Anouilh.

Someone summed up the spirituality of St. Vincent de Paul as "simple, Christocentric, oriented toward action." The "Apostle of Charity" put his basic principles into four simple and direct statements. Pope John Paul was thinking of them, perhaps, when he proposed St. Vincent as a role model for priests:

My friend, you belong to God. Let this reality color your entire existence. Give yourself up to God ceaselessly with every beat of your heart.

We are commissioned not only to love God, but to cause Him to be loved. It is not enough to love God, if our neighbor does not love Him also.

Only through the charity of Our Lord can we transform the world. The wonderful thing is that in letting His love pass through us, we are ourselves converted.

The poor are our masters; they are our kings; we must obey them. It is no exaggeration to call them this, since our Lord is in the poor.[4]

Those principles still inspire the work of the more than 750,000 men and women in 112 countries throughout the world who revere St. Vincent de Paul as their heavenly patron as they carry on their person-to-person apostolate.

The St. Vincent de Paul Society was born in 1833, when a few Catholic students under the leadership of Antoine Frederic Ozanam, living in a hostile anti-Catholic atmosphere at the Sorbonne in Paris, were challenged to show how their religion made any difference in the France of their day. The students decided to "go to the poor" in Paris, as Vincent de Paul and his sisters of Charity had gone in their time. The American Society came to St. Louis in 1845. There are more than 36,000 active in the Society in the United States now.

Saint John Bosco
(1815-1888)

A ceremony, unprecedented in living memory, occurred in the piazza of St. Peter's in Rome on May 11, 1959. Two canonized saints who had been friends in their lifetimes were venerated by Pope John XXIII in a four-hour service. Their remains had been brought together in the piazza and their embalmed bodies were visible in their glass coffins behind the altar. The unusual rites attracted 200,000 people. In his address Pope John emphasized the humble origin and pastoral achievements of both saints.

One of the saints honored by Pope John was his predecessor, Pope St. Pius X, born Giuseppe Sarto in 1835, who died in 1914 and was canonized in 1954. The other saint who, you might say, met his friend Pope Pius in the piazza that day was born in 1815 to a poor family of the Piedmont section of Italy. He died in 1888 and was canonized in 1934. His name was John Bosco.

St. John Bosco (Don Bosco) was born in a tiny village near Turin. One hundred thousand people came to his funeral seventy-three years later. We might ask "Why?" Part of the answer lies in the titles of articles I have read about him. He was the "first friend of modern youth," a saint for the young, the poor. Called "the Saint who took the boys off the streets and into the Church," he was interested above all in spreading the charity of Christ to poor and neglected boys and girls. He was an eloquent preacher and a popular writer of great skill and diligence. He also had a reputation as a visionary, with an extraordinary gift for handling difficult youths without punishment, but with a gentle firmness. Donald Attwater in *A Dictionary of Saints* describes his innovative philosophy of education: "His genius with boys was partly inborn, partly the fruit of experience; he disclaimed having any system of education, while emphasizing that his methods were preventive as opposed to repressive. He sought to make things attractive, whether school subjects or religious practice."[5]

A hundred years before the coffins of Don Bosco and Guiseppe Sarto lay side by side in the piazza of St. Peter's, St. John put the name and spirit of St. Francis de Sales into a new religious foundation. He organized, with the approval of Pope Pius IX, the Society of St. Francis de Sales, popularly known as the Sons of Don Bosco or the Salesians, who work all over the world as missionaries and teachers of youths.

John Bosco was born in the Piedmont in northern Italy near Turin. He was the youngest son of a peasant farmer who died when John was only two years old. His mother Margaret brought him up rigorously and lovingly in their poor cottage. John walked twelve miles a day to go to school and decided at age nine, on the strength of a dream, to become a priest and devote himself to children. In a British Broadcasting System radio talk in 1932, Father C.C. Martindale, S.J., spoke about a boyhood apostolate of his: "He haunted every caravan and fair; learnt to walk tightropes, to become an acrobat and conjuror at the cost of an often-broken nose ... and provided fascinating entertainments, which he wound up with the rosary and a sermon."

After his ordination in 1841, Don Bosco was persuaded by St. Joseph Cafasso, the rector of the seminary, to abandon his dream of foreign missionary work; he went instead to Valdocco, a suburb of Turin, where in time he had hundreds of youths attending his chapel and evening classes. With his saintly mother as housekeeper, he opened a boarding house for apprentices, followed by workshops which taught tailoring, shoemaking, and other trades. In 1872, together with a woman from Genoa, St. Mary Mazzarello (canonized in 1951), he began a new congregation for similar work among girls, the Daughters of Mary, Help of Christians.

When Don Bosco died in 1888, there were nine hundred Salesian priests and almost that many nuns in sixty-four foundations. Almost half of them were in South America. As of December 31, 1985, there were 17,702 Sons of Don Bosco. With their Sisters, they minister to young people in eighty-four countries. The Salesian priests and brothers are the third largest religious order and the second largest missionary society of men. The Salesian Sisters are now the largest society of women religious in the Church.

A Salesian priest once summed up Salesian spirituality for me as "joyful service to the Lord," which is expressed by devotion to the Eucharist, Mary, and the Pope.

Earlier I asked why a poor peasant boy born in a tiny town in northern Italy would have a hundred thousand to mourn him at his Requiem Mass. Perhaps the answer could be put quite simply in the words of Pope Pius XI when he canonized Don Bosco in 1934: "In his life the supernatural almost became natural and the extraordinary, ordinary."

In one of his letters to the Salesians St. John Bosco gave them excellent advice, born of his experience, on the care and training of the adolescents he brought to the Church. It is also a fine piece of advice for priests in their communication with their parishioners and for all teachers in the schools:

First of all, if we wish to appear concerned about the true happiness of our foster children and if we would move them to fulfill their duties, you must never forget that you are taking the place of the parents of these beloved young people. I have always labored lovingly for them, and carried out my priestly duties with zeal. And the whole Salesian society has done this with me.

My sons, in my long experience very often I had to be convinced of this great truth. It is easier to become angry than to restrain oneself, and to threaten a boy than to persuade him. Yes, indeed, it is more fitting to be persistent in punishing our own impatience and pride than to correct the boys. We must be firm but kind, and be patient with them.

I give you as a model the charity of Paul which he showed to his new converts. They often reduced him to tears and entreaties when he found them lacking docility and even opposing his loving efforts.

See that no one finds you motivated by impetuosity or willfulness. It is difficult to keep calm when administering punishment, but this must be done if we are to keep ourselves from showing off our authority or spilling out our anger.

Let us regard those boys over whom we have some authority as our own sons. Let us place ourselves in their service. Let us be ashamed to assume an attitude of superiority. Let us not rule over them except for the purpose of serving them better.

This was the method that Jesus used with the apostles. He put up with their ignorance and roughness and even their infidelity. He treated sinners with a kindness and affection that caused some to be shocked, others to be scandalized, and still others to hope for God's mercy. And so he bade us to be gentle and humble of heart.

They are our sons, and so in correcting their mistakes we must lay aside all anger and restrain it so firmly that it is extinguished entirely.

There must be no hostility in our minds, no contempt in our eyes, no insult on our lips. We must use mercy for the present and have hope for the future, as is fitting for true fathers who are eager for real correction and improvement.

In serious matters it is better to beg God humbly than to send forth a flood of words that will only offend the listeners and have no effect on those who are guilty.[6]

When Pope John Paul urged priests to take Don Bosco as a model, he could have emphasized the petition in the opening prayer of the Saint's feast on January 31: "Lord, you called John Bosco to be a teacher and father to the young. Fill us with joy like his: may we give ourselves completely to your service and to the salvation of all people."

Saint John Baptist Vianney

(1786-1859)

A few miles down the road from where I write this is a former convent, now called "Vianney Residence for Retired Priests."

I suspect many who pass by it may be puzzled by that name, "Vianney." The puzzlement disappears if one spoke instead of the Cure D'Ars or spelled out the full name of St. John Baptist Vianney, who was canonized by Pope Pius XI in 1925 and named patron of parish priests in 1929.

St. John Baptist Vianney was born in 1786, three years before the French Revolution began to change the history of the Church in France. He grew up on a farm in Dardilly near Lyons; his parents were extremely poor, and it was a time most unpropitious for the fostering of religious vocations. He received no religious instructions except from his parents, who would not attend their parish church because the pastor had joined the "state religion" introduced by the Revolution. John went to Mass infrequently in out-of-the-way places like barns and hayricks. He received his First Communion in a house shuttered against the police. He received no formal education as a child. When he was sixteen, he started to think about becoming a priest, but his father would not let him go until three years later.

Even then he could not go to a seminary. The professors would have hooted at him. A saintly priest, the Abbe Balley of a nearby parish at Ecully, took him into a preparatory class where he was the oldest and most stupid boy in the class. He had a pathologically weak memory, little proficiency in French, to say nothing of Latin.

When Napoleon ousted the revolutionary regime and re-established the Catholic religion in France, John Vianney was conscripted into the army, but lost his way in the Pyrenees as he struggled to catch up with his regiment. He was sheltered

for two years by a family opposed to Napoleon, since techni-
cally, he was a deserter.

After the amnesty of 1810, he was twenty-five years old, with
no education beyond that of a freshman in high school, but
the Abbe Balley helped him get into a minor seminary, where
he ranked last in a class of two hundred students. After two
years of theology at Lyons, where he continued to struggle with
Latin, he was finally ordained in 1815.

The Abbe Balley at Ecully took him as an assistant priest and
helped him continue his studies. The Abbe, who deeply ap-
preciated the holiness of his companion, died in 1817 and the
bishop was faced with a problem. What could they do with
John Baptist now? He sent him to the most undesirable parish
in the diocese, which nobody else wanted, at Ars-en-
Dombes; in this remote and unimportant village of about two
hundred fifty inhabitants, most of whom liked to drink and
dance to forget their miserable poverty and could not have
cared less about the practice of their religion, everything
seemed against success for Abbe Vianney as a parish priest —
except God. Today the name of the village of Ars is known and
cherished around the world because it was the locale of the
moral miracle that was Jean-Baptiste Vianney, the parish
priest of Ars.

As I try to sum up the life and works of the Cure of Ars, some
sayings come to mind. The Prophet Isaiah reminded his hear-
ers that God tells them that "My ways are not your ways." For
the theme sentence of his *Grammar of Assent*, Cardinal John
Henry Newman quoted a line from St. Ambrose: "Not by logic
alone hath it pleased God to save his people." And there is the
statement I once saw embroidered into a piece of cloth on a
wall: "God works in mysterious ways his wonders to perform."

The life of St. John Baptist Vianney is a bundle of paradoxes, even contradictions. At the academic level he had so little
talent that he was not ordained a priest until he was twenty-
nine. He broke down at his final examination and the examin-
ers would not accept him for ordination; they told him to try
another diocese. Abbe Balley convinced one of them to examine him again at his rectory. This time he passed. They put
the case of "the most unlearned and the most devout seminarian in Lyons" to the Vicar General. "Is M. Vianney good?" he

asked. "He is a model of goodness," was the answer. "Let him be ordained," said the Vicar General. "The grace of God will do the rest ... the Church needs not only learned priests, but, even more, holy ones."

There was a further humiliation for the struggling Vianney. The authorities would not let him hear confessions. The Abbe Balley coached him again, and when the permission was given, the pilgrimages to Ars soon began. People who heard of his sanctified common sense in the confessional streamed in by the thousands from France and beyond and forced him to spend eleven to sixteen hours a day in spiritual counseling and absolution of their sins.

Some of his fellow priests misjudged him and called him over-zealous, ignorant, a charlatan, even mad. His bishop told his priests during their annual retreat, "I wish, gentlemen, that all my clergy had a touch of the same madness."

People still make pilgrimages to that little village of Ars. Catholics come from around the world to revere the priest who was its pastor. They do not wonder about his lack of talent in the classroom but about the profundity of his sanctity. Strange events swirled about him at Ars — diabolical obsessions, even miracles, but the schoolmaster at Ars, echoing words said about St. Bernard of Clairvaux, saw the greatest miracle of them all in his life. He said, "The most difficult, extraordinary, and amazing work that the Cure did was his own life."

In the opening prayer of the feastday of St. John Vianney on August 4, the Church, which has made him patron of parish priests, singled out his priestly zeal: "Father of mercy, you made Saint John Vianney outstanding in his priestly zeal and concern for your people. By his example and prayers, enable us to win our brothers and sisters to the love of Christ and come with them to eternal glory."

In one of the Cure's catechetical instructions to his people, most of whom he had brought back to the church, he spoke of their glorious duty to pray and to love:

This is the glorious duty of all: to pray and to love. If you pray and love, that is where one's happiness lies. Prayer is nothing but union with God. When one has a heart that is pure and united with God, one is given a kind of serenity and sweetness that makes a person ecstatic, a light that surrounds him or her with marvelous brightness ... My little children, your hearts are small, but prayer stretches them and makes them capable of loving God ... When we pray properly, sorrows disappear like snow before the sun.[7]

In his annual Holy Thursday letter in 1986 to more than 400,000 priests around the world, Pope John Paul II described St. John Vianney as an example of courage for the priest today. The French bishops had invited him to visit Ars in October, 1986, during his visit to France to mark the second centenary of John Vianney's birth, he said, and he intended to use that occasion to highlight the ever-relevant witness of a parish priest whose life was a model of strong will in the face of obstacles and difficulties.[8]

The Tablet of London commented on the pope's message:

The pope emphasized three particular areas of priestly life where St. John Vianney's example was relevant. His concern for preaching was lively and showed clear conviction. His dedication to the Eucharist was the very center of his spiritual life and pastoral work and his devotion to the sacrament of reconciliation untiring. The pope once again urged priests to devote the necessary time and care to the sacrament of reconciliation.[9]

In the eyes of the world it may seem passing strange that a pope could recommend, as a model for priests, a French peasant young man who barely scraped through his seminary studies, but, as St. Ambrose said, "Not by logic alone hath it pleased God to save his people."

Brother Charles Eugene de Foucauld

(1858-1916)

One of the most disturbing sentences I have ever read is this: "The only Gospel some people may hear is YOU!" Charles de Foucauld, whom Pope John Paul II recommends as a model for priests, imagined Jesus telling him at Nazareth in 1897: "Your vocation is to shout the Gospel from the rooftop, not in words, but with your life." He spent the last thirty years of his life — the same length of years Jesus lived hidden in Nazareth — following Christ closely and "living always with him." His life shouts the Gospel now to thousands of Christians who live in the spirit of the rule he wrote for himself. He is a supreme example of a man who lived the central Christian paradox: to lose your life is to find it, to gain your life is to lose it. He is almost a legend now, one of the most fascinating of modern mystics. Like Jesus, his own life is full of paradox, which my dictionary defines as "a person, situation, or action exhibiting inexplicable or contradictory aspects."

In 1902 he wrote a rule for a religious congregation he called the "Little Brothers of Jesus of the Sacred Heart." Ten years later he added "and Sisters" to its name. During his lifetime he did not attract a single person to join him in living the rule, but fifty years after his death there were well over two hundred fifty "Little Brothers of Jesus" (founded by Father Rene Voillaume in 1932 in Algeria) in twenty-five countries living in absolute poverty. In 1980 there were over one thousand one hundred dred "Little Sisters of Jesus," an order founded in the Sahara Desert in 1939.

The little Brothers of Jesus live in small communities and work in factories and fisheries and among the poor; everything not needed to sustain them is given to the poor. The Little Sisters live in ordinary houses in small groups of diverse races and nationalities; they are in cities such as Boston and Chicago, but mostly they witness to Christ in Moslem countries.

In the United States small groups of diocesan priests meet in small support groups called *Jesus Caritas*, to pray and study together in the spirit of Father Foucauld, the hermit of the Sahara, the "universal brother." They try to embrace his spirituality — living in the presence of God and at the same time living in the midst of men and women; they try to observe how the spirituality of Foucauld can fit into their lives as priests. Throughout the world thousands of Sisters, priests, singles, and married people meet in other small groups in that same spirit; they live in a context of poverty and prayer and availability to all who come for help, combined with adoration of the Blessed Sacrament. Father Foucauld always kept a consecrated host exposed in his hermitage compared to which, he said, everything else is "as dry as dust." All these men and women consider themselves members of the "Brother Charles of Jesus Family."

Charles Eugene Foucauld, whose cause for beatification is being considered in Rome, was born in Strasbourg, France, in 1858 and orphaned at the age of six. His grandfather directed him toward a military career. He had lost his faith at the age of sixteen; he proved himself disastrously irresponsible and dissolute; he was dismissed from the army in Algeria for "indiscipline and notorious misconduct."

For two years he lived in the desert disguised as a Jewish servant of a Rabbi. The desert solitude and the religious spirit of the Moslems he met there and the fervent piety of his cousin, Marie Bondy in Paris, brought him to Abbe Henri Huvelin and back to God and the Church in 1886.

It was a complete conversion. With his usual intensity he joined the Trappist monastery of Our Lady of the Snows in Nazareth. Soon he sought the greater poverty of a monastery in Syria, then the even greater poverty and self-sacrifice of an abbey in Algeria. His superior sent him to Rome to study theology, but he left the Trappists and went back to the poverty of Nazareth as a hermit. In 1901 he was ordained a priest.

Soon he was back in the Sahara in a hermitage on the frontier of Morocco. In response to the call of Jesus "to shout the gospel" by his life, he tried to bring Christianity to the Moslems in the desert by good example, not by preaching, but by being a man of God, a "universal brother" in what he called "pre-evangelization" to prepare the way for later missionaries. In 1905 he took his hermitage deeper into the desert in the mountains near Tamanrasset among the nomad Tuareg tribe.

At his hermitage at Beni-Abbes in the desert he continued his unique apostolate, depending not so much upon "good works" as upon bringing the "presence" of Christ to the desert tribes.

The paradox continued. The Tuaregs respected him as a profoundly holy man, but a fanatic group of a Moslem sect murdered him (we might even say martyred him) as an intruding Frenchman and Christian on December 1, 1916.

With the Vatican II Council in the Sixties, we came in the Church to a spirituality deeply influenced by liturgical, biblical, ecumenical, and social justice movements. Brother Charles de Foucauld, a twentieth-century prophet, anticipated all these dimensions, someone has said, by "practicing a spirituality in the midst of people without any particular apostolate except that of being Christ where Christ most needs to be, where he is not yet — or is no more."

Saint Maximilian Mary Kolbe

(1894-1941)

By the count of the Catholic Church in Poland, 2,647 Polish Catholic priests died at the hands of the Nazis during World War II. One of them was Maximilian Kolbe, who was canonized by Pope John Paul II on October 10, 1982. A dispatch from the Reuters News Agency summed up his life in a few terse lines: "Father Kolbe died at Auschwitz on August 14, 1941, after taking the place of one of the ten prisoners the Nazi camp commander selected to starve to death in an underground bunker to avenge another prisoner's escape."

Franciszek Gajowniczek, the Polish sergeant whose life was saved to spare him for his family, was at Rome for the canonization of the saint who had taken his place at Auschwitz. He was also at the concentration camp when Pope John Paul II came to visit the infamous camp in Poland in 1979.

On June 7, 1979, a few months after his election as Pope, John Paul prayed for peace at Auschwitz from an altar erected over the train tracks which bore millions to their death at the camp. He was making what he called a pilgrimage of peace to the heart of cruelty and hatred, he said. "No more war!" he cried to the hundreds of thousands listening along the barbed wire fences. "Peace! only Peace!"

John Paul walked down the rock-strewn alleys between the brick barracks to Cell Block 11 and stepped into the dungeon cell of Father Kolbe. The Pope then walked to the "Wall of Death," where the prisoners were whipped, clubbed, and shot to death where knelt to pray. Then he flew by helicopter to the concentration camp at Birkenau (called Auschwitz II) a few miles away. Of the four million murdered there, about 2.5 million were Jews. In twenty languages a monument commemorated them and those other millions who died along with them.

St. Maximilian Kolbe was born at Zdunska-Wola, near Lodz, Poland on January 7, 1894. He was baptized Raymond. He joined the Conventual Franciscans, taking the name of Maximilian when he pronounced his temporary vows in 1911. In 1917 he founded the Militia of Mary Immaculate. He received doctorates in philosophy and theology at Rome and was ordained a priest there in 1918. His Militia of Mary Immaculate, which he first established among his Franciscan confreres, received the approval of the Church as a "pious union" in 1922. Father Kolbe described its purpose as a crusade against the forces of evil in society and the conversion of the Church's enemies. Its members consecrated themselves as Knights of the Immaculate Mary and practised a special devotion to Our Lady of the Miraculous Medal as a symbol of their dedication.

The particular work of the Militia was the use of the communications media, especially the printed word. Its magazine appeared in Polish, Japanese, English, and Latin (for seminarians and priests). Father Kolbe went to Japan as a missionary in 1930 and the "City of the Immaculate" he established in 1933 was an astonishing success. Many professionals of the press joined him; many became Franciscan brothers.

Because of failing health he was recalled to Poland in 1936. When the Nazis overran Poland, he was sent to a prison camp for a few months in 1939. He went back to the Franciscan headquarters at the Polish "City of the Immaculate" in the city of Niepokalanov to care for refugees; among them were many Jews. The Nazis arrested him again in February, 1941, on a trumped-up charge of "political interference" and sent him to hard labor in Auschwitz.

It was at the beginning of August, 1941, that the Nazi commandant of the camp, angered by the escape of a single prisoner, sentenced ten of the prisoners to die of starvation. Father Kolbe volunteered to take the place of one of them and was entombed with nine others in a bunker to die of starvation. There is testimony that during the horror he tried to keep up his companions' spirits and faith. After two weeks he was still alive. The Nazis needed the bunker for storage space; they killed the priest by an injection of carbolic acid. They burned his body in the gas chamber at Auschwitz.

On that June day in 1979 Pope John Paul II spoke at the concentration camp at Birkenau: "It would have been impossible for me not to have come here as pope ... I have come here, and I kneel on this Golgotha of the modern world, on these tombs, largely nameless, like the great tomb of the unknown soldier."

At the end of World War II the famous war correspondent, Dorothy Thompson, visited one of the liberated Nazi prison camps and asked a survivor, "Who held up best?" The answer was one word: "Priests." It was certainly true of St. Maximilian Kolbe. He will perdure in the annals of the Church because, like Jesus, he gave his life and his love for others. The text for the Gospel reading might well have been from John's Gospel: "For God so loved the world that he gave his only son, that everyone who has faith in him may not die but have life eternal."

Maximilian Mary Kolbe climbed his Golgotha, not on a hill named Calvary near Jerusalem, but in a hell called Auschwitz.

Saint Philip Neri

(1515-1595)

The Saint Who Loved Laughter

To the six priest-saints Pope John Paul II suggested to the priests of Switzerland as role models, I would add two more — Philip Neri and Charles Borromeo. The ministry of Philip Neri proves that a saint need not be a gloomy and dour ascetic but can bubble merrily with laughter and wit and draw people to God with a highly unconventional approach. Charles Borromeo, although it seems that he did not laugh much, was a leading figure in the implementation of the reforms decreed by the Council of Trent; he could teach pastors and people the need for a continuing spirit of reform in the Church after Vatican II.

One biographer of Philip Neri called his book, *Mystic in Motley.* His favorite reading was the Bible and a book of jokes and riddles. At times he would don outlandish clothes and floppy white shoes and shave off half his beard. He was dismissed as a fool or a "crazy." There were many more, however, who recognized him as a very holy man, a saint of God. He told his jokes and did the unconventional things because he did not want people to think of him as a saint, but his holiness kept shining through.

Philip was called the "Second Apostle of Rome" and the "Herald of the Counter-Reformation." Popes and cardinals consulted him, and he was the confessor of St. Ignatius of Loyola. Yet he was the most unpretentious of persons. He was years ahead of his time in the way he treated the young people he gathered around him in an age of gross immorality when some priests and high prelates of the Church led scandalous lives. He anticipated one of the basic tenets of progressive education when he said that "If you wish to be obeyed, you must not appear to be giving orders."

Philip Neri was born in 1515 into a poor family in Florence, although his father was a notary of good family. His mother died when he was quite young. His father was a dreamer who earned little and spent his evenings experimenting with ways to turn lesser metals into gold. Philip received a good education and was attracted to and influenced by the Dominican friars at San Marco, where Savonarola had been burned at the stake.

At eighteen, Philip was apprenticed by his father to a relative in Gaeta, a city half-way to Rome. He soon found that Uncle Romulo was not that rich and, indeed, that he himself was not too welcome in Gaeta. Philip also experienced an intense conversion of heart at that time. He packed a few possessions and set out for Rome, where he spent more than sixty years. He died at Rome in 1595. His apostolate extended from the lowly poor and sick to popes and cardinals at the Vatican. His influence in every part of Rome was incalculable. He was a joyful joker whose pursuit of holiness inspired many indifferent and irreligious citizens of Rome to return to the Church and the Gospel way of Jesus.

Philip's apostolate in Rome was an informal one. As he talked to the young men and women of the city, his cheerfulness kept breaking through; his attractive personality won him many friends, whom he inspired to spend their time in serving the sick in hospitals and visiting churches with him. Soon he founded a confraternity of Brothers who cared for the thousands of pilgrims who flocked to the city, especially during the Holy Year of 1550. They then turned to help the poor convalescents of the city. Philip Neri sometimes spent the whole night praying in the catacombs; he often enjoyed mystical experiences. And always he dipped into that book of jokes and riddles he carried with him in his apostolate.

St. Philip was ordained a priest in 1551. He soon acquired a reputation as an extraordinary insightful confessor at the Church of San Giralamo. He continued to walk the streets evangelizing the young people of Rome. He built what he called an "oratory" over the church where he spent many afternoons with them in religious services and discussions. He had composers (among them the famed Palestrina) set the words of the Bible to music at the Oratory. Philip called these compositions "oratorios" and thus gave the name to a later kind of music like Handel's *Messiah.*

In 1575, Philip founded the "Congregation of the Oratory," a loosely organized religious society of priests and others who did not take the usual religious vows. At one time he was inspired by St. Francis Xavier, his contemporary, to go to the "Indies," but a holy monk told him that his Indies were the streets of Rome.

St. Philip Neri is the patron of joyous Christians, and the readings of his Mass on May 26 radiate that joy. In Galatians 5, Paul eloquently preaches the Christian law of love and beautifully describes the ideal life in Christ: "The fruit of the Spirit is love, joy, peace, patient endurance, kindness, generosity, faith, mildness, and chastity." In John 15, Jesus gives his disciples — and us — his farewell gifts of joy and peace: "You will live in my love if you keep my commandments and live in my Father's love. All this I tell you that my joy may be yours, and your joy may be complete." Philip Neri's joy was complete.

At the end of his account of St. Philip in *A Dictionary of Saints*, Donald Attwater writes a summary:

> *The path of perfection was for lay people as much as for clergy and monks and nuns. He preached more about love and spiritual integrity than about physical austerity; the virtues that shone in him were impressed on others: Love of God and people, humbleness and gaiety. Like Thomas More, he is notably marked by the cheerfulness that is supposed to distinguish every saint.*[10]

I suppose there may still be some Catholics who think that their religion, with its history of more "don'ts" than "do's" should be a joyless, even melancholy, exercise. St. Thomas More, St. John Bosco, and above all, St. Philip Neri would tell them, "Don't you believe it."

Chesterton said that men and women "marked of the cross of Christ go gaily in the dark."

Saint Charles Borromeo

(1539-1584)

Leader of the Reform after Trent

Many high schools, colleges, and seminaries have borne the name of St. Charles. Many readers might not know, I suspect, that his last name was Borromeo, and that it is a most appropriate name for a school and seminary because, in implementation of the decrees of the Council of Trent in the late sixteenth century, Charles Borromeo was a most important originator of the Catholic seminary system which remains in existence in our own times.

St. Charles Borromeo was born in 1538 of an aristocratic and wealthy family in the castle of Arona on Lake Maggiore in northern Italy. He died as Cardinal Archbishop of Milan in 1584 and was canonized in 1610. When he was twenty-two, though not yet ordained as a priest, he was made a cardinal and administrator of the See of Milan by his uncle Pope Pius IV, who heaped many other honors upon him. (The pope was the brother of Charles' mother, Margaret Medici.) The pope kept him in Rome, where he was in practice the pope's "secretary of state." It was not until 1564 that he was ordained priest and consecrated a bishop.

Charles actively supported Pius IV in his successful attempt to reopen the Council of Trent for its third and final session. At the Council he was outstanding for his energy, diplomacy, and vigilance. To a great extent he was responsible for bringing the often-interrupted council to its conclusion, when it enacted its most important decrees. Charles was important in drafting the Catechism of the Council of Trent and in reforming liturgical books and church music.

The Council of Trent was called to respond to the Protestant Reformation, but it was more than a negative condemnation of some of the key Protestant doctrines. For years a movement for reform of the Church "in head and members" swelled up from the ranks of the faithful which encouraged bishops, cardinals, and popes to pursue a corporate reform of the Mystical Body of Christ. Perhaps the thorough renewal of the Catholic Church after Trent should not be called the Counter-Reformation but rather the Catholic Renewal.

The council defined nothing new, but did clarify the traditional faith in opposition to Protestant dissent. It decreed a series of reforms in church life, worship, and discipline, which, when accomplished in the following decades, gave new confidence to a shaken Church. Charles Borromeo was a superb leader in putting those reform decrees into practice in northern Italy.

Borromeo was named Archbishop of Milan at the end of the Council and received permission from his uncle's successor to go there as the first resident archbishop in eighty years. He began by giving away much of the rich revenue he had received in various assignments in Rome. For the last twenty years of his life, "his life was a textbook of pastoral theology" for bishops, as one biographer put it. In his *A Dictionary of Saints*, Donald Attwater summarizes Borromeo's efforts at reform in a diocese which needed it badly: he set his clergy an example of virtuous and selfless living, of caring for the needy and sick, of making Christ a reality to society. His influence was felt outside his own archdiocese. During the plague year of 1576, in particular, he worked unceasingly for his flock and used up much of his means in relieving sufferers.[11]

The efforts of Borromeo to reform the immoral lives of many of the laity and clergy in the archdiocese met with stiff opposition and conflict with the civil authorities. One discontented religious order priest even tried to assassinate him.

It is not possible to list here all his activities in implementing the reforms of Trent, but I should single out his concern for the education of learned, holy, and dedicated priests. He founded three seminaries in the archdiocese and initiated a positive program of intellectual and cultural formation of priests in a setting designed to promote the seminarians' spiritual growth. The principles Borromeo developed for clerical education and in catechizing had a profound and immediate effect; they were a principal source of inspiration for seminary training across hundreds of years. With adaptations in the Church after Vatican II, they have validity today.

One biographer summed up his life: "Above all he gave a conspicuous example of an utterly devoted, reforming pastor in an important archdiocese in the very time it was most needed." In his Image Book *Dictionary of Saints,* John J. Delaney concluded his treatment by saying that "he was one of the towering figures of the Catholic Reformation, a patron of learning and the arts and though he achieved a position of great power, he used it with humility, personal sanctity, and unselfishness to reform the Church of evils and abuses so prevalent among the clergy and nobles of the times."[12]

In her delightful and witty book, *Saint Watching,* Phyllis McGinley remarks that "Charles Borromeo is too steely for my taste," but she does quote a story about him which reveals a lighter side. "Charles enjoyed chess. He was once criticized for the pleasure he took in his skill. 'And what would you do if you were playing away and the end of the world suddenly arrived?' 'Keep on playing chess,' said St. Charles."[13]

St. Charles Borromeo died at the young age of forty-six, worn out by his efforts to repair the ravages of a world split apart by the Reformation in Italy and his attempts to root out its causes by forming his own clergy. Phyllis McGinley conceded that "it did not give him much time for games."

Chapter 3
Missionary Martyrs

Introduction

On February 14, 1969, Pope Paul VI approved a revision and reorganization of the liturgical year and the calendar of saints' feast days for the Roman Rite. It was part of the implementation of the directives from the Second Vatican Council that the liturgical and sacramental life of the Church should be renewed. The Pope began by stating the principle that "the Paschal Mystery of Christ should receive greater prominence in the revision of the liturgical calendar."

The liturgical calendar is an arrangement through the Church year of a series of liturgical seasons and feasts of saints for the purpose of divine worship. "Within the cycle of a year," said the *Constitution on the Sacred Liturgy*, "the Church unfolds the whole mystery of Christ, not only from his incarnation and birth until his ascension but also is reflected in the day of Pentecost, and the expectation of a blessed hoped-for return of the Lord."[1] The emphasis in the new calendar is on the saving events by which Christ won salvation for all people. These events are summed up in the term "Paschal Mystery" and are "in some way made present at all times, and the faithful are enabled to lay hold of them and become filled with saving grace."

In its section on the saints, the Liturgy Constitution puts special stress on the veneration of Mary, the Mother of God, and goes on to say of the feast days of the saints: "The Church has also included in the annual cycle days devoted to the memory of the martyrs and other saints ... the Church proclaims the Paschal Mystery as achieved in the saints ... she proposes them to the faithful as examples who draw all to the Father through Christ, and through their merits she pleads for God's favors."[2]

In the decree of Pope Paul VI approving the general norms

for the revision of the liturgical year and the new Roman Calendar, he wrote about the celebration of saints' days as

> ... *proclaiming the wonderful works of Christ in his servants... The Catholic church has always believed that the feasts of the saints proclaim and renew the Paschal Mystery of Chriss ... Asthe Council properly pointed out, over the course of centuries more feasts of the saints were introduced than necessary. Lest the feasts of the saints overshadow the feasts which recall the mysteries of redemption, many of these should be celebrated by local churches, countries, or religious communities. Only those which commemorate saints of universal significance should be kept by the universal Church.*[3]

Twenty-five years ago, it was widely believed that the accumulation of saints in the calendar over many centuries had led to an over-emphasis on their importance at the expense of the more important "Temporal Cycle" of the calendar composed of the Advent, Christmas, Lent, Easter cycles, and the "ordinary Sundays" throughout the rest of the year. In the 1962 edition of *The Saint Andrew Bible Missal* there were two hundred eighty saint's names in its index.[4] The new Calendar reduced the number of saints to be celebrated worldwide to sixty-three obligatory memorials and ninety-five optional memorials, i.e., those which, at the discretion of the presiding priest at the Mass, may be observed.

When the drastically reduced calendar was announced in 1969, there were howls of protest from those who discovered that their favorite saints were abolished or reduced in rank. (The editor of the diocesan paper in New York said that his telephone had never rung so frequently in protest.) When the feast of St. Christopher, the popular patron of motorists, was reduced to the dimension of a merely local cult, for example, there was a sharp reaction in various countries, led in Italy by popular film stars.

In *The Oxford Dictionary of Saints* David High Farmer explained the principles — especially the principle of universality — which the authors of the new Calendar used in selecting the saints it included:

> *Saints were selected for universal veneration by deliberate choice from each century of the Church's history and from every country. Their historical significance as representatives of particular types of*

the apostolate were duly considered. Others who had long been venerated elsewhere in Christendom were approved for particular countries, churches, or religious orders.5

Early in this century the Catholic author, Hilaire Belloc, published a book called *Europe is the Faith; the Faith is Europe*. It was a prime example of the "Eurocentrism" of which the Church of previous generations (and of today, too) was often accused. The earlier calendars, with some exceptions, limited the feast days of the saints to those who had lived in Europe, especially Western Europe. Now, Pope Paul noted in his decree, the names of martyrs and saints born and raised in regions to which the Gospel was later carried have been added. "These representatives of every group of people are given equal prominence in the lists of saints because they shed their blood for Christ or showed extraordinary signs of virtue."[6] (The Litanies of Saints used in various liturgies were also revised to conform to the same principles of universality and geographical distribution of the saints.)

The new Calendar of Saints was an example of what Vatican Council II was all about — bringing the practices and pieties of an older Europe-centered Church up to date. The Calendar today is more adapted to modern attitudes toward those practices and pieties.

Under the sub-title, "Making the Calendar Universal," the official commentary on the new Calendar reviews the history of the veneration of saints and martyrs and explains why some names were dropped and why some were added:

The cult of the saints began with the veneration of martyrs. To the Roman saints in the general calendar were added many saints from the East and from North Africa, quite a large number from Italy, France, and Spain, and some from other European countries. The time has now come to include in the calendar some saints from other areas, especially martyrs, for whom the Church's liturgy has always shown a special predilection. Today all the continents have been sanctified by the labors of the preachers of the Gospel and by the blood of martyrs. And so into the new calendar have been inserted the memorials of Paul Miki and his companions from Japan, the first canonized martyrs of the Far East (February 5, 1597); Isaac Jogues and his companions, martyred in Canada and the United States (October 18, 1647); Peter Chanel, the first martyr of Oceania (April 28, 1841); and Charles Lwanga and his companions from Uganda, the first of Central Africa (June 3, 1886).

"Rose of Lima was already in the calendar (August 30) and now there have been added Turibius of Mogrovejo, Archbishop of Lima (March 23, 1606), who established the hierarchy in Latin America, and Martin de Porres (November 3, 1639), very popular among black people and those of mixed color."[7]

In pages to come I want to write the life-stories of some of those martyrs and saints who brought the Good News to those far-away places like Oceania, Uganda in Africa, Nagasaki in Japan, and Peru in South America.

Saint Charles Lwanga and Companions

The First Martyrs of Central Africa

This is about martyrs, both ancient and modern. When I think of martyrs, my mind goes back to some statements about them. St. Justin Martyr, who died in 165, once observed: "Nobody believed Socrates until he died for what he taught." A recent article about modern martyrs in Central America was called, "You bet your life." The most famous quote of all is by Tertullian, who died in 240, when he challenged the persecutors of Christianity: "We multiply whenever we are mown down by you; the blood of Christians is seed." St. Jerome, who died in 420, wrote in a letter, "The Church of Christ has been founded by shedding its own blood, not that of others, by enduring outrage, not by inflicting it. Persecutions have made it grow; martyrdoms have crowned it."

The thought of Tertullian has been put into the prayer in the Mass of St. Charles Lwanga on June 3: "Father, you have made the blood of martyrs the seed of Christians. May the witness of St. Charles and his companions and their loyalty to Christ in the face of torture inspire countless men and women to live the Christian faith." Some of the companions were St. Kizito, St. Matthias Kalemba Murumba, and St. Joseph Mukasa. You may well ask, "Who?"

The Catholic Martyrs of Uganda in East Central Africa were twenty-two Bantu tribesmen, martyred for their Catholic faith by Mwanga, a debauched king, who burned most of them to death on a flaming pyre on June 3, 1886. Half of them were teenage pages at the royal court.

In the homily he preached on October 18, 1964, during the Mass in which he proclaimed them saints, Pope Paul VI said: "The African martyrs add another page to the martyrology — the Church's roll of honor ... This is a page worthy in every way to be added to the annals of earlier times ... Who could have predicted that to the famous confessors and martyrs such as Cyprian, Felicity, Perpetua, and — greatest of them all — Augustine, we would one day add names so dear as Charles Lwanga and Matthias Mulumba Karemba and their twenty companions?" Pope Paul then added, with a fine ecumenical touch: "Nor must we forget those members of the Anglican Church who also died for the name of Christ."[8]

When the Missionaries of Africa, once called "The White Fathers," came to evangelize Uganda in 1879, they were welcomed by King Mutesa, but he was soon succeeded by King Mwanga, who despised Christians and feared them as a threat to his power. Joseph Mukasa, a twenty-six-year-old convert, was the head of the King's household. He dared to reproach Mwanga for his seduction of some of the young pages at the court and for his murder of a Protestant missionary bishop. The King had him burned alive on November 15, 1855.

After Mukasa's death, the Christians looked to Charles Lwanga, an ardent apostle and twenty-year-old chief of the pages. He continued to protect them and encouraged them to embrace the Faith. The King's mounting rage against Christians came to a murderous violent climax on May 25, 1886; he savagely attacked Sebuggwawa, his personal attendant, for daring to teach catechism to one of his favorite pages.

The King assembled all the pages before him. The Christians were ordered to form a separate group. Charles Lwanga was the first to step forward, together with Kizito, a thirteen-year-old page, one of those he had baptized the night before. Fifteen, all under twenty-five, joined them; so did two others and two soldiers. The King asked them if they wished to remain Christians. Their answer was "Until Death!" The twenty-two were taken to Namugongo, a village thirty-seven miles away, wrapped in mats of reeds, and burned alive on June 3, 1886. (In that year alone Mwanga martyred two hundred fifty Catholic and Anglican Christians.)

In 1900, sixty-two generations after Christ, the world was 34.4% Christians (81.1% of them whites) and 51.3% evangelized. In that year Africa had a population of about one hundred thirty-three million, of whom only nine million (7%) were Christians. In 1960, the year many African countries gained their independence from colonial rule, Africa's population was nearly three hundred million, of whom eight-six million (30%) were Christians. In 1978 the population of Africa was four hundred and twenty million and 45% were Christians. Since then Christians have outnumbered Moslems. The figure of nine million in 1900 will have grown, it is estimated, forty-five times as much in a period of a hundred years. Never before in the history of Christianity has such a rapid growth been observed on such a large scale.[9]

In his 1957 encyclical, *The Gift of Faith,*[10] Pope Pius XII said that the African Church was rapidly gaining a position of world significance. In 1979 there were more than 739 million Catholics in the world. Fifty-two and a half million were in Africa; that was 12.4% of the total. In 1982 there were almost fifty-five million Catholics in Africa in a total population of some four hundred forty-three million.

There are many factors which would have to enter into any attempt to explain that stupendous surge of Catholics and other Christians in what used to be called "The Dark Continent." But surely one of them would have to quote Tertullian and say that "the blood of martyrs is the seed of the Church."

Saint Peter Mary Chanel

(1803-1841)

The First Martyr of Oceania

Peter Chanel was born in France, but he died in Oceania at daybreak on April 28, 1841, when aborigines on the island of Futuna beat him to death with war clubs.

Not many Americans had heard about Oceania, the Island World of the Pacific, before Japan attacked the Pacific Fleet at Pearl Harbor. But soon after that they began to read the exotic names in the headlines — Tahiti, Samoa, the atolls of the Carolinas, the Fijis, and the Solomons. They learned that Oceania, lying off Australia and Asia, was a name for thousands of islands scattered across three million square miles. The islands were discovered and explored by traders and whalers from the West in the late sixteenth century.

For two centuries no Catholic missionaries, for a variety of reasons, had made their way to the islands on the other side of the European world. That disturbed Pope Gregory XVI, who ruled the Church from 1831 to 1846. He knew that thousands of pagans in Oceania had not received the saving Good News of Christ.

At about the same time a zealous group of seminarians and diocesan priests in the area of Lyons in France under the leadership of Jean Claude Colin received permission from their bishop to form a missionary band to care for rural districts in France. They called themselves the Society of Mary, now better known as the Marist Fathers. With Father Colin as their founder they asked permission of the pope to form a religious community. He asked them to send missionaries to Oceania.

Peter Chanel was one of those professed in the first group to make their religious vows before Father Colin. He was born in 1803 of peasant stock at Cluet, near Belley in France, and was a shepherd in his youth. The parish priest of nearby Cras, the

Abbe Trompier, took him as a pupil because of his unusual intelligence and piety. Peter was ordained a priest in 1827.

A year later the young Father Chanel was sent to be the pastor of the unpromising parish at Crozet. Within three years he had revitalized it, but Peter Chanel longed for the life of a foreign missionary. He joined the recently founded Marist Fathers. For five years he taught at the seminary in Belley, but in 1836 he was sent with a few companions to the Marist mission in the New Hebrides Islands of Oceania.

It was a rugged voyage for the eight Marist missionaries who accompanied the newly consecrated Bishop Pompallier, Vicar Apostolic of western Oceania. Their ship, the *Delphine,* was at sea more than six months, and Father Chanel was seasick much of the time. They made the last leg of the voyage on an American brig, the *Europa*, and finally landed at Tahiti.

Ten years after he was ordained, Father Chanel and a Marist lay brother reached the island of Futuna on November 12, 1837. His apostolate was to last little more than three years, during which time he seemed to accomplish very little. There were two warring factions on the island and the missionaries were caught in the middle.

In a sermon in Holy Cross Cathedral in Boston shortly after the canonization of Peter Chanel in 1954 by Pope Pius XII, Archbishop Richard J. Cushing summarized the terrible trying hardships which the missionaries from France had to endure:

> *The three short years that were allotted to Father Chanel beggar description in hardships. A strange and uncomfortable climate for those reared in temperate lands; harsh and primitive conditions of living; a revolting religion entwined in social customs; a new, unusual language; everything so unfamiliar and so arduous that not even one daily customary act of existence recalled the home of his childhood.*[11]

For three long years the Marist missionaries toiled incessantly under the tropical sun, and only on the eve of death did Peter Chanel begin to see signs that their preaching had begun to bear fruit. Then the chief's son asked to be baptized. This so infuriated the chief that he sent his warriors with orders to kill. One of them clubbed Peter to the ground and the others cut up his body with axes and knives. As they were about to split open

his skull, he spoke to them in their own language which he had
learned in order to preach the Word of God to them ... "Malie
fuai — it is good for me that you are doing this."

One can hear the voice of Jesus from the cross in the background. One can hear the last words of Stephen the first martyr, "Lord, do not lay this sin against them."

The Marist lay brother who was with him at the end wrote a
eulogy of Peter Chanel's last years in Futuna:

> *Because of his labors he was often burned by the heat of the sun,
> and famished with hunger, and he would return home wet with perspi-
> ration and completely exhausted. Yet he always remained in good
> spirits, courageous, and energetic, as if he were returning from a
> pleasure jaunt, and this would happen almost every day.*
>
> *He could never refuse anything to the Futunians, even to those who
> persecuted him; he always made excuses for them and never rejected
> them, even though they were often rude and troublesome. He dis-
> played an unparalleled mildness toward everyone on all occasions
> without exception. It is no wonder then that the natives used to call
> him the 'good-hearted man.'* [12]

On the day before his martyrdom, the account quotes what
he said, "It does not matter if I die. Christ's religion is so
deeply rooted on this island that it cannot be destroyed by my
death."

Less than a year later the whole of Futuna became Christian.

Saint Paul Miki and Companions

The First Canonized Martyrs of the Far East

This is the opening prayer of the liturgy of Saint Paul Miki and Companions, Martyrs, which the Church celebrates on February 6:

> God our Father,
> source of strength for all your saints,
> you led Paul Miki and his companions
> through the suffering of the cross
> to the joy of eternal life.
> May their prayers give us the courage
> to be loyal until death in professing our faith.

Behind that prayer is a story of faith and fidelity, of rare courage. It is a fascinating tale of persistence under savage persecution and death on the cross for the twenty-six saints we call the Japanese Martyrs.

Put briefly, it is the story of Paul Miki, who was born in Japan between 1564 and 1566. Entering the Society of Jesus, he preached the Gospel with great success. But when persecution against Catholics became oppressive, he was arrested along with twenty-five others. After enduring torment and derision they were taken to Nagasaki and there suffered crucifixion on the vigil of their present Saints' day in 1597.

Paul Miki was of a Japanese aristocratic family; the other twenty-five were two Jesuit lay brothers; six Franciscans, of whom four were Spanish, one from Mexico City, and one from Bombay; sixteen Japanese lay persons, and one Korean. They included catechists, interpreters, a soldier, a physician, and three young boys.

Their story begins with the first Christian apostle of Japan, St. Francis Xavier, who landed in Japan in 1549. When he left a few years later, the Christians of Japan numbered perhaps two thousand. Francis Xavier was one of the six original disciples of St. Ignatius Loyola. Ignatius had given his *Spiritual Exercises* to his associates in Paris. With them he took the vows of religion and founded the Society of Jesus, which was approved by the Pope in 1540. The next year Ignatius sent Xavier to Goa, a Portuguese enclave in India. Eight years later Francis Xavier opened up the hitherto tightly closed society of Japan.

By the 1580's Catholic Christians could be counted in the hundreds of thousands. In 1587 the first anti-Catholic ferment broke out. After that there were intermittent persecutions and periods of relative peace until the last priest in Japan died of starvation in a prison cell in Tokyo.

It is possible to list several complex factors to explain the bitterness and savagery of these persecutions — the clash between Japanese culture and the European version of Catholicism brought by the missionaries, the religious opposition of Shinto (a religion which identified religion and the State), and of Buddhism. There was also the fear that Christianity would undermine the authority of the Shoguns and the deep suspicion that the religion of the foreigners represented political and economic aspirations of the Spanish and Portuguese.

There were thousands of martyrs for the Faith in what has been called the "Christian Century of Japan." Our interest centers here on the twenty-six who died on crosses on the hill above Nagasaki on a clear and cold Wednesday in February of 1597.

The martyrs had part of their left ears cut off and were paraded through various towns to terrify the other Christians. They were chained to crosses on the ground first; these were planted in a row, and each martyr was killed by the thrusts of a lance by twenty-six separate executioners.

I quote from an account of the deaths of St. Paul Miki and his companions by a writer who was their contemporary:

The crosses were set in place. Father Pasio and Father Rodrigues took turns encouraging the victims. Their steadfast behavior was wonderful to see. Our brother, Paul Miki, saw himself standing now in the noblest pulpit he had ever filled. To his "congregation" he began by proclaiming himself a Japanese and a Jesuit. He was dying for the Gospel he preached. He gave thanks to God for this wonderful blessing and he ended his "sermon" with these words: "As I come to this supreme moment of my life, I am sure none of you would suppose I want to deceive you. And so I tell you plainly: there is no way to be saved except the Christian way. My religion teaches me to pardon my enemies and all who have offended me. I do gladly pardon the Emperor and all who have sought my death. I beg them to seek baptism and be Christians themselves."

The account concludes:

Then, according to Japanese custom, the executioners began to unsheath their spears. At this dreadful sight, all the Christians cried out, "Jesus! Mary." And the storm of anguished weeping then rose to batter the very skies. The executioners killed them, one by one. One thrust of the spear, then a second blow. It was over in a very short time.[13]

The Martyrs of Nagasaki were canonized by Pope Pius IX in 1862. Five years later he beatified 205 martyrs who died between 1617 and 1632. In 1970 in Manila Pope Paul VI beatified sixteen more.

Few Christians remained in Japan at the end of the eighteenth century, and they were isolated in small pockets in Nagasaki and Kyushu.

The story does not end there.

On the morning of August 8, 1853, the Japanese at Edo Bay in Japan were astonished to see a United States naval squadron under the command of Matthew Perry lying in the bay. The courteous Japanese received the Americans, who came with greetings from President Fillmore. Six months later, Japan opened its ports to American commerce. The nations of Europe quickly followed. The great door of Japan, closed to all Christians for more than two centuries, suddenly swung open again.

Ten years later, in the dusk of St. Patrick's Day, a French priest named Bernard Pettitjean looked at a chapel newly erected on Oura Hill. A group of men and women struggled up the hill. The priest invited them to enter with him. He knelt for a brief prayer; so did two middle-aged women. One said, "All of us have the same heart as you." One lady asked, "And where is the Santa Maria?" The priest led them to the Blessed Virgin altar. They cried out, "Look, there she is! There is the Santa Maria and she is holding her infant in her arms." Then all knelt down and cried for joy.

Through two centuries of constant and cruel persecution the "hidden Christians" of Japan kept the flame of faith alive. Soon the French priest found ten thousand other Christians scattered throughout Japan. Now he could bring the Mass of Christ back to the Land of the Rising Sun.

Blessed John Mazzucconi

The Martyr of Woodlark Island

On February 19, 1984, Pope John Paul II announced to the whole Church that one hundred persons who gave their lives for Christ should be declared "Blessed" — that word used by Jesus as he spoke the Eight Beatitudes at the beginning of his Sermon on the Mount. Ninety-nine of those whom the Pope beatified that day were French, victims of the Reign of Terror in 1793-1794 during the French Revolution. The French martyrs included twelve priests, three women religious, and eighty-four lay persons, a few of the immense number of the victims of the Reign of Terror.

The hundredth person whom John Paul declared a Blessed Martyr that day was a young Italian priest named Giovanni Mazzucconi, a priest of the Pontifical Institute for Foreign Missions. Its members are known as the P.I.M.E. Fathers because those are the initials of the Italian name of the Institute. Father Mazzucconi was savagely murdered in 1855 at his mission on the island of Woodlark in what is now Papua-New Guinea, a part of that immense number of islands, collectively known as Oceania, in the central and south Pacific Ocean.

The Pontifical Institute for Foreign Missions is an international society of secular priests, bound together by an oath of stability, who work under the direct jurisdiction of the Congregation for the Propagation of the Faith. (This agency of the Vatican is now also called The Congregation for the Evangelization of Peoples.) It is exclusively dedicated to mission work and places special emphasis on training local clergy and establishing a local hierarchy in foreign mission territories.

The society is the result of a merger effected by Pope Pius XI in 1926 of the Institute for Foreign Missions of Milan and the Pontifical Seminary of SS. Peter and Paul for Foreign Missions in Rome. The Milan branch, which was larger, was founded in

1850 by Angelo Ramazzoti at the request of Pope Pius IX. The Roman branch was also founded at the request of the same Pope in 1871 by Pietro Avanzini.

Father Mazzucconi was a charter member, a co-founder of the Milan society. In his retreat in preparation for his priestly ordination on May 25, 1850, he drafted a letter asking to be one of the first students of the Missionary Institute that Bishop Ramazotti of Pavia was founding in Milan. "The missions have been the secret desire of my heart for several years already," he wrote, "and this is a vow that I wish to offer to God the first time that he descends into my hands." He also wrote, among his many contributions to the Institute, the moving missionary prayers still in use among the P.I.M.E. Fathers. In them he reveals an ardent desire for martyrdom as the crown of his apostolate.

Blessed John Mazzucconi was born in Rancio di Lecco in the diocese of Milan on March 1, 1826, the ninth of twelve children born to Giacomo Mazzucconi and Anna Maria Scuri. Three of the children were ordained priests and four of the girls became Sisters. John entered a seminary in the diocese in 1840 for his first studies. From 1844 to 1846 he was a student in the Philosophical Seminary of Monza, where he was noted for the extraordinary gentleness of his ways with everyone, his easy forgiveness, and profound devotion to the Holy Eucharist and the Blessed Virgin. His theological studies took him to Milan from 1846-1850. The professors praised him for his brilliant intelligence and as a "mirror of virtue." The Rector of the seminary summed him up as "gentle, pious, distinguished for his attitude to studies, both scientific and literary, and possessing a very pronounced ecclesiastical spirit."

The young priest volunteered for the most difficult and remote mission frontier. With six other pioneers, he left London for the missions of Melanesia and Micronesia in Oceania, to which the young Institute had been assigned by the Roman authorities. They made their way to London and on March 16, 1852, embarked on a 105-day, eighteen thousand mile journey to Sydney, Australia. It was a dangerous voyage. Two of the ship's masts were shattered in a storm and the vessel, which was little more than one hundred feet long, came at long last to Sydney with only two sails left.

It took fifteen more days of sailing to bring the six P.I.M.E. missionaries to the little islands of Woodlark and Rook, where they had been assigned. Mazzucconi went to Rook, whose natives were practicing unheard-of depravities; this made the preaching of the Good News of Christ practically impossible. Father Mazzuconi was stricken with an uncontrollable fever which opened up painful sores all over his body and caused him great numbness and fatigue. The missionary suffered from extreme poverty, lack of medicine, isolation from all that was familiar, and unremitting hostility from the islanders. Through it all he accepted everything "with incredible patience," as one report put it, "with serenity and abandoned completely to the will of God." He offered his sufferings for the conversion of the natives. After two years he had to fear for his life and his superior sent him back to Sydney to recover his health, with the understanding that he would return to his mission. After four months, John took a schooner to Woodlark, not knowing that the mission had been abandoned. When the ship foundered on the Woodlark barrier reef, he was murdered by a native who climbed into the ship and struck him dead with one blow of the hatchet he had concealed. He was twenty-nine years old.

Father Nicholas Maestrini, P.I.M.E., (the first superior of the Society in this country) has just published a book which he calls *Mazzucconi of Woodlark*. In it he acknowledges that from the human point of view the pioneer expedition of the P.I.M.E. fathers was "a total and unmitigated disaster," but, Maestrini continues, one does not measure a spiritual profit by statistics; "the number of souls who gain a spiritual profit from the sufferings of Blessed John and his companions is known only to God."[14]

The *Decree on the Missionary Activity of the Church* published by Vatican Council II declares that the missionary "enters upon the life and mission of him who 'emptied himself and took the form of a slave' ... he bears witness to his Lord, if need be, to the shedding of his blood."

Father John Mazzucconi was such a witness.

Chapter 4

Missionaries to the Americas

Saint Martin de Porres

The Fifth Saint of Lima

In early 1962 Pope John XXIII spoke to a newly ordained young priest and his mother during an audience. The young man was the first black priest from tiny Montserrat Island in the West Indies. The Pope said to his mother: "There is no color bar in the Church, you know. We have a Negro Cardinal, Negro bishops, many good Negro priests."

Two months later Reuters news agency announced in a dispatch from Rome: "Martin de Porres, seventeenth-century illegitimate son of a Spanish knight and a Negro woman, will soon join the Catholic Church's roll of canonized saints." Pope John canonized Martin on May 6, 1962. St. Martin is the patron of interracial justice and, especially in the United States, is invoked as the patron of all who work for harmonious race-relations.

Few citizens of the United States have been canonized. There is no St. Catherine of Chicago, no St. Robert of Rochester, but the city of Lima in Peru can boast of five saints, men and women who walked its streets at the beginning of the seventeenth century. All of them died within a few years of each other. All of them are known for their compassion to the poor and the oppressed blacks and Indians who were under the heel of the Spanish conquerors. All of them are excellent examples for us to follow in our duty of compassion for the poor and downtrodden minorities in our own country.

One was the pioneer archbishop of Lima, St. Toribio de Mogrovejo (1538-1605), the first American man to be canonized. Three times he trekked the eighteen thousand square miles of his archdiocese to bring the healing waters of baptism to native Peruvians before he died, worn out by his apostolic adventures.

A second saint was Rose of Lima (1586-1617). She was

confirmed by St. Toribio and came to him for counsel and confession. At fifteen she received the habit of a Third Order Dominican. In obedience to her parents Rose did not enter a convent, but lived at home as a recluse in a shack in the garden. She experienced extraordinary mystical gifts and visions. The people of Lima heard of her holiness, and her garden became the spiritual center of the city. She spent long hours in prayer and cruel penances and found an outlet for her sympathy for the sufferings of others in her care for the sick, poor, Indians, and slaves. Today she is considered the originator of social service work in South America. She was the first saint of the New World and was canonized in 1671. She died on August 24, 1617, after a three-year illness. She is patroness of South America.

The third saint of Lima was St. Francis Salerno, a Franciscan priest and collaborator with St. Toribio. The ship on which he sailed from Spain had to be abandoned in a storm. Francis insisted on staying aboard with the black slaves who were left to their fate and helped most of them escape from the sea. For twenty years he preached the Good News to thousands of Indians and Spanish colonists. When he was buried in 1610, the Jesuit who preached at the Requiem Mass proclaimed him "the hope and edification of all Peru, the example and glory of Lima."

St. John de Massias (1585-1645) was a Dominican brother, a native of Spain. He entered the Dominican friary at Lima in 1622 and served as doorkeeper until his death. He was beatified in 1837 and canonized in 1975. He is buried in the Church of Santo Domingo in Lima.

Saint Martin de Porres, canonized by Pope John XXIII in 1962, was the fifth saint of Lima. He was a humble black Dominican lay brother born in Lima in 1579. His mother was Anna Velasquez, a freed black slave from Panama. His father was a Spanish grandee, Don Juan de Porres of Burgos in Spain, Knight of Calatrava, Grand Cross of the order of Alcantara.

Don Juan's nobility did not prevent him from abandoning the mother and child after a brief period. At twelve, Martin was a barber's apprentice picking up a rudimentary knowledge of medicine, which stood him in good stead later in life. At fifteen, he became a Dominican tertiary and nine years later took the vows of a Dominican lay brother at the Convent of the Rosary.

Then he began an almost incredible mission of charity to the poor people of Lima. Most of his hours he spent begging for needy families, for poor students and clergy, for special help to blacks and Indians. Many cures of the sick were traced to him. His hours of prayer and charitable work gave him hardly any time for sleep. Thousands thronged to him for spiritual counseling and prayer. Miracles, visions, and penitential practices were attributed to him.

In the convent he held various positions — almoner for the poor, barber, infirmarian, wardrobe keeper, caring for the sick throughout the city. He founded an orphanage and foundling hospital. He was a close friend of St. Rose of Lima. His holiness, penances, and prodigious efforts to help the poor brought him the veneration of the whole city.

When he died at Rosary Convent on November 3, 1639, he was acclaimed a saint by the people. The formal canonization took place much later.

In their 1979 pastoral, *Brothers and Sisters to Us*, the National Conference of Catholic Bishops proclaim the responsibility of all American Catholics to rid themselves of the sin of racism:

"Racism is a sin, a sin that divides the human family, blots out the image of God among specific members of that family and violates the fundamental dignity of those called to be children of the same Father. Racism is the sin that says some human beings are inherently superior and others essentially inferior because of race. It is the sin that makes racial characteristics the determining factor for the practice of human rights. It mocks the words of Jesus: "Treat others the way you would have them treat you." (Mt. 7:12) ... Indeed, racism is more than a disregard for the words of Jesus; it is a denial of the truth of the dignity of each human being revealed in the mystery of the incarnation."[1]

The bishop's pastoral asks us to examine our consciences and work to cure the cancer of racism wherever it exists:

"Racism is not merely one sin among many; it is a radical evil dividing the human family and denying the new creation of a redeemed world. To struggle against it demands an equally radical transformation in our minds and hearts as well as in the structure of our society."

In the Liturgical Constitution at Vatican II the bishops of the world wrote that "the feasts of the saints proclaim the wonderful works of Christ in his servants and offer fitting examples for the faithful to follow." St. Martin de Porres is pre-eminently a "fitting example" to follow in the quest for social justice for blacks, Hispanics, native Americans, Asians, and other minorities in our country.

Saint Turibius of Mogrovejo

The Bishop on Horseback

I suspect that very few Catholics have any notion of who St. Turibius was. This brief account is in answer to the question, "Who was St. Turibius?"

One of America's first saints, St. Turibius de Mogrovejo was the first archbishop of Lima in Peru.

Turibius (his Spanish name is Toribio Alfonso de Mogrovejo) was born at Mayorga in Spain; he died in Peru on March 23, 1606; he was canonized in 1726, fifty-five years after the canonization of Rose of Lima, whom he had confirmed. He also confirmed St. Martin de Porres and St. John Messias, both Dominicans. In Peru he worked with the Franciscan missionary, St. Francis Salerno, a Franciscan.

Turibius was a lay professor of law at the University of Salamanca. King Philip II appointed him principal judge of the Court of the Inquisition at Granada, an unusual post for a layman. It was more unusual that he was named Archbishop of Lima. Despite his protests, he received holy orders and was ordained bishop. He came to Peru in 1581.

The vast Archdiocese of Lima stretched four hundred miles along the coast and many miles inland to the Andes — eighteen thousand square miles in all. In his twenty-five years as archbishop, Turibius visited every corner of it three times — every seven years. They called him the "Bishop on Horseback." He baptized, it is estimated, five hundred thousand and confirmed eight hundred thousand and worked unceasingly for the Indians and the Spanish colonists. His twenty-five years as archbishop were full of accomplishments; he built churches, religious houses, schools, hospitals, and roads in the trackless jungle.

Even more difficult was his attempt to eradicate the abuses and scandals among the clergy and his battle against the

Spanish conquerors, who had little regard for religion and were interested only in the riches they could amass. In his *The Oxford Dictionary of Saints*, David Hugh Farmer writes that immense numbers of baptized knew nothing of the Christian religion, partly because of the shortage of suitable clergy, also because, "above all, the Spanish conquerors gave appalling examples of tyranny, oppression, and cynical disregard for Christian moral teaching, and they were there to make their fortunes by any means in their power."[2]

Archbishop Turibius corrected the worst abuses and disciplined the most notorious of the clergy. He was persecuted because he protected the poor from oppression and because with patient courage he confronted the people in power who fought him. He overcame their opposition in the end.

Turibius took more positive steps. In 1591 he founded the first seminary in the New World. Even in his old age he studied the Indian dialects and converted many by speaking in their own languages. He often stayed in the jungle for several days without sufficient food. He visited every part of his huge archdiocese and celebrated Mass every day with great fervor, even during his rough journeys. He gave his possessions to the poor and was tireless in the leadership he gave by his example of Christian charity to the Indians and to poor Spaniards, who did not know where the help came from.

After a quarter-century of unremitting missionary work he fell ill at Pacasmayo. Toiling to the last, he struggled as far as Santa, where he knew he would die. He made his will, gave his personal belongings to his servants, and the rest of the property to the poor. After receiving Viaticum and the Sacrament of the Sick, he died while those about him sang from the psalms, "I was glad when they said to me, we will go into the house of the Lord." It was March 23, 1606. He was sixty-eight years old. David Farmer says of him: "His cult has long been strong in the Americas ... but he was recently selected as a type of a pioneering missionary and reforming bishop and as a representative of South America, whose immense Christian population is often forgotten."

Saint Peter Claver, S.J.

The Slave of the Black Slaves

There was another seventeenth-century saintly missionary to South America who worked for fifty years, not in Peru, but in Colombia.

On the "Mausoleum of the American Saints" at St. Joseph Cemetery south of Columbus, Ohio, there is a portrait of one of them. The inscription reads: "St. Peter Claver, 1580-1654, Canonized 1888," followed by this summary of an extraordinarily courageous and compassionate missionary.

Braving the horrible odors, the sickly atmosphere, and overwhelming anxiety within the slave ships of South America, Claver not only gave the slaves spiritual comfort and guidance but cured their sores, bandaged their wounds, and cared for the sick.

Peter Claver was born at Verdu in Catalonia, Spain, in 1580. He studied at the University of Barcelona, and took his vows as a Jesuit in 1600 at Tarragona. He was sent to the Jesuit College in Parma in Majorca. There he began to doubt his vocation as a Jesuit. It was the old hall-porter at the College, St. Alphonsus Rodriguez (also canonized in 1888) who counselled him and helped him overcome his nervousness at being a priest and spoke to him of the need for missionaries in the New World. In 1610, he went "to the Indies" — to Cartagena, a seaport on the Caribbean in what is now Colombia; it was the most fearsome slave market in South America. There he met Father Alonso de Sandoval, a Jesuit priest who had devoted his life to the slaves. Peter was ordained a priest in 1616 and began a thirty-three year heroic career which he summed up when he called himself "the slave of the black slaves."

In the early seventeenth century the seaport town of Cartagena was the center of the incredible cruelties and indignities of the profitable slave trade in the Americas. There the slave-ships put in, packed with men and women wrenched from their homes in Africa, chained together in bundles of six, wedged under decks where neither sun nor moon could penetrate, in a stench into which no white officer could put his head for fear of fainting. The description comes from Father Sandoval, who had already spent forty years caring for the slaves. It is estimated that ten thousand slaves were shipped from Africa to the seaport town of Cartagena. Many of the slaves died during the long voyage; those who survived were starving, stinking, covered with sores, and more than half-crazed with fear.

The curious crowd of whites who stood on the shore as the slave-ships came into port would stand back as the little Jesuit priest bustled among the slaves with fruit, bandages, medicine, and brandy. Peter's face would beam as he moved gently among them — and they never knew how sick he became at the task, how he almost fainted daily at the horrors of his ministry. But he did it for thirty-three years. To conceal his physical disgust, he would kiss the running sores. Peter Claver baptized the dying, then washed and fed the sick. As he took them to the yards where they were penned like cattle, the slaves crowded around him with pathetic demonstrations of affection for the one white man in Cartagena who was kind to them.

For thirty-three years, he continued to wash them, dress their putrid wounds, make their beds for them, and mother the whole pitiful crowd of them. It was Peter who told them of a God whose love for them was unbounded. One biographer comments:

The poor outcasts fell on their knees and through a mist of tears worshipped the God who made the slave-trader in his image, the God of the white men who had torn them from their homes, the God of the brutes who had treated them as brutes. God was all this, but he was also the God of Father Claver.[3]

By 1650 the slave of the black slaves was old and broken. From Havana had come the plague. Claver and the other Jesuits flung themselves into the attempt to help those who were struck down by it. Peter caught the plague; he recovered but found himself almost helpless. Strapped to his horse, he visited the harbor, his house of lepers, and the hospitals. Often he fainted as he went, and finally they put him in a sick room of his own. During his last four years he was practically alone. His fellow Jesuits were too busy with the plague to visit him. They appointed a black slave, Joachim, to feed Father Claver, who lay there all day in the steaming heat and the flies. Joachim became a bully; he grew more and more contemptuous of the silent, helpless old man who could not feed himself. Often, toward the end of the bullying, Joachim would not come at all. There were days when Father Claver would lie alone, very still and uncomplaining, without food and without help.

On September 8, 1654, Our Lady's birthday, Peter Claver died in Cartagena. In 1888 he was canonized and named the official patron of those who bring the Gospel to their black brothers and sisters.

In every century since Christ was born there are a few persons with a special holiness about them, special glory. St. Peter Claver was one of them.

In 1932 Father Cyril C. Martindale, S.J., gave an inspiring talk on St. Peter Claver over the B.B.C. radio. Reprinted recently in *What Are Saints?* I have relied on it for much of this account. I have also used the book about St. Peter Claver which Arnold Lunn published under the title, *A Saint in the Slave Trade*.[4]

Father Martindale ended his radio talk with two questions and an answer: "Do you want a hero? Do you want a man co-crucified with Christ? You have him. Peter Claver."

Fray Junipero Serra, O.F.M.

Founder of California

Of all the missionaries from abroad who brought the name of Mary and unleashed great waves of devotion to the Mother of God, probably the best known is Franciscan Friar Junipero Serra, even though one commentator calls him "the most overlooked man in America." His statue is in the Hall of Statuary in the Capitol in Washington, D.C., placed there by the people of California.

Franciscan Friar Junipero Serra attracted the attention of the news media in 1985. Under the headline, "Pope to visit United States again," *The Tablet* of London stated that Pope John Paul had expressed a desire to visit the United States again, probably in 1987. At a Mass in August, 1984, celebrating the 200th anniversary of Father Serra's death, the eighteenth century founder of nine of the famous twenty-one missions in California, Archbishop Pio Laghi, the Apostolic Pro-Nuncio to the United States, gave a strong hint, the *Tablet* wrote, that "in the near future" the pope might come to proclaim Serra's beatification at Carmel, California, where Serra died.[5]

Junipero Serra was officially declared "Venerable" on May 9, 1985. This title is given to one whose cause for beatification has been accepted by the Congregation for Saints at the Vatican. Beatification, a preliminary step toward canonization, as the *Catholic Almanac* says, begins with an investigation of the candidate's life, writings, and heroic practice of virtue. There must be certification of at least two miracles worked by God through the intercession of the "Blessed," as the candidate for canonization is called. If the findings of the investigation so indicate, the pope decrees that the "Venerable Servant of God" may be honored locally or in a limited way in the liturgy. Additional procedures may lead to canonization.

The investigation of alleged miracles has already begun. In its issue of May 31, 1985, Boston's *The Pilot* quoted Bishop Thaddeus Shubsda of Monterey, who said the Church is studying one possible miracle attributed to Father Serra. He set up a tribunal in February, 1985, to question witnesses and doctors in the case of a woman allegedly cured of cancer due to Father Serra's intercession. Two more in the Los Angeles diocese also are under review by tribunals, Bishop Shubsda said.

St. Bernadette is linked to Lourdes; Thomas Becket is linked to Canterbury. Junipero Serra is linked to the coast of what was once known as Upper California. As leader of the Franciscans who were both missionaries and colonizers, Serra worked there from his arrival in 1769 at the age of fifty-seven until his death in 1784 at the Carmel mission in Monterey.

On May 19, 1985, the National Broadcasting System aired a documentary called "Father Serra and the American West." In a review entitled, "California's Founding Father" by John W. Donohoe in the weekly, *America,* the author states that the film so accurately captures the association of the man with the place that it may be said to have two principal characters: Fray Junipero Serra and California.

The documentary begins with Edwin Newman inspecting the statue of Serra in the Capitol in Washington and remarking, "If you had to nominate the most overlooked man in America, you might choose this man, Father Junipero Serra." The scene shifts to California, where the ignorance is not total, as Newman says, "To Californians Serra is a founding father." Then he shows glimpses of a "Junipero Serra Road" traffic sign overarching a freeway, of a "Junipero Serra County Park" and a "Father Serra's Restaurant and Deli."

Jose Miguel Serra was born at Petra, Majorca, Spain, on November 24, 1713. His parents were farmers. He took the name Junipero, who was a companion of St. Francis, when he joined the Franciscan order in 1730. In 1743 he was appointed to the Duns Scotus chair of philosophy at Lullian University in Palma; however, he had always wanted to be a missionary with the Franciscans in New Spain. In 1749 he was sent to San Fernando College in Mexico City. From 1758 to 1769 he was an itinerant preacher throughout Mexico and a teacher at San Fernando College.

It was not until he was fifty-seven, with a lame leg, that he received the assignment for which he is famous. In 1767 he was chosen *"presidente"* of the Lower California missions. Two years later he and his Franciscan companions pushed north with the military expedition under Gaspar de Portola to San Diego, where he founded his first mission in Upper California on July 16, 1769. A year later he established his permanent quarters at Monterey-Carmel in the San Carlos mission.

Father Serra became *presidente* of the Franciscans who took over the missions of the banished Jesuits in Lower California and led them to present-day California in 1769. By the time of his death in 1784 he had personally founded nine missions from the first at San Diego, to Sonoma, his last foundation, six hundred miles to the north. Ultimately, the Franciscans would found twenty-one missions in California. The names read like a litany of saints. Those founded by Serra himself were San Diego, San Carlos, San Antonio, San Gabriel, San Luis Obispo, San Francisco de Assisi, San Juan Capistrano, Santa Clara, and San Buenaventura. Each of California's four largest cities — Los Angeles, San Diego, San Jose, and San Francisco — has a name originating in one of the Spanish missions of the eighteenth century.

Spanish Franciscans went to California for two reasons: first, with the expulsion of the Jesuits in 1767 from Lower California where they had established their missions, the Franciscans took their place; secondly, with the expansion of Russian exploration into Alaska, the Spanish rulers feared that California might be lost to them. They ordered the fortification of two places on the coast. Serra was placed in charge of the missionaries who always accompanied Spanish colonization.

The sixth of the nine missions founded by Junipero Serra himself was San Francisco, named for the founder of the Franciscan order. The name of the mission later was changed to Los Dolores because a Spanish general came upon it on the feast of Our Lady of Sorrows. Father Serra celebrated Mass there on June 29, 1776, five days before the signing of the Declaration of Independence.

Junipero Serra baptized some six thousand Indians and confirmed almost five thousand more. He is so well known for the spiritual aspect of his achievements along the Pacific Coast that his help in fostering the material progress of the Indians tends to be forgotten. He was a pioneer in helping the Indians to an amazing development in agriculture, the raising of cattle, arts and crafts. He was beloved by the Indians, defended their rights against exploitation by the Spanish governors. He was the one man who held California for Spain and a source of inspiration for all. Although he was a frail man with a persistent leg injury, he supervised an incredible network of missions.

It was his humanitarian and cultural leadership which led the California legislature to erect the bronze statue of Father Serra in the Hall of Statuary in the Capitol in Washington.

At the end of his television documentary, Edwin Newman suggested that the life of Serra might be miracle enough for beatification. "And so, too, might the cardinals for the Causes of Saints if 'Father Serra and the American West' were to be screened at their next meeting," wrote Father Donohoe at the end of his review of the documentary on Fray Junipero Serra.

Venerable Joseph de Veuster

Father Damien: The Leper Priest of Molokai

Father John Bannister Tabb, a poet-priest of Maryland, wrote a well-known quatrain about Father Damien:

> Oh, God, the cleanest offering
> Of tainted earth below,
> Unblushing to Thy feet we bring—
> "A leper white as snow."

When he died in the leper colony of Kalaupapa on the Hawaiian island of Molokai on April 15, 1889, the whole world paid tribute to him.

When I visited Honolulu and Molokai in 1980, I saw the unconventional — and controversial — statue of Damien outside the state capitol building; it is the work of artist Marisol Escobar in 1969. In the *Homiletic and Pastoral Review* in 1980, Robert J. Curran described the statue: "The statue depicts the priest in the advanced stages of leprosy, with ruined facial features, wired spectacles, and battered black hat, with a diseased hand holding a walking stick, and a squared, but sturdy body draped in a black cape that could serve as a burial pall."[6] The statue is a copy of the original bronze work which the State of Hawaii chose to place in the Hall of Statuary in the Capitol in Washington.

Father Damien began life as Joseph de Veuster, but took the name of St. Damien, a seventh century bishop of Pavia in Italy, when he joined the Sacred Hearts Fathers. St. Damien, the story goes, once healed a leper with a kiss.

Joseph de Veuster was born on January 3, 1840, in the town of Tremeloo, about six miles from the famous old University of Louvain or Leuven (Flemish) in Belgium. His parents were farmers. When he was eighteen he joined the Fathers of the Sacred Hearts of Jesus and Mary, where his older brother had gone before him and taken the name Pamphile. (The Society was also known as the Picpus Fathers and Brothers; it was founded by a Father Coudrin in 1805 in the Rue Picpus in Paris.)

After a few months in Leuven, Joseph decided to join the missionary society. He began his studies for the priesthood. One day a visiting bishop, the Vicar Apostolic of Tahiti in Oceania, spoke to the seminarians about the need for and the life of missionaries in Polynesia. Damien, who had wanted to go as a missionary to the Indian tribes of North America, now felt called to work in the South Pacific.

In 1825, Pope Leo XII had entrusted the missionary efforts in the archipelago of the Sandwich Islands (presently Hawaii) to the Sacred Hearts Fathers. The first priests and brothers went there in 1827, but after three years of persecution, they were forced into exile. In 1839 the Hawaiian government signed a treaty with France, granting Catholics freedom of worship and the same privileges as Protestants.

Father Damien volunteered to go to the Islands when his brother, who had been appointed to go, fell ill with typhus. He arrived in Honolulu in 1863 and was ordained a priest the next year. For the next nine years he worked in various mission parishes. Something of a rough and ready physician, this young priest from Tremeloo soon saw his reputation as a healer spread through the islands. The exotic diseases of the tropical islands intrigued him and he spent many hours studying their causes and searching for means to alleviate them. The lepers especially interested him.

At that time leprosy (or Hansen's disease) left hideous deformities in its victims; it was the scourge of the islands. The Hawaiian government under King Kamehameha had designated a thin strip of land on the rocky island of Molokai, to which lepers were exiled. The lepers on Molokai set up a colony governed after a fashion by themselves. While their strength lasted, they spent their days in dancing, card playing, and licentiousness, then crawled away to die. The lepers were torn from their families, herded into boats, and dumped onto Molokai. There they had no medical care, little food, no sanitary facilities, no hope — nothing but a grinding despair and sullen apathy while their bodies rotted away. Often the others were too uninterested even to bury the dead. There was no doctor or priest to care for their physical and spiritual needs.

Joseph de Veuster stepped into that horror in 1873 when he volunteered to live with the lepers on Molokai. He remained there for the rest of his life. In a fine phrase of Robert Louis Stevenson, "he was the man who shut with his own hands the door of his own sepulchre." He ministered single-handed to the spiritual and physical needs of six hundred lepers of all religions, dressing their wounds, building houses and a church with them, and digging their graves. He fought with the government (and even his own religious brothers) for them.

For the last three years of his life, Damien did get some help. Ira Barnes Dutton (1843-1931) of Vermont and Wisconsin, who had served in the Civil War as a Union lieutenant, became a convert to Catholicism in 1883 and joined the Trappists as a lay brother with the name of Joseph. In 1886 he came to Molokai to work with Father Damien among the lepers. When Damien died, Brother Joseph became administrative assistant of the colony.

One Sunday Damien began his homily at Mass with the words, "My fellow lepers." For the rest of his life he shared everything with his beloved lepers, even their disease. Even after he became a leper himself, he continued his work for them. He was assisted toward the end by Brother Joseph and some priests of his own Order. Shortly before his death a group of American Franciscan Sisters from Syracuse, N.Y. came to Molokai to help. Led by Mother Marianne Kopp, they were to continue Father Damien's apostolate.

The renowned English novelist, Robert Louis Stevenson, who had visited Molokai, wrote a stinging rebuttal of charges of moral laxity made against Damien by a Protestant minister named Hyde.[7] Stevenson predicted that Father Damien de Veuster would be canonized by the Catholic Church. On July 7, 1977, one hundred fifty years after the Sacred Heart Fathers came to Hawaii, Pope Paul VI called Damien "Venerable" — a step on the road to canonization. Stevenson's prediction might come true before the hundred years he had prophesied in his prediction.

Mother Marianne of Molokai

Successor to Father Damien

In the summer of 1980 there was a news item in Catholic papers about Mother Marianne Kopp of Molokai. Bishop Scanlan, bishop of Honolulu, it said, had named an official historical commission "to investigate the sainthood of Mother Marianne, a German-born American who spent thirty-three years among the lepers of the Hawaiian Islands before her death in 1918. For thirty of those years, she and the Franciscan Sisters had continued the work of the famed Father Damien de Veuster at the leper colony of Kalawao on Molokai.

I was especially interested in that news item because I had prayed at her grave two months before I read it. In the summer of 1980 I was one of the thousands of tourists who flocked to the islands of Hawaii. In the blaze of beauty on the islands, I could understand why Mark Twain could call them "the fairest fleet of islands anchored in any ocean."

I remember, of course, the white beaches and gorgeous flowers and the warm breezes that make Hawaii a magnet for tourists. I remember better the priests and laypeople who showed me the rich spirit of welcome summed up in that fine word, "Aloha." Most of all, I remember the day when, through the courtesy of Father Daniel Dever, the superintendent of schools of the Honolulu diocese, I flew with him in a small plane to the two settlements of Kalawao and Kalaupapa where Father Damien achieved world fame as the leprous Apostle of the lepers. I felt his continuing presence.

There is no one living at Kalawao now, but the Church of St. Philomena built by Father Damien and his lepers still stands. It is empty now, but it was full that drowsy first Sunday of June in 1888 when Damien walked to the communion rail to give his homily. All the congregation was shocked to attention when, instead of his usual, *"My brothers and sisters,"* he began slowly and clearly *"We lepers."* It was his way of telling his people he had the dread disease. What happened that day will be part of the documentation for the process of beatification of Father Damien, now underway.

The grave beside the church is empty now, for his body was returned to his native Belgium in 1936. But the body of the woman who came to continue his work a few months before he died rests in another grave not far away in a cemetery beside her Sisters' hospital at Kalaupapa. The tombstone is inscribed, "Mother Marianne Kopp." There are still Sisters of her order caring for the lepers still living at Molokai.

The story of Mother Marianne could begin at the motherhouse of the Third Franciscan Order, Minor Conventual Sisters, founded in 1860 by Mother Bernadine Dorn in Syracuse, New York. Mother Marianne succeeded her as superior general. One day in 1883, Father Leonor, at the request of his bishop in Honolulu, came to the motherhouse to ask for volunteers to continue Father Damien's work for the lepers in the fearsome exile of Molokai. The priest had toured the United States and spoken to fifty religious communities, but not one had responded to his plea. He had all but given up the quest. Mother Marianne called the nuns of St. Anthony's convent in Syracuse together and Father Leonor tried again. She explained just what the mission would mean. Thirty-six Sisters and almost all the novices volunteered at once. Mother Marianne soon sailed with six of the Sisters and landed at Honolulu to a royal welcome on November 8, 1883. She had intended to return to Syracuse, but soon decided to stay and devote the rest of her life to the lepers. "I am hungry for the work," she wrote. "I wish with all my heart to be one of the chosen ones. ...I am not afraid of any disease; hence, it would be my greatest delight to minister to the abandoned lepers... Waking and sleeping, I am on the Islands. Do not laugh at me for being so wholly absorbed in that one wish, one thought, to be a worker in that large field."[8]

After a three-year whirlwind of work amid the incredible squalor and neglect in which the lepers of Oahu lived, Mother Marianne turned over her responsibilities to three of her Sisters and sailed to Molokai with two others in November, 1888. She gave the Sisters a solemn promise that if they shared her faith and followed her instructions to the letter not one of them would ever contract the disease from which Father Damien lay dying in his rude home at Kalawao. None of the many Sisters who served with her and after her ever did.

Mother Marianne was in charge of the leper settlement for thirty more years. On April 15, 1889, Father Damien — Joseph de Veuster — died happy with the knowledge that his beloved lepers were in good hands. Because of the heroic faith and love which drove her through the horrors of Kalawao, we may someday celebrate the feast of Saint Marianne of Molokai.

Bishop Frederic Baraga

The Bishop on the Postcard

The headline in the *National Catholic Reporter* was intriguing: "How many bishops does it take to mail a postcard? One — and the church-state separatists object."

In early 1984 the Postal Service of the United States announced that it would issue a commemorative postcard on June 29 honoring Bishop Frederic Baraga, a Slovenian missionary known for his linguistic achievements and humanitarian work with American Indians. He was the first bishop of Marquette, Wisconsin, from 1853 to 1868.

W. Melvin Adams, the executive director of the Americans United for Separation of Church and State, vehemently protested. He said that Bishop Baraga may possibly be beatified and canonized as a saint, and that his picture on the postcard might possibly help the process and thus would constitute state interference in an "internal process of the Roman Catholic Church." To which Agnes Rufus of Marquette, a leader in the Bishop Baraga Association, replied in effect, "Come off it, Mr. Adams." She said, "When are people going to learn that you can look beyond Catholicism, beyond the priesthood, and see his goodness and humanity? If a daisy can get on a stamp, why can't Baraga, who did so much for people?"

Frederic Baraga was one of the greatest of the missionary priests who brought the Faith to the United States in the early nineteenth century; he preached the Good News to the Indians of the Upper Peninsula of Michigan and in Northern Wisconsin.

Bishop Baraga was born June 29, 1797, of a wealthy Austrian family of Slovenian extraction at Malavas, Carniola (now a province of Jugoslavia). His devout parents died when he was a child. A lay professor took him into his home and directed his classical studies. At nineteen he was a law student at the

University of Vienna. There he met St. Clement Mary Hofbauer, a Redemptorist priest, who was known as the "Apostle of Austria." Under the influence of St. Clement he decided to become a priest. After graduating from the University in 1821 he broke off his engagement to marry, renounced his inheritance, and entered a seminary at Laibach (now Ljubljana, Yugoslavia). He was ordained a priest in 1823 at the age of twenty-six. As an assistant in a small, neglected parish in his diocese, he soon became famous as a preacher, confessor, and spiritual writer. A prayer book he wrote quickly ran through ten editions.

Through the Leopoldine Society, Frederic learned of the desperate plight of American Indians. This society, founded by Emperor Franz I of Austria and named for his daughter, the Archduchess Leopoldine, Empress of Brazil, focused on mission activity in the United States and Canada. With the French Society for the Propagation of the Faith, founded by laypersons in Lyons in France and the Ludwig Society, founded by King Ludwig of Bavaria, it played a highly significant role in the development of Catholicism in the Midwest by its financial largesse.

Frederick decided to volunteer to go to Cincinnati. On January 18, 1831, Father Baraga presented himself to Bishop Fenwick in Cincinnati. After a three months' study of Indian dialects, he was sent to Arbre Croche (now Harbor Springs) in Michigan. For the next thirty-seven years he preached the Good News to the Indians of the Upper Peninsula and northern Wisconsin. He found his happiness in ministering to the Indians, whom he loved. He sought them out unceasingly in their hidden haunts; he built churches, and established Christian communities. Within twenty-eight months he baptized 547 members of the Ottawa tribe at Arbre Croche and changed a deteriorating mission into a thriving Christian settlement. It was the same wherever he went: from Arbre Croche to Beaver Island, from Indian Lake to Grand River (1833), to La Pointe (1835), to L'Anse (1843).

The Indian tribes in L'Anse were the Chippewas, among whom he spent much of his time. (The Chippewa tribe, known in Canada as Ojibwa, is the largest Algonquian-speaking tribe of North American Indians, inhabiting a region stretching

from Lake Superior and Lake Huron west to North Dakota
across the northern tiers of those states. They still number
55,000 living along the United States-Canada border.)

In his fascinating book, *Sanctity in America*, the late Cardinal Amleto Giovanni Cicognani, then Apostolic Delegate to
the United States, followed Frederic Baraga across those
northern trails: "On and on, through the woods, on snow
shoes or dog-sleigh, over the choppy waters of the lakes in
birch-bark canoes, this dauntless missionary made his way
with only one intent — to bring the Gospel to the red man."9
Archbishop Cicognani quotes from his letters a theme which
re-echoes in them often: "The snow was very deep and the
temperature bitterly cold; but 'oh, the salvation of a single
soul is more than all the millions of this world.' " In each
place, Baraga wrote, "chapel, house, and school have to be
built." And during those long and grueling cold journeys he
was composing a *Practical Grammar of the Otchipwe Language* (published in Detroit in 1850) and a dictionary of the
same language. He wrote numerous other books in Indian dialects, German, and Slovene, about the history and culture of
the Indians, and numerous catechisms and prayerbooks for
the Indians in their own languages.

In 1853 he was named Vicar Apostolic of the Upper Peninsula and ordained a bishop in Cincinnati. Four years later the
vicariate became the diocese of Sault Ste. Marie, which he later transferred to Marquette. His new role did not stop him
from continuing his work for his beloved Indians. Cardinal Cicognani quotes some random entries in his diary: "I lay down
on the cold sand and spent the night shivering with cold.
...From four in the morning until ten this evening, I worked incessantly — many confessions, five sermons, twenty-three
baptisms, and three Confirmations."

In his *Dictionary of American Catholic Biography*, John J.
Delaney described his ardent zeal and incessant activity:

*He spent the last fifteen years of his life administering his far-flung
see, traveling incessantly through it. He had a voluminous correspondence ...He was passionately devoted to the spiritual, material,
and intellectual needs of his people and gave tirelessly of his considerable energy to them. He made thousands of converts to Catholicism and was a popular figure, not only among the Indians but among*

all with whom he came in contact; he is remembered in Michigan by the county named after him."[10]

In the fall of 1857 Bishop Baraga suffered a stroke at the Second Provincial Council of Baltimore. Though he was critically ill, he insisted on returning to Marquette to await his co-adjutor bishop and to fulfill his vow to die among the Indians. He lived on for another decade and died on January 19, 1868, still preaching, writing, sacrificing his life for the Indians to whom he brought the Word and Sacraments. The preliminary steps for his beatification have been taken.

Father Jean Pierre Aulneau, S.J.

Minnesota's Forgotten Martyr

On December 9, 1985, the *New York Times* published an article with the headline: "Minnesota Corner Joining Civilization." The dateline was Angle Inlet, Minnesota, which is a tiny settlement on the shore of the Lake of the Woods in what is called the Northwest Angle, a 150-square-mile tract of bogs and woods. Only sixty people lived there. The *Times* article describes its history briefly: "The Angle's first inhabitants were Chippewa and Sioux Indians. In the 1730's explorers and Jesuits came to the Angle in search of the Northwest Passage, a waterway thought to connect the Atlantic and Pacific Oceans."

I write here about one of those Jesuit missionaries. I first read about him in an article by Father James Plough, entitled "The Forgotten Martyr: The Story of a Jesuit Priest and a Sioux Tomahawk." This was his first paragraph: "On the morning of June 6, 1736, the sun rose quietly over the blood-stained shores of an island in northern Minnesota's Lake of the Woods. The blood was that of 31-year-old Father Jean Pierre Aulneau."[11]

Father Aulneau was indeed a forgotten martyr. I could find only three brief references to him in the 15-volume *New Catholic Encyclopedia*. One spoke of "historic Fort St. Charles, founded by the French explorer Pierre La Verendrye in 1732, which was reconstructed by the Minnesota Knights of Columbus in memory of Jean Pierre Aulneau, a Jesuit martyred by the Sioux Indians in 1736." Another reference was to another Jesuit missionary in New France: Pierre de Lauzon, who was named in 1732 the superior of the Jesuits in Canada and Rector of the College of Quebec, where he remained for seven years. After a visit to his native France in 1733 to seek help, "he brought back Rev. Jean Pierre Aulneau, who was martyred at the Lake of the Woods." The third reference was about La Verendrye, who explored North America. Born in Trois Rivieres in Canada in 1685, he set out to explore the West after a soldier's career. He was accompanied by fifty-nine men. "Advance was slowed by lack of funds and skirmishes with the Indians — Cree, Assiniboines, and Saulteaux, on the one hand, and the Sioux, on the other; and by the Sioux's massacre (1736) of his eldest son, Jean Baptiste, a Jesuit missionary, Jean Pierre Aulneau, and twenty-nine of his men."

A few weeks before he died on what has been called "Massacre Island" in the Lake of the Woods, Father Aulneau wrote to his superior in Quebec from Fort St. Charles about his future plans: "After all, what the issue of all these projects will be is known to God alone, and who can tell, perhaps instead of receiving the announcement of these plans, you may hear the news of my death."[12] Eventually, his superior did hear the grisly detail's of Aulneau's death by beheading by a Sioux tomahawk.

On September 17, 1736, Pierre La Verendrye buried the remains of his son Jean Baptiste and Father Aulneau in the chapel of Fort St. Charles, the westernmost outpost of his exploration, from which he sent his son to lead the expedition which ended when the Sioux hacked all twenty-one men to death. Aulneau's premonition was fulfilled that day: they found his headless body on "Massacre Island."

In his article Father Plough explained how, 150 years after it happened, the knowledge of Minnesota's Forgotten Martyr's death came to light in his home town in France.

"On the last day of an Advent mission at Vendee, France, an aged and venerable descendant of the old Aulneau family approached one of the Jesuits who were giving the mission. 'You won't believe it, Father,' he stammered, 'but you're the first Jesuit Fathers I've ever seen — even if the blood runs in the family.'"[13]

An old heirloom he produced showed that some members of the Aulneau family in years past had been Jesuits and that one of them met death at the hands of Indians on a lake in the wilds of North America. Various letters told of the piety and zeal of this forgotten saint.

Father Jean Pierre Aulneau was born in Vendee, France, in the manor of the wealthy Aulneau family on April 21, 1706.

Two of his brothers were priests and one sister became a nun. He joined the Jesuits and at the age of twenty-nine was sent as a seminarian to serve as a missionary in New France. With other Jesuit priests he sailed from La Rochelle in France for eighty long days and nights to Quebec. A plague broke out on the ship *Ruby* and he was so zealous in caring for the sick (twenty of whom died on the way) that a companion Jesuit wrote home, "God preserved his health for the consolation of those aboard." In Quebec he himself fell ill. Many weeks later he recovered his health and spent a year preparing for his ordination in the spring of 1735.

Aulneau's first mission assignment was to accompany Pierre La Verendrye's expedition to Fort St. Charles. This assignment, wrote a fellow Jesuit, was "the longest, most painful and dangerous journey ever undertaken by a missionary in Canada." Leaving Montreal with the expedition on June 21, they reached Fort St. Charles on September 6, 1735. Father Aulneau spent that winter preparing for his mission — to go to a tribe no white man had ever seen. Verendrye had heard about them and called them *Quant Chipouanis* — "those who dwell in holes." Father Aulneau never could preach the Good News to them. He was beheaded a few weeks after beginning his quest to find them.

After the death of Pierre La Verendrye in 1749, Fort St. Charles was abandoned. A few years later, the French and Indian War and the surrender of Canada to the British ended French fur trade in the West. Fort St. Charles was forgotten; its meager records were lost in governmental archives. The stockade and buildings of the fort were obliterated by nature and the northland weather. Knowledge about it existed only in the confused lore of the Indians for one hundred fifty years. Then came the Advent mission of the Jesuits at Vendee in 1889 and the recollections of the old descendant of the Aulneaus.

The Jesuits at St. Boniface College in Manitoba read the Aulneau letters (they had been published in *The Canadian Messenger*) with great interest. In 1889 they organized an expedition to the Lake of the Woods but did not find the forgotten Fort St. Charles. In 1908 another exploration, led by the Archbishop of St. Boniface, discovered it. The fort was fully restored by the Minnesota Knights of Columbus in 1951; they built a memorial altar there. It has two names on it: Father Jean Pierre Aulneau, S.J., 1705-1736, and Pierre G. V. La Verendrye, 1685-1749. At the bottom was another inscription: Fort St. Charles, founded 1732; rediscovered 1908. It is a place of pilgrimage now where the Eucharist is celebrated.

Father Pierre Jean de Smet, S.J.

Missionary and Peacemaker

At its beginning Jesus gave his Church its "Great Commission" to go to the people of all nations, "baptizing them ... teaching them to observe all I have commanded you."

Missionaries fill the pages of the Church's history; over the centuries this has not changed. Vatican II said, "The Church is missionary by its very nature" and defined mission work as "the planting of the Church among those people and groups where she has not yet taken root."

I once spent some hours on a lake with the unusual name of Priest Lake. The priest with me told me it had previously been named Roothan Lake to honor Johannes Philip Roothaan, the twenty-first Superior General of the Jesuits (1785-1853). The Jesuit missionary, Pierre Jean de Smet, who explored, evangelized, and helped pacify much of the American West, named that lake in Idaho to honor his General. For reasons I do not know (perhaps anti-Catholic sentiment) the name was later changed to Priest Lake. But in the Selway-Bitterroot Wilderness in western Montana there are two mountains named by Father de Smet which are still called Mount Saint Mary and Mount Saint Joseph.

Francis Parkman, the famed historian of the exploration of the United States and Canada, remarked somewhere that in that exploration "not a river was crossed, not a corner was turned but a Jesuit led the way." That is an exaggeration, but it is true that European Jesuits were in the forefront of that gallant band of priests, nuns, brothers, and layfolk who came from Europe to bring the Good News and help in the education of Indian tribes throughout Canada and the American Northwest.

Father de Smet was a pioneer who pushed west from St. Louis, through the Plains States and the American Rockies to the far Northwest, leaving churches and mission schools in his wake.

Pierre de Smet was born in 1801 in Termonde (Deudermonde), Belgium; he died in St. Louis in 1873. After meeting Father Charles Nerincks, an early missionary in Kentucky, he came to the United States in 1821. He entered the Society of Jesus and was ordained in Florissant, near St. Louis, in 1827.

The story of the Indian missions in the Pacific Northwest began in St. Louis in 1831 when an Indian delegation from the Flathead and Nez Perce tribes of the distant Columbia River valley came to ask Bishop Joseph Rosati of St. Louis for priests to come to them. They were led by "Old Ignace" LaMousse, a Catholic Iroquois from near Montreal who had intermarried with a Flathood woman. Old Ignace made the long trip over the mountains again in 1835 and 1837 to ask for the "Blackrobes," but no priest came; he was murdered by the Sioux Indians on his third journey. His son came again to St. Louis; on the way he was met by Father de Smet. The Jesuit superior at St. Louis agreed with the bishop that a survey of possibilities should be made and chose de Smet to make it. He had found his life-work. He left for the Rockies in 1840 to begin his ministry to the Indians there.

A year later, he went by wagon train with five companions, one of whom was a French priest, Nicholas Point, whose collection of sketches depicts the first years of the Jesuit missions in the Northwest. In Montana's Bitterroot Mountains they established a base at St. Mary's Mission and worked among the Flathead, Coeur d'Alene, and Blackfeet tribes. They opened missions among various other tribes. But Father de Smet was soon called back to St. Louis.

Pierre de Smet no longer spent most of his time as an active missionary, but he did travel the Great Plains and the Rocky Mountains as an occasional government peace commissioner. His principal work now was to act as a chronicler and publicist for the missions. Between 1843 and 1863 he wrote four books about the Western missions and missionaries.

This Jesuit priest knew the magnitude of the missionary task in the American West. In 1843 he went to Europe to solicit funds and workers. He returned in 1844 around Cape Horn to land at Astoria on the Columbia River with new missionaries;

among them were six Sisters of Notre-Dame de Namur. The account of de Smet's tremendous labors among and for the various Indian tribes of the American West is outlined in the *Dictionary of American Biography:*

> *In carrying out his great projects he traveled 180,000 miles. He crossed the Atlantic sixteen times ... He touched with his unique regenerative influence nearly all the native populations of the Columbia Valley ... He was a personal friend of all whom he met. And to the Indians of the great West he was the ambassador of Heaven — he was "Blackrobe."* [14]

John J. Delaney summed up de Smet's relationship with the Indians: "More than any white man, Father de Smet was trusted by the Indian tribes west of the Missouri and he worked unceasingly for them with the United States Government. He made several trips to Europe, visiting practically every European country seeking aid for the Indians." [15]

During the fifty-two years Pierre de Smet travelled the Western United States in response to that call, first heard in Belgium, to evangelize the American Indians, the white people pushed west, following the Frontier as it moved from East to West; and the Indians resented and resisted this great migration across their territories. Because of the esteem of the Indians for de Smet and his great influence with them, the Government frequently asked him to act to bring peace between the whites and the Indian tribes. De Smet also intervened successfully to bring peace to the tribes when they warred against each other.

In 1851 the authorities in Washington asked de Smet to attend a conference of the tribes who were restless over the influx of white settlers into California and Oregon; at Fort Laramie he succeeded in pacifying them. In 1858 he was chaplain on an expedition against the Mormons (the "Mormon War") and acted as a peacemaker in the matter. (He is said to have advised Brigham Young where to settle with his Mormons and his name is on part of a Mormon monument.)

His most notable intervention in Indian diplomacy occurred in June, 1868, when he visited in the Bighorn Valley. Hostile Indians in Sitting Bull's camp had vowed to kill the first white man to appear among them. As usual, by keeping a just

balance between the two races, he paved the way for a conference and eventual peace.

After reading a dozen accounts of the life of the peripatetic
Belgian Jesuit priest and the many different facts of his career
in the Northwest, I find it difficult to summarize such a crowded and fruitful life. His life reminds me of the words of another
great missionary, St. Paul. His autobiography is found in the
last three chapters of Second Corinthians. There are many
echoes of it in the life of Father Pierre Jean de Smet.

Saint Marguerite Bourgeoys

A Tale of a Valiant Voyager

In 1975, the International Year of Women, the Postmaster General of Canada issued a stamp in her honor at Montreal to honor the 275th anniversary of her death. This stamp pictured her with four young children and acknowledged her dominant role in the educational and social history of Canada. On the stamp were the dates of her birth and death: 1620-1700.

She was called the "First Schoolmistress of Montreal" and the "First Lady of Canada." The day after she died, a priest wrote: "If saints were canonized, as in the past, by the votes of the people and of the clergy, tomorrow we would be celebrating the Mass of Saint Marguerite of Canada."

In 1950 Pope Pius XII beatified her. On October 31, 1982, 282 years after her death, Pope John Paul II canonized her. Her name is Marguerite Bourgeoys. She was the foundress of the Sisters of the Congregation of Notre Dame of Montreal. She was born in 1620 in the city of Troyes in the Champagne district of France.

The first French settlement in North America, on an island called Ville-Marie, dates back to 1608. It is now Montreal, named for the mountain that overlooks the city. The first French governor was Paul de Maisonneuve. In 1653 he was in Troyes to visit his sister in a convent there. He told her that the colony of the City of Mary needed a young woman to instruct the handful of children of the colonists and Indians. She introduced her brother to a twenty-three-year-old member of the congregation of young women she directed. The purpose of the congregation was to bring young women together for prayer and to prepare them for teaching the poor children of the city.

Marguerite Bourgeoys had heroic courage and ardent zeal. She responded to the Governor's plea and set sail on the long and dangerous sea voyage across the North Atlantic on June 20, 1653. In November she arrived at Ville-Marie. She found there a few houses and a fort to guard the few colonists against marauding Iroquois Indians. In the forty-seven years till her death Marguerite became the "Mother of the Colony." She was a contemplative in action, who manifested a mixture of mysticism and realism.

In many ways this pioneer woman of Montreal was ahead of her times. Prayerfully, she would read the "signs of the times," a phrase used by Jesus Christ which has returned to the vocabulary of the Church in the documents of Vatican Council II; and she would respond with appropriate action. In 1658 she opened her first school and lived in a stone stable given to her by Governor Maissonneuve. There she organized a group of young women along the lines of the one she had known in Troyes. They called themselves the "Congregation." Soon she was organizing courses of preparation for marriage and taking care of "The King's Wards," who were young women brought from France to marry and establish homes in the colony. At great risk she and her Congregation taught Indian girls to teach their own people at a time when French politicians frowned on the idea of educating the Indian natives.

Her most lasting contribution to the Church of Canada — and to the world — was the founding of the Congregation of the Sisters of Notre Dame in 1653. In need of recruits to help her innovative work in education and social services, she had crossed the North Atlantic several times and returned with young women who were to form the nucleus of her teaching Sisters. It was a time when the hierarchy of the Church could not understand a religious order of women who would not be cloistered in a convent but active in the world. Bishop Laval of Quebec was in Paris when she made her third trip to France in 1680 and he forbade her to bring back any new recruits to Canada. In God's providence, the Canadian-born girls who had entered the Congregation assured the future of her work.

In her meditations on the mystery of the Visitation of Mary to Elizabeth, Mother Bourgeoys found the essence of her spirituality and the life-style she worked out for herself and others. She found in the Blessed Virgin her inspiration, her desire to comfort those in distress. One of her Notre Dame

Sisters today summed it up: "The essence of Marguerite's spirituality is the spirituality of compassion. The spirit of compassion never failed her in the trials of her life, great or small; it grounded her relationships with her Sisters, her voluntary work for the settlers."

Someone has written an epitaph about a man to the effect that "nothing was so fitting in his life as the way he ended it." The same is true of the valiant woman, St. Marguerite Bourgeoys. In the night of December 31, 1699, the Sisters of the Congregation were called to pray at the deathbed of Sister Catherine Charly, a young mistress of novices. Marguerite had her own prayer: "Lord, why not take me instead of this poor Sister who can still do great things for you?" That night she became critically ill with a high fever. Twelve days later she died. Sister Catherine survived.

The contribution of Marguerite to the Church continues in the missionary works of several thousand of her Sisters, some of whom are in the United States, around the world in schools, colleges, universities, and in diocesan and parish social and family ministries. She still is a *Valiant Voyager* through the Catholic world — a title given to the biography of her life.

Saint John Neumann

America's Unspectacular Saint

On June 19, 1977, a huge crowd watched in St. Peter's Square in Rome as Pope Paul VI celebrated a Mass during which he canonized the first American male saint. In his homily the pope described him as one who was close to the sick, at home with the poor, a friend to sinners, the honor of all immigrants and, from the viewpoint of the Beatitudes, the symbol of Christian success. Just before, Pope Paul had presided at a fifteen minute ceremony where he proclaimed John Neumann, the fourth bishop of Philadelphia, a Saint. The proclamation concluded: "We declare **that** Blessed John Nepomucene Neumann is a saint and we **inscribe** his name in the Calendar of the Saints and establish that he should be devoutly honored among the saints in the Universal Church."[16]

In the modern Mass there is a procession in which people bring bread and wine and other gifts to the presiding priest at the beginning of the Eucharistic Prayer. In Rome that day the gifts included a porcelain bowl filled with rice, symbolizing the Bishop's concern for the poor, a scale model of Bishop Neumann High School in Philadelphia (Neumann established the Catholic school system in the United States), medicines, symbolic of his work for the sick, and bouquets of the state flowers of Pennsylvania, New Jersey, and Delaware, portions of which made up the Diocese of Philadelphia when he served there from 1852 to 1860.

The life of St. John Neumann (pronounced "Noy-mun") divides into four divisions of unequal length. He was born in Prachatitz, a small town in Bohemia (now a part of Czechoslovakia), on March 28, 1811, the third child of Agnes and Philip Neumann, a German father and a Bohemian mother. He was a voracious student of a wide variety of languages and sciences, with a strong inclination to a religious life. He went to the diocesan seminary of Budweis in 1831 and then, two years later, to the theological school at Charles Ferdinand University at Prague. In 1835 he finished his studies for the priesthood, but the diocese of Budweis had a surplus of priests and the bishop would not ordain him. He had always wanted to be a missionary to the United States and was helped by a society in Vienna which sponsored priests for the increasing number of immigrants to that country. He wrote to various bishops in the United States with little response, so he left his home and family and boarded a ship at Le Havre on April 20, 1836, to make the forty-day crossing to New York in search of a bishop who would ordain him. The story is that he arrived at New York harbor with a dollar in his pocket. This ended the first phase of his life.

Bishop John Dubois welcomed the young seminarian and to Neumann's grateful surprise, ordained him after a few weeks, because he had many German immigrants in his diocese, which at that time covered the whole state of New York. Two days after his ordination Bishop Dubois sent him to minister to the many German immigrants around Buffalo and upstate New York. He was to spend four years as a missionary there among the grateful immigrants. By 1840 he wanted to deepen his spiritual life, so he became a member of the few Redemptorists in the United States at Pittsburgh and was the first Redemptorist priest to be professed in the United States. Thus he began the third era of his life.

The 29-year-old Neumann plunged into an unremitting round of pastoral work in Maryland, Ohio, Pennsylvania, and Virginia. After four years as a Redemptorist missionary he became an American citizen and was named the provincial of the Redemptorists. He built St. Peter and Paul Church in Baltimore, and was appointed the rector of St. Alphonsus Church in that city in 1851.

The last stage of St. John Neumann's short life began a few weeks before his 41st birthday. He returned to his room one evening after a busy day of ministry and found on his desk the ring and pectoral cross which Archbishop Francis Patrick Kenrick had worn for twenty-one years as bishop of Philadelphia. (The archbishop had paid a visit that afternoon.) Neumann was aghast. He realized that Pope Pius IX had named him bishop of the sophisticated city of Philadelphia, which had more Catholics than any other — many of them Irish immigrants and some of them the elite of Catholic society in the city — who did not welcome the idea that a roughly clad priest with a pronounced German accent would be their bishop.

The beginning of the account written by *Time* magazine in the week John Neumann was canonized was this: "He stood but 5 ft. 4 in., so they called him the little priest.' He was a shy sort, not much of an orator, and enough the awkward immigrant from Bohemia that some of his colleagues lobbied in vain with Rome to keep him from becoming the bishop of cultured Philadelphia."

When he died at 48, the carvers misspelled his name on the tombstone. When Neumann heard that Kenrick was recommending him as his successor at Philadelphia, he beseeched nuns to pray against such an appointment which he considered "a grave calamity for the Church."[17]

Pope Pius IX thought otherwise, and in 1842 he was ordained Bishop of Philadelphia.

In the eight years of his brief term as bishop, the implausible John Neumann from Bohemia raised a revolution in the diocese of Philadelphia and inaugurated movements which still have impact today. Of necessity he was a brick-and-mortar bishop who had to provide schools and parish churches for the ever-increasing flow of Catholics of different ethnic origins into the diocese, which stretched across thousands of square miles. He spoke to them in their own languages.

He was distressed to find that there were only five hundred children in Catholic schools; the rest went to public schools which often had a bigoted anti-Catholic bias. He met with priests and laity to plan changes. Within a few weeks he made history by establishing the first central diocesan school board in 1852; other dioceses soon followed and the board became the model of parochial school education throughout the nation. Within a year the students in the Catholic schools numbered five thousand and two years later he reported nine thousand. Shortly before he died he said, "Almighty God has so wonderfully blessed the work of Catholic education that nearly every church in my diocese now has its school." He

himself invited several orders of religious women to the diocese and wrote two catechisms, which were widely used. When
he found that black children had no religious training, he built
a school for them. The "little bishop" achieved other distinctions. By the time he died of a stroke on a Philadelphia street
in 1860 he was revered and renowned for his holiness, charity,
spiritual writing, pastoral work, and preaching.

The campaign to have Bishop Neumann declared a Saint —
to be "raised to the honors of the altar," as they say — soon
began, but, as usual, Rome was not hurried about that process.
The bishop was almost overlooked as a serious candidate for
many years; in fact, the case was put on hold in 1912 because,
they said, they doubted whether he had the necessary "heroic
virtue"; he was "too ordinary" a man to be a candidate. In
1921, however, Pope Benedict XV and a board of Cardinals
listened to the persistent pleas. (Just a few hours before their
meeting, the main opponent of Neumann's canonization col-
lapsed and died in a barber chair.)

The article in *Time* magazine in the week the pope canonized him was called "The Saint They Almost Overlooked." It
went on to say,

> *Benedict subsequently designated Neumann as Venerable (worthy
> of veneration and a proper recipient of private prayers) — the begin-
> ning of the long process to sainthood. In doing so the Pope set a
> precedent for the future judgment of possible saints by declaring:
> "Even the most simple works, performed with constant perfection in
> the midst of inevitable difficulties, spell heroism in any servant of
> God."*[18]

Pope Paul VI made the same point in his homily at the ceremony on October 13, 1963, the day he beatified Bishop Neumann. He referred to the "ancient biographers" of saints ...
who sought the unusual and miraculous aspects of the lives of
the saints, perhaps too much so, the Pope admitted, "but they
had understood that the life of a Christian who is really moved
by faith and grace cannot but be wonderful."[19]

The sainting of Bishop John Neumann was a triumph and a
model for the millions of men and women who live unspectac-
ular lives in persistent patience and quiet virtues every day before the God whose will they strive to follow.

Chapter 5
Nine Foundresses

Introduction

Luisa Hensel and Her Three Students

The contributions which the Catholics of Europe have made to the religious life of the United States were enormous. In his book, *Religion in America,* Winthrop Hudson wrote that "the most spectacular development in American religious life in the latter half of the nineteenth century was the growth of the Roman Catholic Church."[1] In *American Catholics,* James Hennesey, S.J., says that immigration transformed American Catholicism: "The effect was massive. Over a million Catholics poured into the country in each decade between 1880 and 1920, and over two million in the years 1901-10. The Catholic population grew from 6,259,000 in 1880 to 16,363,000 in 1910 in a national population that went from 75,995,000 to 91,972,000. Until 1896, most immigrants had come from south, northern and western Europe."[2] Nearly forty percent of the immigrants were Catholic.

German immigrants in the nineteenth century numbered more than six million; a great proportion of them were Catholic. The largest number came from 1850 to 1860 and from 1880 to 1890. Some became farmers but many headed for cities in the Cincinnati — St. Louis — Milwaukee triangle. Mostly poor, with only an elementary education, they soon were building well-organized parishes and schools in the cities and villages of the Midwest. The American Church looked desperately to Europe for the priests, sisters, and brothers who would assist in the assimilation into American Catholic life of the massive torrent of newcomers from Europe.

In 1899, Frances Xavier Cabrini, the Foundress of the Missionary Sisters of the Sacred Heart, sailed from her native Italy to New York with some of her Sisters. She came there to minister to the thousands of poor Italians who had come to this country. She had wanted to work in China, but several prelates advised her to devote herself instead to the Italian immigrants in the United States and to a rapidly growing American church. She became a United States citizen and is the first citizen to be canonized. When she died in Chicago in 1917, her nuns numbered one thousand five hundred in sixty-seven houses in eight countries. They continue to serve in education, nursing, and the care of orphans.

Mother Cabrini was canonized in 1946 by Pope Pius XII. This is the opening prayer of the Mass celebrated in her honor in this country on November 13:

> God our Father,
> You called Frances Xavier Cabrini from Italy
> to serve the immigrants of America.
> By her example teach us concern for the
> sick and the stranger.

The same prayer, with different names, could be said in honor of many women who founded religious orders in the countries of Western and Southern Europe and sent their members to serve the immigrants from their native countries, in thousands of schools, hospitals, parishes, and orphanages in the United States. They came at the urgent request of American bishops who needed their help in staffing the schools and hospitals, built to minister to the needs of the immigrants from Europe.

This is not about Mother Cabrini, however; it is about three other women who founded religious orders of women in Germany in the middle of the nineteenth century. What prompts me to treat them together is a single sentence in an article about Aachen in Germany in the *New Catholic Encyclopedia:* "Three pupils of Luisa Hensel, a teacher at St. Leonhard School in Aachen from 1827 to 1832, founded religious orders: Clare Fey (1815-94), Franziska Schervier (1819-76), and Pauline von Mallinckrodt (1818-81)."[3]

In that small city of Aachen, in Rhine-Westphalia, Luisa taught her three students more than poetry when she gathered her pupils in her classroom. She taught by her example a loving concern and compassion for the poor and sick; she led them into the streets of Aachen to help "the sick and stranger." She taught the three girls to implant that compassion in the Sisters of the Orders they founded.

There are a few lines about Luisa Hensel in *Das Grosse Brockhaus*, a standard German encyclopedia. It mentions her birth on March 3, 1798, at Linum and her death on December 18, 1876 in Paderborn; it tells of her conversion to Catholicism in 1818, how she helped bring back Clemens Brentano, a well known poet, to the Catholic faith, and her refusal of his offer of marriage. "Her published poems," the article says, "were pearls of Catholic poetry inspired by a deeply sensitive Catholic spirituality." [4]

Luisa was a captivating teacher who infused that deep spirituality into her pupils. Nineteen of the thirty-four girls she taught at St. Leonhard's entered religious life. One of them was Clare Fey, the foundress of the Sisters of the Poor Child Jesus, whose American headquarters are in Columbus, Ohio, where they operate Our Lady of Bethlehem early childhood center.

Clare Fey

Marie Louise Christine Clare Fey, the fourth child of Ludwig and Catherina Fey, was born on April 11, 1815, in Aachen, where she spent most of her life. The Fey Family was wealthy, but not attracted to an affluent life-style. They became involved, socially and politically, in fighting for social justice for those in need. Under the inspiration of her mother, who instilled a deep love of neighbor in her children from their earliest years, Clare and the other children soon found themselves helping the poor in the slums of Aachen; she was shocked to find in the inner city a world of social injustice, poverty, despair, hate, and misery.

Clare Fey wanted to establish her belief in every child's right and need to be educated, a principle taken for granted now, but not implemented in early nineteeth-century Germany. At St. Leonhard's, Luisa Hensel helped her to fix it more firmly in her compassionate heart. Clare voluntarily left her family and relatives to dedicate herself completely to the poorest children and to supply them with a home and an education.

After she left school, she and some other zealous women opened a school for poor children in Aachen in 1837. She founded the Sisters of the Poor Child Jesus (a name that met with some opposition) in 1844 to extend the apostolate to the poor. Despite frail health, frequent illnesses, and exile in Holland for her order, she was Superior General of the Sisters for fifty years. She was noted for her industriousness and deep interior life. Her Sisters first came to the United States in 1923.

In 1888 Rome approved the rule of her congregation. The rule stressed the Sisters' purpose of caring for and educating children and young people, especially the poor and the spiritually abandoned and endangered. The rule specified that there would be no distinction of classes among the Sisters. In

1982, that revised rule, updated according to Vatican II, was approved by the Church. A few years ago, their foundress was named a candidate for beatification.

The Congregation of the Poor Child Jesus founded in 1888 is an Apostolic Religious Community whose members publicly take simple vows of virginity, poverty, and obedience. It is a Religious Institute of papal right whose constitutions are based on the Rule of St. Augustine.

A love for children, especially those in greatest need, was the special charism of Mother Clare. Her choice of a name for her Congregation reflects this charism, and her motto — "Lead the children to Jesus" — is the epitome of the apostolic mission of the Sisters. Today that charism is still alive in different parts of the world where her Sisters are actively present among children and youth.

One of the Sisters of the Poor Child Jesus has written a brief description of the spirituality of Clare Fey, which is still the heritage of her Sisters today:

But all true apostleship is rooted in contemplation and Clare's mission was only possible because it flowed from a vital source: the presence of the Lord. In her longing for union with God, Clare developed, under the spiritual guidance of Father Sartorius, a way of life which she calls "The Practice of walking in the presence of God." This too is her charism. The words of Jesus: "Manete in Me" — "Remain in Me" are the well-spring of this Practice and form the key-concept of the spirit of the Congregation. In one of her meditations on Mary, Clare explains the basic principle: "Mary had only one thought — one single, simple, sublime thought: the thought of Mary was the Lord." The spirit of Clare Fey is clear and well-defined. It is finding God in all things, not least at the heart of the human condition. To live in this spirit requires a constant waiting on God, an "opening up" to his gifts so that distractions turn into an awareness of his presence and self-centeredness becomes freedom to love and to give.

The mission and name of the Congregation led Clare to a deep awareness of the mystery of the Incarnation and the childhood of Jesus. In the joyful proclamation of Christmas: "Do not be afraid. Listen, I bring you news of great joy... " (Luke 2:10) she finds expressed that basic spiritual attitude of joy which springs from a life lived in the spirit of "Manete in Me".

"MANETE IN ME": This is the spiritual heritage left us by Mother Clare. It is our vocation and privilege to make it our own, so that we may witness with joy to the Lord's continuing presence in our world.[5]

Blessed Frances Schervier

Clare Fey founded the Sisters of the Poor Child Jesus in 1844. Blessed Pauline von Mallinckrodt founded the Sisters of Christian Charity in 1849. Blessed Frances Schervier founded the Franciscan Sisters of the Poor in 1851. What ties them together is the fact that all three sat in the classroom of Luisa Hensel in the late 1820's. All three were inflamed with a love of the poor; all three zealously let that love spill over into their lives in the practice of the corporal and spiritual works of mercy. These three and the Sisters in the congregations they founded admirably responded to what Jesus called his "New Commandment." They loved others as Jesus loved them.

Frances Schervier was born on January 3, 1819, in Aachen, not far from Belgium, of a German father and a French mother, both of whom taught her a deep religious spirit. Her ancestors suffered for their Catholic faith during the 1790's in the French Revolution; she herself suffered so much during Bismarck's *Kulturkampf* that these difficulties helped cause a physical collapse.

Frances' father was a prominent and well-to-do citizen of Aachen. Her godfather at her baptism was the Emperor of Austria. As a child she showed an extraordinary love for the poor. She wanted to become a contemplative Trappistine nun, but decided instead to serve the poor as a laywoman. She became a Secular or Third Order Franciscans where she met other women who shared her interest. Inspired by her faith and charity, she and four companions formed a congregation they called the Sisters of the Poor of St. Francis. Frances named the feast of Pentecost of 1845 as "the day on which the Congregation was conceived." In 1850 they established their first hospital and in 1851 the Sisters, now numbering twenty-four, received the habit of St. Francis. A separate, cloistered

branch of the Community, with a limited number of Sisters
was founded in 1849; it was devoted exculsively to works of
prayer and penance. Mother Schervier's congregation was
recognized by the apostolic authority of Pope Pius IX in 1870,
and received final approval in 1908.

In a booklet written by Archbishop John T. McNicholas,
O.P., of Cincinnati, there is a short life of Frances Schervier.
The archbishop wrote about the inspiration she gave to other
congregations:

> *Mother Frances, the Foundress and Superior General of the Con-*
> *gregation, was called "Mother" not only by her Sisters, but by all who*
> *were treated kindly by her Institute. The founders of the "Poor Broth-*
> *ers of St. Francis" received their inspiration from Mother Schervier.*
> *With the cooperation of this "Mother of the Poor," the Community*
> *of Sister nurses known as the "Franciscan Sisters of the Holy Family"*
> *was instituted. Mother Frances was also helpful in founding the*
> *"Sisters of St. Francis Seraph of Perpetual Adoration," who are dedi-*
> *cated to education and hospital work.*[6]

In 1858 Mrs. Sarah Worthington Peter, acting on a suggestion of Pope Pius IX, helped bring six Sisters of Mother
Frances' order to Cincinnati, where they established St. Mary
Hospital. Mrs. Sarah Peter of Cincinnati (1800-1877) was the
daughter of Thomas Worthington, the first senator in Congress from Ohio. She was born at Adena near Chillicothe
where her father, who is called the "Father of Ohio," lived.
The Worthingtons were an ancient family who retained their
Catholic faith through the persecutions of the English Reformation, but lost it in colonial Virginia. Sarah was a beautiful,
rich, well-educated young woman who often traveled abroad.
She had audiences with the pope on her stays in Italy. In an article on "The Early Days of St. Francis Hospital in Columbus"
in the *Bulletin of the Catholic Record Society* of the Columbus
diocese, Donald Schlegel writes, "After a long life as an active
member of the Episcopal Church, Mrs. Peter was received
into the Catholic Church in 1855 while on her second trip to
Europe."[7] He tells how she first met Pope Pius IX in 1852 and
how the pope told her that he had heard of her works of charity
and mercy. Archbishop Purcell of Cincinnati, Schlegel says,
considered her, quite literally, a saint.

Mrs. Peter sought to bring to America small groups of nuns

to help the poor, orphans, and prisoners. She failed with the Little Sisters of the Poor and told Pope Pius IX of her disappointment. He suggested that she apply to the Archbishop of Cologne for some Sisters of the Poor of St. Francis. There she succeeded.

Mother Frances sent six Sisters in 1858 to Cincinnati, where they founded St. Mary Hospital. The first Provincial House in America was the Convent of St. Clare, built on Sarah Peter's property. In 1862 another group founded St. Francis Hospital in Columbus.

During the American Civil War, Mother Frances herself brought a fourth group of Sisters to this country. She toured the great military hospitals and her Sisters volunteered to nurse the sick and wounded in three Cincinnati hospitals and on hospital boats which brought the wounded from the battlefield. Archbishop McNicholas described the work of the nursing Sisters during the War:

> *The group arrived on June 26, 1863, five days before the battle of Gettysburg. The Annals give only a glimpse into the actual work accomplished during Mother Frances' visits to the great military hospitals. One day a physician asked another doctor if he could tell him the name of the newly appointed "night nurse." "Yes," was the reply, "the saintly lady who just entered the Chapel is Mother Schervier, the beloved foundress of this Community." In a letter from Cincinnati Mother Frances says, "I visited all the sick in the large hospital ... Oh, how necessary is the exercise of charity! Here is the place to aid the poor by the corporal works of mercy. The poor people in their abandoned state are very well disposed to grace and as docile as children.[8]*

Frances Schervier died on December 14, 1876, in her fifty-eighth year. The name of Jesus was on her dying lips. The whole city of Aachen mourned her death; twenty thousand people, rich and poor, church dignitaries and government officials, marched in her funeral cortege. A floral tribute from the Empress Augusta lay at her feet. She was buried in a vault under the sanctuary of the motherhouse in Aachen. The tomb has this inscription: "Come, Bride of Christ, and possess the crown which God has prepared for you in eternity."

In 1948, Cardinal Amleto Cicognani, Apostolic Delegate to the United States at that time, wrote in an Introduction to *Mother of the Poor*, a biography of Frances Schervier:

> *When we examine the long story of the fruitful zeal of the Franciscan Sisters of the Poor, we find therein another illustration of the age-old story of God's chosen works: Great results from circumstances and surroundings which at first sight appear almost in contradiction with the accomplishment of any worthwhile works. According to worldly standards, her life was not spectacular. But when we view her accomplishments in the light of the spirit of faith we see once more how "to those who love God all things work together unto good."[9]*

The same thing could be said of all three of Luisa Hensel's students: Mother Clare Fey, Mother Pauline von Mallinckrodt, and Mother Frances Schervier.

On April 28, 1974, Pope Paul VI beatified Frances Schervier. The Church calls her "Blessed" now.

Blessed Pauline
von Mallinckrodt

Foundress of the Sisters of Christian Charity

On January 29, 1963, in the St. Conrad chapel of a mother-house in Paderborn, Germany, the Archbishop presided at the forty-second session of the Apostolic Process for the beatification of Blessed Pauline von Mallinckrodt, foundress of the Sisters of Christian Charity. Her body was interred in the cemetery of that motherhouse. When they opened her grave, they found her religious habit in good condition and the skeletal remains intact. Soldered to the zinc rim of the new coffin in which they re-buried her body was a plaque with this inscription:

> The Servant of God
> Mother Pauline von Mallinckrodt
> Foundress of the Congregation of
> the Sisters of Christian Charity
> Daughters of the Blessed Virgin Mary
> of the Immaculate Conception
> Born June 3, 1817
> Died April 30, 1881.

I first heard the story of Mother Pauline long ago in the classroom of the small St. Mary's School in Riverdale on the southern edge of Chicago. The teachers who taught me — Sister Satura, Sister Donavita, Sister Angeline — were members of the Sisters of Christian Charity which Mother Pauline had founded. Some teachers were trained by the Sisters she had sent from Germany to help in schools like St. Mary's.

Pauline von Mallinckrodt was born June 3, 1817, in Minden, Westphalia, in the Rhineland of Germany. Her mother was a devout Catholic; her father was a tolerant Protestant. Her brother Herman was a co-leader of the German Catholic Center Party, which was fiercely opposed to the predominantly

Protestant Party led by Otto Von Bismarck, the "Iron Chan-
cellor" of Prussia. Bismarck had persecuted Catholics during
the 1870's in what he called a *Kulturkampf*, a word which can
be roughly translated as a "clash of cultures." From 1871 to
1877 Bismarck tried to subordinate the Catholic Church to the
German state and passed restrictive laws against it; these laws
drove many religious orders of priests and nuns into exile in
Holland and Germany. The restrictive laws against the Catholic Church were openly resisted by the Center Party led by
Herman von Mallinckrodt. Beginning in 1878 the laws were
gradually repealed. (It has been said that Bismarck was one of
the greatest benefactors of Catholic education in the United
States because he caused so many priests and women religious
to establish their foundations elsewhere.)

Pauline's family wealth and prestige did not close her mind
to the hardships of others. As a young woman she was especially involved with poverty-stricken families on the outskirts
of Paderborn, to which she had moved in 1839. The Mallinckrodt family had moved to Aachen in 1824, where her father became a civil servant. Pauline went to St. Leonhard's
school, where she had Luisa Hensel as a teacher and where she
had been inspired to a compassionate concern for the poor.

At Paderborn in 1839 she plunged into works of charity with
a group of women whom she had organized; soon she founded
a day nursery and a school for blind children. At her request
St. Madeleine Sophie Barat, Foundress of the Society of the
Sacred Heart, was about to take over this school, but the Prus-
sian government would not allow the French order into Germany. By 1849 Pauline's works of charity had become too ex-
tensive for her to manage alone, so the Bishop of Paderborn
advised her to found a religious community. She founded the
Congregation of the Sisters of Christian Charity in August,
1849. The new congregation soon expanded to include elementary and secondary schools. When Bismarck's laws forced
her and her Sisters to close seventeen of their houses in Germany, they moved to a new motherhouse near Brussels in
Belgium.

The Congregation spread rapidly to North and South America and several European countries, where education became
its chief apostolate. The pioneer sisters to the United States

arrived in New Orleans in 1873. Mother Pauline herself was soon there to visit them.

Like so many other German religious congregations, the daughters of Mother Pauline von Mallinckrodt made their own rich contribution to the booming Catholic growth of the European immigrants to the United States by developing schools, hospitals, orphanages, and other institutions.

Mother Pauline visited her Sisters in America once more in 1879. By that time the congregation had grown to 150 Sisters and many women were entering the order. The 1985 *Catholic Directory* listed 403 professed Sisters in the Eastern Province with their motherhouse in Mendham, NJ, and 242 in the Western Province, whose motherhouse is in Wilmette, IL.

The Sisters of Christian Charity, who have the additional name of Daughters of the Blessed Virgin Mary of the Immaculate Conception, have been praying for the beatification and canonization of their foundress, Mother Pauline. The formal opening of her cause took place in 1926 at Paderborn in Germany. After the ordinary informative process from 1926 to 1938, and interim procedures from 1938 to 1958, Pope Pius XII signed the decree authorizing the cause of Mother Pauline on May 23, 1958; this decree gave her the official title of Venerable Servant of God. After several other processes from 1961 to 1982, six theologian-consultors and their chairman met at another stage of the beatification process in Rome; they were to present their opinions and cast their votes on the heroicity of Mother Pauline's virtues. They met on January 26, 1982. The concluding paragraphs of a document from the Sacred Congregation for the Causes of Saints reads:

We see before us a woman of towering spiritual stature, endowed with the ability of forming others even from earliest childhood. Admired and esteemed because of the magnetism of her individual virtues, she instantaneously became part of charitable and apostolic activity on behalf of the many suffering aged. During the last century she was second to none in this field in Germany, disturbed as it was by nationalistic unrest and by violent storms against the Church.

A heroine of charity, strong and humble, rich in a deep interior life built on a conscious and active faith, a woman of unparalleled leadership, Pauline von Mallinckrodt was truly a mirror of holiness in her own time; and today she is regarded by both her daughters and those who know her as a model to follow and imitate in the fulfillment

*of their own duties along the way traced for each one by Providence.
The immediate official recognition of her heroic virtues and her
eventual glorification (through beatification) will be a stimulus and an
encouragement for all who find themselves in the forefront of apostolic work. As we look up above and place before ourselves such a
model, we too shall have greater strength to overcome the calumnies
and contradictions that are not wanting to those who pursue the way
of holiness.*

*The unanimous, enthusiastic affirmative vote of all the participants
of the commission opens the way to the final goal.*[10]

On January 14, 1983, Pope John Paul II signed the decree
proclaiming the heroicity of Mother Pauline's virtues. She was
beatified by him on April 14, 1985. She is now Blessed Pauline
von Mallinckrodt and on the way to canonization. The next
step will be to authenticate another "answer to prayer beyond
human control." The Vatican has already accepted one such
answer to prayer — the instantaneous cure of a German Sister
with a severe case of multiple sclerosis. That Sister was among
the Sisters of Christian Charity in St. Peter's Square when the
pope beatified Mother Pauline.

The Church's official opening prayer in the Mass honoring
her is:

> Father, all powerful and every-living God,
> you gave Blessed Pauline, your virgin,
> as an outstanding sign of your goodness.
> Grant that, inflamed with the fire of your love,
> we may, through her intercession,
> always seek after you
> and become witnesses of your love in the world.

In 1876 the leadership of Otto von Bismarck was failing and
the oppressive anti-Catholic laws were repealed. Mother Pauline could return from exile in Belgium to Paderborn in 1879.
On April 20, 1881, at the age of sixty-four, she succumbed to
pneumonia and died a holy death in the motherhouse of the
congregation in Paderborn. At her death the congregation
numbered forty-five houses with four hundred twenty Sisters in
Europe, North America, and South America. Her ministry
continues today in Germany, Switzerland, Italy, the United
States, Chile, Uruguay, and Argentina.

Mother St. John Fontbonne

The Sisters of St. Joseph of Baden

The *Official Catholic Directory for 1985* lists three hundred sixty-seven religious orders of women in the United States; fourteen of them bear the name of St. Joseph in their titles. Here I describe the history and spirituality of one of them: The Sisters of St. Joseph who trace their beginnings to 1650 in France and one of whose independent motherhouses is in Baden, near Pittsburgh.

One of the sixteen documents promulgated at Vatican II by Pope Paul VI is a Decree on the Appropriate Renewal of the Religious Life *(Perfectae Caritatis)* promulgated on October 28, 1965. In it the bishops speak of the renewal of religious life in each religious community after the Council without abandoning its original purpose (or "charism," as it is called):

> *It serves the best interest of the Church for religious communities to have their own special character and purpose. Therefore, loyal recognition and safe-keeping should be accorded to the spirit of the founders, and also to the particular goals and wholesome traditions which constitute the heritage of each community.[11]*

The same document also says of the Renewal:

> *It is more than a simple return to the religious zeal of its founder.... The original spirit of the institute becomes effective through ministries ever incarnated afresh, according to the changing circumstances and tasks of the times.[12]*

My source for this account is a Master's dissertation by Sister Mary Evelyn, C.S.J., a member of the community.[13]

The Sisters of St. Joseph were founded by a Jesuit missionary priest, Jean-Pierre Medaille, in 1650 at Le Puy in southern France. He was inspired by St. Francis de Sales to establish an active order of non-cloistered religious women; this was a new idea at the time. He was an exceptional preacher and spiritual director; his obituary noted that he was acclaimed by people who knew him as an "apostle" and a "saint." The Eucharistic theme in Father Medaille's "Eucharistic Letter," Sister Mary Evelyn writes, represents the spirituality in the congregation of the Sisters of St. Joseph which he founded. The theology of the Eucharist is his underlying message. He chose St. Joseph as patron because he wanted the Sisters to have a manner of apostolic service to what he called the "dear neighbor" which characterized the devotion of Joseph as he cared for Jesus and Mary at Nazareth.

The Congregation grew rapidly across France. Each of the new houses established elected its own superior and began its own novitiate, with the local bishop as superior and a priest as a "spiritual father" appointed by him. Sister Mary Evelyn explains how the Congregation developed: "From each motherhouse sisters were, from time to time, sent to new missions, which, when they were able to maintain themselves, became independent of the original house. They, in turn, gave rise to other houses in similar sequence."

During the French Revolution, the Sisters of St. Joseph were dispersed, their property was confiscated, and they had to return to their homes. Some were arrested and dragged through the streets and imprisoned. At the end of the Revolution in 1794 four of the Sisters survived; seven had been executed. Under the leadership of Mother St. John Fontbonne, the order was reconstituted in 1808; a small remnant once more could lead the common life, and the order began to flourish. Before Sister St. John died she saw the Congregation firmly established again; it had grown to world-wide proportions.

The first foundation in the United States was at Carondolet, St. Louis, Missouri, in 1840. From there it spread to practically every state and across Canada. Under the influence of Prince Demetrius Gallitzin (1770-1840), the missionary priest-pioneer of the Allegheny district in western Pennsylvania, who built his headquarters at Loretto, the Congregation established a motherhouse near that settlement in 1869. Toward the end of the century that motherhouse was moved to Beaver County, near Baden, about twenty miles west of Pittsburgh, where it remains to this day.

The essence of Jean-Pierre Medaille's spirituality, as ana-
lyzed by Sister Evelyn, is found in the "Consecration to the
Two Trinities" which he wrote. (The "two" trinities are the
"holy and uncreated Trinity" and the "created trinity of Jesus,
Mary, and Joseph.")

Six virtues, the founder says, should characterize the Sisters
in his order. They are 1) *Excellence* — "The Sisters should
profess in all things to seek whatever is most perfect." (This is
the "more" in the motto of St. Ignaius: "For the greater glory
of God.") 2) *Abnegation* — "generosity in responding to
grace, peace, and gentleness that comes from self-denial, the
death to self that is the price of this generosity." (It does not
mean despising one's self or the world). 3) *Love* — that "in
honor of the Holy Spirit, who is all love, they make profession
of the greatest love of God in daily practice." 4) *Zeal* — "the
Sisters shall manifest great zeal for the advancement, as far as
possible, of the greater glory of God and the salvation and
perfection of their neighbor." 5) *Docility to the Holy Spirit* —
"in honor of the glorious Virgin Mary ... they shall let themselves be led with great obedience to the most adorable Holy
Spirit," 6) *Service of the neighbor* — that "in honor of
St. Joseph ... they shall profess the most perfect unity and
charity possible among themselves, as well as complete charity and mercy ... towards everyone."[14]

After Vatican II and in response to its call for renewal of
their spiritual life in the spirit of its founder, the Baden Sisters
of St. Joseph met in General Chapter and published their de-
liberations in a document which indicated that their spirituality today is really that of Father Medaille and that his
spirituality is relevant for apostolic women today in spreading
the Good News. These are the two conclusions of Sister Mary
Evelyn Hannan in her dissertation. She quotes the 1977 document of the General Chapter which met in obedience to the
guidelines of Vatican II:

> *We experience ourselves as called to make known and to apply His*
> *Gospel to all realms of human life. This renewed understanding of*
> *our charism resonates with the two-fold orientation toward the glory*
> *of God and perfection of the neighbor. This has been ours since our*
> *foundation.*[15]

Three Dominican Congregations and How They Grew

The *New Catholic Directory* for the United States lists, in the order of their seniority, thirty congregations of Dominican Sisters of the Third Order of Saint Dominic in the United States. The first, founded in 1822, is the Congregation of St. Catharine of Siena, whose general motherhouse is in St. Catharine, Kentucky, near Springfield. The second is the Congregation of St. Mary of the Springs, founded in 1830, in Somerset, Ohio, with headquarters now in Columbus, Ohio. The seventh is the Congregation of St. Cecilia, founded in 1860, whose motherhouse is in Nashville, Tennessee.

The history of these three congregations is intertwined: St. Catharine's gave birth to St. Mary's, which gave birth to St. Cecilia's.

The story of the three congregations begins early in the nineteenth century, when Marie Sansbury as a little girl came with her family from Prince Georges County in Maryland to a Catholic settlement on Cartwright Creek near Springfield, Kentucky. One Sunday in February, 1822, Dominican Father Samuel Wilson preached on the call to the religious life at St. Rose Church in Springfield. At the end he asked any young woman at the Mass who felt called to the religious life to speak to him. He asked for one or two volunteers and was delighted when eight young women came forward. One of them was Marie Sansbury. On Easter Sunday of that year he gave her the Dominican habit. She took the name Sister Angela. Others were invested later. All of them, accustomed to the hardships of wilderness life, became the nucleus of the first Dominican Sisters in the United States.

The other six Sisters — all like Angela, born in the United States — elected Angela as their Mother Prioress after she made her profession of vows early the next year. Her father gave her a tract of land on Cartwright Creek, where the Sisters built a new convent and school — the first Dominican school in the country.

It is impossible to compress into a page or two the courage and tenacity — and holiness — of the pioneer Sisters in the face of severe difficulties and utter poverty in the wilderness. Writing about Mother Angela in the *Dictionary of American Biography*, John J. Delaney gives a taste of the frustrations of the small community when Father Raphael Munos, a Dominican from Spain, replaced Father Richard Miles, their first chaplain. Munos knew only the cloistered lives of the Sisters in his home country. The American nuns had to earn their own keep not only by teaching girls, who came in increasing numbers to their school, but also by weaving, sewing, tilling the soil, and chopping wood. Father Munos disapproved; he wanted them to leave the active life or disband. The Sisters strenuously refused. There was a protracted struggle till 1830, when Father Stephen Montgomery, O.P., was sent to be their chaplain.

The story of the Sisters of St. Mary's of the Spring begins in 1808 when Father Edward Fenwick, O.P., of Kentucky came to a small settlement of Catholics in Perry County in Ohio, in response to urgent appeals by Jacob Dittoe, who for several years had written to ask Archbishop John Carroll of Baltimore to send a priest to minister to the Dittoe and Finck and other families of Somerset. The first Catholic church in Ohio was dedicated in 1818. Edward Fenwick, O.P., was named the first bishop of the new diocese of Cincinnati in 1821.

In 1830 Bishop Fenwick asked Mother Angela Sansbury in Kentucky to send some of her Sisters to Somerset to start a school. Despite his many duties as bishop of the whole of Ohio, the bishop never forgot the families of Somerset. Jacob Dittoe donated the land and built a little log cabin and rectory for the parish of St. Joseph's at Somerset, Ohio.

Holy Trinity Church in Somerset, built in 1827, welcomed the four Sisters sent by Mother Angela from Springfield in response to the bishop's request. Their prioress was Sister Emily Elder; one of them was Sister Benvin, the sister of Mother Angela.

On April 23, 1833, Mother Angela herself came to

St. Mary's in Somerset. She was elected prioress there in 1834. She remained in Somerset till her death on November 30, 1839.

In his history of the Columbus diocese Bishop James J. Hartley tells how the Somerset Sisters came to Columbus at the invitation of the first bishop of Columbus, Sylvester Rosecrans.[16] A fire had destroyed their buildings in Somerset. The new location, generously donated by Mr. Theodore Leonard of Columbus, became their new academy and convent. They took possession of the property and on September 7, 1868, opened their school to thirty-five pupils. Bishop Rosecrans suggested that they name their new Columbus motherhouse St. Mary's of the Spring because of the number of springs on the grounds.

In 1860 Bishop James Whelan, O.P., asked the Dominican Sisters in Somerset to come to his diocese of Nashville in Tennessee. On August 17 four of them — Sister Columba Dittoe, the superior, Sister Lucy Harper, Sister Philomena McDonough, and Sister Frances Walsh — arrived in Nashville after a journey by stage coach, steamboat, and rail. They opened St. Cecilia Academy in a two-story frame building in October.

Five months later, the Confederate States were organized. In May, 1861, Tennessee joined them. The Confederates evacuated from Nashville the troops camped around the Academy; Union sentinels guarded the school as classes continued during the War.

Throughout the War the pioneer Dominicans were plagued with financial and other problems. When General Robert E. Lee surrendered in April, 1865, St. Cecilia's, like the South itself, was bankrupt. There were attempts to take over the property, but the Bishop intervened each time to save the Sisters' school. Despite all their problems, the Sisters opened a novitiate: this is now a separate Dominican Congregation of St. Cecilia.

In the summer of 1873 the Nashville Dominicans won the hearts of many people in Nashville by nursing the sick poor through cholera and yellow fever epidemics; one of the Sisters died. Their heroism broke down generations of hostility toward Catholics in Nashville.

In 1927 they organized at their motherhouse a Normal

School for the education of the young Sisters of the Community; it was the first Community Normal School to be affiliated with the Catholic University of America.

Over the years, these three Dominican congregations, whose history I have briefly sketched, have sent their Sisters to open Catholic schools in many cities and many states. The Catholic people of the United States have profited immensely because of them. All three would agree with the tribute paid to Mother Angela Sansbury in a book called *Great American Foundresses*: "The ever-increasing number of Dominicans in America who are carrying on the work she began in the wilderness of Kentucky is the truest monument to the greatness of this woman."[17]

Mother Angela Sansbury, the foundress in Kentucky, did the difficult work of organizing the Congregation of St. Mary's in Somerset. After the move to Columbus, Mother Vicentia Erskine was administror, builder, and conserver of funds. Then came Mother Stephanie Mohun, a woman of vision who extended their work. The terms of these three valiant women covered sixty-five years.

I learned these details from Katherine Burton's *Make the Way Known*, a history of the Columbus congregation.[18] Sister Monica Kiefer, O.P., also wrote the history of St. Mary's Congregation in a series of eight booklets which she called "historiettes." In the thirteenth century St. Dominic told the Order of Preachers which he founded, "Speak only to God or of God." The three congregations I have described have followed that injunction faithfully — in many a ministry and in the example of their lives.

The Song at the Scaffold

The Carmelites of Compiegne

I once saw a picture of the radiant face of Frederica von Stade, the famous soprano, in an announcement that the Metropolitan Opera in New York would produce Francis Poulenc's opera, *Dialogues of the Carmelites*. Miss Van Stade, dressed as a Carmelite nun, was Blanche de la Force, the heroine of the opera.

Francis Poulenc (1899-1963) was a deeply spiritual French composer. His opera captures the pathos and sacrificial ecstasy which the Catholic writer, George Bernanos (1888-1948) put into his screen scenario, *Dialogues des Carmelites*, which in turn was based on the short novel, *Die Letzte am Schafott* ("The Last on the Scaffold") by Gertrud von Le Fort, which was published in English under the title *The Song at the Scaffold*.

I remember reading that novel long ago. The final scene at the Place de la Revolution in Paris is one of the most thrilling — and most poignant — pieces of literature that I have ever read.

Gertrude von Le Fort, who wrote her novel in 1931, found inspiration in the true story of sixteen Carmelite Sisters of Compiegne who were guillotined in Paris on July 17, 1794, during the Reign of Terror of the French Revolution. The central events of the novel are presented within the framework of a letter written in 1794 by a French nobleman, Henri de Villeroi, to an aristocratic friend of pre-revolutionary days. In his letter Villeroi describes an event he witnessed during the closing days of the Revolution — the deaths on the scaffold of the Carmelite nuns and that of a young noblewoman Blanche de la Force.

Blanche, the daughter of the free-thinking Marquis de la Force, is depicted by Le Fort as a girl full of nameless fears and obsessions. At seventeen, she decides to enter the Carmelite community at Compiegne near Paris. She feels a genuine vocation to the religious life, but she also is seeking protection from the harsh world outside. In the convent Blanche comes to terms with the strange, obsessive fear which has haunted her since birth by accepting it as a part of her personality and a burden given to her by God.

The Carmelite contemplatives, who elect the life of the order founded by St. Teresa of Avila, devote their lives to prayer and in particular to acts of expiation for evil done by other people living in the world. Carmelites have been known to think of their Community as a kind of "spiritual lightning rod," down which, as George Schuster states in the introduction in *The Song at the Scaffold*, "what would otherwise be wrathful flames of retribution pass harmlessly."[19]

For Blanche de la Force and the sixteen Sisters at the convent, the regime of terror that was the climax of the Revolution soon swirls around their community. The fanatics at the helm decree the dissolution of religious houses; the shadow of the guillotine pervades their home. The Carmelite Sisters face death calmly. They make a solemn vow to accept the sacrifices that may come to them, even death, in order that France may be preserved from a prolongation of the reign of terror.

Blanche, however, does not make the vow because she fears death above everything else. She flees from the convent and returns home. The revolutionaries murder her father, take over her home and make her their captive — finally they bring her to the Place de la Revolution to force her to watch the execution of the nuns of Carmel.

The last scene at the Place de la Revolution is a miniature masterpiece in both the novel and the opera. In Georges Bernanos' *Dialogues des Carmelites* (translated into English with the title, *The Fearless Heart*) the scene begins with the Carmelites climbing down from the tumbril or the wagon which had brought them to the foot of the guillotine. A priest in the front row of the mob furtively makes the sign of the cross and gives absolution to the nuns. The Sisters immediately begin to sing the *Salve Regina* and then the ancient chant, *Veni Creator Spiritus*, in clear and firm voices. The mob, gripped with wonder, becomes silent spectators.

Only the foot of the scaffold is visible. One by one the sixteen Carmelites mount it, still singing. As they disappear the volume of sound decreases. Only two voices remain; then only one as the guillotine slashed down on the last of the nuns. Suddenly, in one part of the large plaza, a new voice sounds out above the crowd. Here is how Georges Bernanos gives the directions for this last scene in his movie script: "And toward the scaffold, through the crowd, which, astounded, makes room, one sees approaching the slight figure of Blanche de la Force. Her face seems stripped of all fear. She sings the last verse of the *Veni Creator.*"[20]

It is a moment of grace and God-given strength. With a crowd of women pushing her toward the foot of the place of execution, she finishes the Song at the Scaffold which her sisters had begun but could not finish. It was a hymn to the glory of the Holy Trinity:

Deo Patri sit gloria
Et Filio qui a mortuis
Surrexit ac Paraclito
In saeculorum saecula.
And then her voice, too, falls silent.

The main theme of Gertrude von Le Fort's *Song at the Scaffold* is embodied in the biblical paradox in Corinthians, "My strength finds its full scope in Thy weakness ... When I am weak, then I am strongest of all." Or it could be in the *Hymn of St. Teresa* with which Le Fort prefaced her novel:

I am Thine, I was born for Thee,
What is Thy will with me?
Let me rich or beggared,
Exulting or repining,
And comforted or lonely... .
O Life! O Sunlight shining
In stainless purity;
Since I am Thine, Thine only,
What is Thy will with me?

In his *Divine Comedy* Dante Alighieri was succinct: "In his will is our peace."

Saint Elizabeth Ann Seton

America's First Native-Born Saint

When Pope John XXIII beatified her on St. Patrick's Day in 1963, he said of her: "God led this woman through many experiences and to profound decisions concerning her spiritual life, so that faith became a habit with her, like her life breath; and he made her the object of her neighbor's love, particularly in a very sad moment in her life, so that she could feel the tangible presence of God."[21]

The woman of whom he spoke is one of the glories of American Catholic history. In her relatively short life — she died at 46 — she was many things: an Episcopalian, a Catholic, a wife, a working mother, rich, then poor, a widow, a nun, a social pariah whom her family and friends drove into exile from the place of her birth, an aristocrat among the top families in Colonial times, a social worker, the foundress of the first American religious order of women, the organizer of what might be called the first Catholic school in the United States — and ultimately — the first native-born American Saint.

In the Mass which we celebrate on her feast day over the past decade the priest prays with the people in the pews on January 4: "Lord God, you blessed Elizabeth Seton with gifts of grace as wife and mother, educator, and foundress, so that she might spend her life in the service of your people. Through her example and prayers may we learn to express our love for you in love for our fellow men and women." The Mass for January 4 was written after Pope Paul VI canonized her on September 14 in the Holy Year of 1975.

Elizabeth Ann Bailey was born in New York City on August 28, 1774. Her father was a prominent physician and first professor of anatomy at King's College (now Columbia University). Her mother was the daughter of the rector of St. Andrew's Episcopal Church on Staten Island.

When Elizabeth was fourteen she stood in the festive throng and saw George Washington sworn in as the first President of the United States in downtown New York. Alexander Hamilton lived a few doors down the street on which she grew up. Her formative years coincided with the first years of the Republic. Her life divides into two phases: New York and Baltimore. In New York she lived in high society; her background was of a staunch French Huguenot ancestry. The New York phase included a French finishing school, dancing, theater, and admirers. Her mother died when she was three and her father married again — to Helena Roosevelt, an ancestress of Franklin Delano Roosevelt, the President. Her father took charge of her education.

Elizabeth Bailey was baptized in 1774 in Trinity Episcopal Church. As she grew up she took her religion seriously. She was a graceful and charming young woman at nineteen when she married William Magee Seton, a successful merchant. She became interested in social work and helped found the Society for the Relief of Poor Widows with Children in 1707. The young couple were to have five children. When her husband was struck down by tuberculosis in 1803, she went with him and her oldest daughter to Italy in a desperate hope for a cure. On December 27 that year he died in Livorno. Elizabeth returned to New York.

When St. Augustine was baptized by St. Ambrose on Easter Day in 387 A.D., he told him: "It was not your sermons which affected me so much. It was the love you showed me." Something similar happened to Mrs. Seton. Will's broken health and bankruptcy forced them to go to Italy. The family of an old business friend, the Filicchis, took them in with genuine hospitality. In Italy Elizabeth visited Catholic churches and talked to priests the Felicchis brought to their home. When she and her daughter sailed home, Antonio Filicchi accompanied them. She had written home that "I am laughing with God" at the attempts to convert her to Catholicism, but back in New York, after a year of indecision, she was received into the Roman Catholic Church at the parish of St. Peter's in the city. She turned to Catholicism because, she said, she believed it to be "the one true Church."

She was exceptionally thrilled by the Catholic doctrine of

the Eucharist and its belief in the Real Presence of Christ in the Sacrament. As an Anglican she had received communion on "Sacrament Sundays," and the possibility of frequent, even daily, communion in her new Church entranced her. She wrote, "To receive the Daily Bread and to do the Sacred Will — that is the fixed point." I take these details from the article by Joan Barthel in *The New York Times Magazine,* "A Saint for all Reasons," which was published on the day she was canonized by Pope Paul VI in 1975.[22] The article had a subtitle: "The making of the first American saint culminates in Rome today."

Her Episcopalian family and friends were outraged and turned on her savagely, cutting themselves off from her completely. (It was a time of bitter anti-Catholic feeling in the country.) Her sister told her that Catholics were "dirty, filthy, red-faced." Elizabeth did not change her faith when she was ostracized, but she was eventually driven to Baltimore, where she was warmly welcomed by the Catholic community.

At the suggestion of a Sulpician superior, Father Louis Du-Bourg, she opened a school for girls in Baltimore. Soon her sisters Cecilia and Harriet, who had become Catholics, joined her. With other women they formed a religious community. Elizabeth took private vows before Archbishop John Carroll, who had confirmed her in New York in 1806. He encouraged her to form a new community, which moved to a farm near Emmitsburg, Maryland, and she took charge of a school to teach poor children. It was the first parochial school in the States.

When they applied to the Sisters of Charity, founded by St. Vincent de Paul in Paris, they were accepted. With some changes, Archbishop Carroll approved their rule. Elizabeth was elected superior and on July 19, 1813, the Sisters of Charity were founded to live under the rule of St. Vincent. The first American religious society was born that day.

From those small beginnings at Emmitsburg the daughters of Mother Seton spread through the country and contributed enormously to the work of Catholic education, social work, nursing, evangelization, and the myriad other things which all the religious have done to enrich the spiritual life of the United States. Not all who call themselves Sisters of Charity trace back to St. Elizabeth Seton, but all of them in some way live by the principles St. Vincent de Paul wrote in the Rule of the first Daughters of Charity.

At the Visitation St. Elizabeth's patroness said to Mary the Mother, "It is well for you, because you believed." Mother Seton, too, was a woman of profound faith and deep courage who lived fully the principles she taught her Sisters: "The first end proposed in our daily work is to do the will of God; secondly, to do it in the manner He wills; and thirdly, to do it because it is His will."

St. Elizabeth expanded the principle that "our daily work is to do the will of God" in a conference she gave her spiritual daughters. It is printed as the Second Reading of the Office of Readings for her feast day of January 4:

I know what his will is by those who direct me; whatever they bid me do, if it is ever so small in itself, is the will of God for me. Then do it in the manner he wills it, not sewing an old thing as if it were new, or a new thing as if it were old; not fretting because the oven is too hot, or in a fuss because it is too cold. You understand — not flying and driving because you are too hurried, not creeping like a snail because no one pushes you. Our dear Savior was never in extremes. The third object is to do his will because he wills it, that is, to be ready to quit at any moment and do anything else to which you may be called...

Be above the vain fears of nature and efforts of your enemy. You are children of eternity. Your immortal crown awaits you, and the best of Fathers waits there to reward your duty and love. You may indeed sow here in tears, but you may be sure there to reap in joy.[23]

We can now pray, "St. Elizabeth of New York, pray for us."

Chapter 6
Eight Jesuits

Seven Students in Paris

The Origin of the Jesuits

It was the dawn of August 15, 1534, the feast of Our Lady's Assumption. Seven students of the University of Paris walked from their rooms in the Latin Quarter across the *Ile de la Cite*, past the cathedral of Notre Dame, and climbed the steep hill of *Montmartre* (the "Mount of Martyrs") to a small chapel which, they knew, was thought to be the burial ground of St. Denis, first bishop of Paris, and of his two companions.

They went to a Benedictine abbey, where the "Ladies of Montmartre" kept the key to the chapel. Sister Perrette Bouillard, the assistant sacristan, hesitated at first to give it to the shabbily dressed young men, but their piety impressed the twenty-two-year-old nun; she handed them the key. (She remembered the shabby seven when she died seventy-eight years later at the age of one hundred.) The seven students went into the chapel.

That visit to the chapel was the beginning of one of the most important movements in the history of the Church. A modes plaque at *11 Yvonne-de-Tac* in Montmartre commemorates the site of the chapel today. It reads simply: *"Crypte de Saint Ignace; Martyrium de Saint-Denis."* The leader of the seven students was a Basque from Spain, Ignatius of Loyola, and the seven young men were the first Jesuits.

In the chapel of St. Denis that morning, Father Peter Faber, 28, who had been ordained a few months before, celebrated the Mass of Mary's Assumption. The oldest student was Ignatius of Loyola at 43. The others were much younger: Francis Xavier of Navarre in Spain, 28; Simon Rodriguez of Portugal, 24; and, from Castile in Spain, Nicholas Bobadilla, 25; Diego Laynez, 22; and Alphonse Salmeron, not quite 20.

Ignatius had taken the six younger students through his "Spiritual Exercises," which he had written during a year of retreat at Manresa in the Basque country. He had gone to Manresa after reading some lives of Christ and the saints which so impressed him that he hung up his soldier's sword and decided to devote himself completely to Christ as a soldier of Christ the King. The other six students were also ready to dedicate their lives to the service of the Lord with Ignatius as their leader. They were the nucleus of what Ignatius called the Company of Jesus — the Society of Jesus.

Simon Rodriguez later recalled what happened after the seven walked down the fifteen step stairway to the small chapel;

> *Peter Faber celebrated the Mass... Before giving the divine food to the companions, he turned toward them with the sacred food in his hand. Kneeling on the ground with his spirits raised to God, each in his own place, they pronounced their vows one by one in a clear voice that all could hear and then together they received the Eucharist. Peter Faber then turned back to the altar and, before receiving the life-giving bread, pronounced his vow in a clear, distinct voice that all could hear.[1]*

The vows of chastity, poverty, and obedience were joined with a fourth vow of a pilgrimage to Jerusalem with the condition that, if the pilgrimage were impossible, they would place themselves at the disposal of the pope to decide their future. The seven went to the chapel of the martyrs on the feast of the Assumption because of their love of the Mother of God.

One might ask, "How did the seven companions spend the rest of that day of consecration and first vows?" Simon Rodriguez told what happened: "After the ceremony they spent the rest of the day in high spirits and exultation near the fountain of St. Denis ... Meanwhile the seven were overflowing with ardor and devotion which stirred them to give themselves to God." At sunset that day "they went home, praising God."

When I was in grade school, the Sisters told us to print A.M.D.G. on the homework papers we turned in. They explained that the four letters meant "For the greater glory of God." I learned later that this was the motto of the Jesuits because it was the motto of St. Ignatius. Those four initials have guided Jesuits across four and a half centuries.

Father Bernard Basset, a beguiling Jesuit spiritual writer from England, in his foreword to *Jesuit Saints and Martyrs*, by

Joseph Tylenda, S.J., wrote about Ignatius' "Spiritual Exercises," by which the seven students had been formed:

> *Every Jesuit, before committing himself, spent a whole month in solitude and silence with the "Spiritual Exercises" as his guide. All the mystery of the Jesuit story may be traced to this little book ... St. Ignatius never taught that the end justifies the means, but he gave us what so many millions long for, a rational, viable developing End to human life... It is impossible to express or explain the Jesuit secret which turns on St. Ignatius and his intimate grasp of the Incarnation; the answer to the quest, "Why did the Son of God become a man."[2]*

Because the seven students from the Latin Quarter of Paris learned what the commitment "to the greater glory of God" meant from their founder and teacher they went home on that day of the Assumption, "praising and thanking God."

Many know something about how Ignatius of Loyola and Francis Xavier spent the rest of their lives. They were canonized as saints. But what about the other five "Companions of Jesus?" After the six Jesuits were ordained in Venice in 1537 and after an unsuccessful attempt to go on pilgrimage to Jerusalem, they went on to offer their services to the pope.

Nicholas Alfonso de Bobadilla, born in Bobadilla, Leon, in Spain in 1509, died in Loretto, Italy, in 1590. He studied theology and completed his studies in Paris. He traveled through more than seventy dioceses as a preacher and missionary. A man of much talent and great contrasts, independent and impulsive, outstanding for both accomplishment and little prudence, he was expelled by Emperor Charles V from Germany. The pope intervened against him when he unsuccessfully demanded changes in the Society of Jesus. He wrote an autobiography that is important for its early history of the Jesuits.

Alfonso Salmeron was born in Toledo in Spain in 1519 and died in Naples in 1585. As a theologian he influenced the Council of Trent; he wrote sixteen volumes on the New Testament — eleven on the Gospels, one on the Acts of the Apostles, and four on the letters of Paul. They are of little value today.

Peter Faber, born in Savoy in 1506, died in Rome in 1546. As a student at Paris he lodged with Francis Xavier. In 1537 he went with Ignatius to Rome, where he was appointed a professor at the Sapienza University. The pope sent him to Germany; he was among the first to respond to the challenge of Lutheranism by promoting a genuine reform and discipline in Catholics. Through the "Spiritual Exercises" and his preaching and spiritual direction he helped save many in the Rhineland for the Catholic Church. He was called to the Council of Trent as a theologian. Peter Faber was beatified by Pope Pius IX in 1872.

Diego Lainez was born in Spain in 1512 and died in Rome in 1565. He became a brilliant theologian and one of the leaders of the Catholic Reform. He is best known for his participation in three periods of the Council of Trent. He intervened in important discussions of the Real Presence, Penance, the Sacrifice of the Mass, and many other theological topics at the Council. He used his prestige to obtain the Council's approbation of the Company of Jesus.

Simon Rodriguez, born in 1520, a friend of Bobadilla, was a student at Paris whom Ignatius recruited for his Company at the University. He was a Portuguese of noble blood. In his *The Origin of the Jesuits*, Robert Brodrick, S.J., writes that he was a headstrong character who joined Ignatius to cause him the gravest anxiety and keep throughout it all his unwavering affection. In her *Saint-Watching*, Phyllis McGinley makes a similar judgment: "He remained forever dear to Ignatius, but a constant thorn in his flesh for the moodiness and will-o'-the-wisp character." He died in 1579.

Saint Ignatius of Loyola

The Founder of the Jesuits

The sixteenth century was decisive in the history of the Church. One of the men who made it so was born in 1491 in the Basque country of northern Spain. He was baptized Iñigu. The Latin word for "fire" is *ignis*, and there was fire in his name and in his life: a consuming zeal for the glory of God and the progress of God's Church. His life ended in a small room in Rome, on July 31, 1556, but not before he had founded the Society of Jesus and offered it to the pope to be used as God willed.

In 1956 some thirty thousand Jesuits remembered the fourth centennial of his death. In 1965 there were thirty-six thousand thirty-eight. Since then the number has declined to less than twenty-five thousand, but the Society still ranks as the largest religious order of men. Of this number about one in four is an American. The Jesuits still direct and educate thousands in high schools, colleges, and universities in the tradition of the early members of the order. They still give retreats and are spiritual directors in retreat houses; they still write scholarly books and edit learned journals; they still go to the foreign missions. But in recent years many have added an active pursuit of justice and peace to their pastoral ministry.

Ignatius of Loyola was born into the Age of the Protestant Reformation, which rejected the authority of the Catholic Church. Half of Germany, the whole of Scandinavia, much of England and her American colonies was lost to the Church. It was also the Age of Exploration when courageous pioneers, Jesuits among them, sailed the unknown seas to India and the Americas and trekked the perilous miles to China and the Far East.

Jesuits formed the advance guard of the Counter-Reformation, the Catholic response to Lutheranism.

235

St. Robert Bellarmine and Francis Suarez compiled a theology that met the challenge of the Reformers and helped lay a foundation for modern democracy.

Men of the Company of Jesus walked along mission trails in the new countries discovered by European explorers: Robert di Nobili in India, Matteo Ricci in China, Peter Claver in South America, Isaac Jogues and the North American martyrs in New York and Canada. St. Ignatius himself sent Francis Xavier to India and Japan. Father Pierre Marquette was one of the first Europeans to see the head of the Great Lakes and with Louis Joliet probed the Mississippi. Father Jean Pierre Alneau was martyred in Minnesota and Father Pierre Jean de Smet explored and evangelized the Northwestern United States and served as a peacemaker with warring Indian tribes, as we noted elsewhere in this volume.

To answer the objections of new philosophies and theologies and to absorb what was good in them, a whole host of scholars was formed in the seminaries and universities the Jesuits founded across the years. Jesuits today are men of modern times, well able to use the heritage of Catholic wisdom in innovative approaches to modern thought in all its branches. There have been great Jesuit astronomers, artists, poets, and scientists of every description.

If I were asked to single out, besides his heroic sanctity, that for which Ignatius should be remembered today, I would not choose to note what the Jesuits have done in education, theology, and the missions. There would be reason enough to remember him for the *Spiritual Exercises*[3] he jotted on a few pieces of paper as he spent a hermit year of prayer at Manresa, a monastery above Barcelona. These simple, but profound, directions for the guidance of his own spiritual life have been used in countless ways as the basis for retreats that have brought millions to a conversion to the Lord.

It was highly appropriate that Pope Pius XI named Ignatius of Loyola the patron of retreats. Through the *Exercises* and the Ignatian spirituality at the heart of his work, untold numbers have been put through the paces of his systematic but also flexible route to prayer and quiet meditation apart from the distractions of the noisy world and have experienced therein a spiritual conversion which changed their lives. Ignatius begins with a "First Principle and Foundation": a simple statement that men and women are created to praise, reverence, and serve God our Lord and by this means to attain salvation. All other things of the world are created to help us attain the end for which we are created.

As St. Ignatius takes the retreatants through his exercises, they begin with an examination of their selfishness and other forms of human sinfulness: they then learn that commitment to Christ the King and not the kingdom of Satan will move them into the condition for conversion. This is followed by meditations on the Mysteries in the life of Christ, especially the saving Passion and Death of the Lord, with which they must personally identify themselves. This process is meant to help the exercitant to realize that salvation is a gift of God's love which they must freely accept. At the end of the *Exercises* the retreatants contemplate the mystery of Easter and its effects on their lives as Christians after they leave the house of retreat.

In his book *Saints Are People*, Father Alfred McBride says that Ignatius was both a mystic and a genius at organization, tough and flexible at the same time, a shrewd judge of people, who became one of the most influential men of modern history. "The rugged romantic soldier of Pamplona became a God-intoxicated religious leader. Few men or women have made the transition so well. Few have ever done so much, as Ignatius liked to say on his own behalf, 'for the greater honor and glory of God.' "[4]

When I think of what Ignatius of Loyola has wrought, I thank God for the cannonball which shattered his leg at the siege of Pamplona in 1521 and turned his dreams of knightly glory to the reality of that army he called the Company of Jesus.

Saint Francis Xavier

Missionary to the Far East

The best known of the seven students who were the first members of the Society of Jesus were Ignatius Loyola, the founder, and St. Francis Xavier, the greatest among the many thousands of Jesuit missionaries.

Three years after the morning Mass on Montmartre in which the seven pledged their lives to the Company of Jesus under the leadership of Ignatius, six of them were ordained priests in Venice. Unable to fulfill their conditional vow of going on pilgrimage to the Holy Land because the Turks, who held Jerusalem, were at war, they went, as they had vowed, to Rome to offer their services to Pope Paul III. After some hesitation, the pope was impressed by the zeal of the unlikely seven and accepted their offer.

Five years later the pope officially established the Society of Jesus and agreed with Ignatius that the new religious order would not be bound to recite the Divine Office together in choir, which was the rule of other orders, because the founder wanted his priests to pray the office in private so that they would have more time for the active ministry.

To the vows of poverty and chastity they had made on Montmartre, the young men added vows of obedience and a fourth vow unique among religious orders — they vowed obedience to the pope, a readiness to go anywhere the pope sent them. Among the earliest Jesuit ideals were works of charity such as teaching the young and uneducated, as well as missionary enterprises. The abandonment of the obligation of the Divine Office in choir, which Ignatius stressed, was a revolutionary step, but Pope Paul III gave his approval to the whole package desired by the Society. Thus they were set free for works of charity and evangelization in foreign countries, which they soon initiated.

Pope Paul III asked Ignatius to send two of his ten priests to Portugal because King John had requested it. Nicholas Bobadilla, "whose brusque manner and fondness for the rich and distinguished," writes McGinley, "gave the Company much amusement"[5] was appointed to go with Rodriguez to the new Portuguese colony of Goa in India, but Bobadilla became ill. Ignatius sent Francis Xavier, his dearest friend, to take his place.

When Xavier and Rodriguez came to Portugal in 1540, they had to wait for a ship to Goa till the next spring. Meanwhile, they preached to the people and ministered to prisoners.

When King John saw their zeal and excellent work among his people, he asked that one of them should remain in Portugal. It was Father Bobadilla who stayed and went on to establish the Jesuit province of Portugal. Francis Xavier became the first — and greatest — of all the Jesuit missionaries who have gone away from their homelands to foreign countries across the four and a half centuries since he boarded that ship for the Far East and the "East Indies" in 1541.

Francis Xavier was born at the castle of Xavier (Javier) in Navarre in 1506; he died on an island off the coast of China in 1551. The Chinese name of the island is Chang-Chuen-Shan. The most famous of the first six disciples of Ignatius, he was a Basque whose family had fought on the other side of the battle when Ignatius was wounded at Pamplona.

The impoverished but proud Francis was a most unlikely disciple and despised what the shabbily dressed Ignatius stood for. He was young and strong, an athlete, expert in Latin, winner of prizes at the University of Paris. Ignatius pursued him quietly and persistently for three years. He kept asking him, "What doth it profit man if he gains the whole world and suffers the loss of his soul?" Francis gave in finally, and the young gallant joined the Company of Jesus.

Francis was to become the closest friend of the founder and before he died, the most generous, irresistibly lovable, and most world-beloved of the long line of Jesuit saints. When he sent Xavier to Portugal and the East Indies, Ignatius knew that he would never see him again.

Francis of Navarre sailed for Goa, fortified by a papal brief nominating him apostolic nuncio in the East, and he became one of the most successful preachers of the Gospel in the history of the Church.

During the ten years left in his life, Xavier was a living flame of zeal and charity flaring across much of the Far East. He began by reforming the notoriously corrupt Portuguese in Goa, upbraiding them for their neglect of the poor, their cruelty to their slaves, and open concubinage. By example, preaching, and writing verses on Christian truths set to popular tunes, he did much to offset the betrayal of Christ and his Church by evil Christians. He went about ringing a little bell to call children to prayer and instruction.

For the next seven years he worked among the Paravas in southern India, in Malacca, the Molucca Islands, and the Malay peninsula:

> *He went among the poor as a poor man himself, sleeping on the ground and eating mainly rice and drinking water. By and large, he met with immense success among the low-caste and almost none among the Brahmins. Wherever he went, he left after him numerous organized Christian communities; a good example of his achievements is the persistent fidelity to Christianity of the Paravas, whom he also probably saved from extinction.[6]*

In 1549 Francis went farther east to Japan. For two years he preached in different cities with great success, although against difficult odds. When he left Japan, the total number of Japanese Christians was about two thousand; within sixty years they resisted fierce persecution, even unto death.

The last act in the high romance that was the life of Xavier of Navarre took him to China. Discovering that the Japanese imitated the superior culture of China, he returned to Goa, where a company of Jesuits was consolidating his pioneer missions. He prepared to go to the emperor of China. But his mission failed. He left for China after a few months, but he fell ill and died on the island of Chang-Chuen-Shan (Sancian) off the China coast while waiting for a ship to take him to the mainland. He was forty-five years old.

St. Francis Xavier died with the name of Jesus on his lips. He had suffered extreme hardship, had worn himself out with ceaseless activity, yet enjoyed a high degree of union with God through prayer.

He was canonized by Pope Gregory XV on March 12, 1622. It was a most remarkable ceremony, for St. Ignatius of Loyola, St. Teresa of Avila, St. Philip Neri, and St. Isidore the Farmer were also canonized that day. It was indeed a noble company!

Matteo Ricci

The Jesuit "Generation of Giants"

A few years ago the English-language newspaper in Peking, the *China Daily,* published a surprising news item. It praised the pioneer scientific work in seventeenth century China of three Jesuit priest-scientists. They were Matteo Ricci (1552-1610) a mathematician from Italy, and two astronomers, Johann Adam Schall (1591-1666) of Germany and Ferdinand Verbiest (1623-1688) of Belgium. They were "once disparaged as carriers of an 'imperialistic culture' during the Cultural Revolution," the paper noted, "but are now recognized as men who made a contribution to China by spreading the understanding of Western science."

These three priests were among many Jesuits who brought the Faith to China during what has been called the Jesuits' "Golden Age." They belonged to those whom Father George H. Dunne, S.J., called a *"Generation of Giants"* — the title of a fascinating history he wrote about the Jesuit presence in the China of the Ming and Manchu dynasties in the sixteenth and seventeenth centuries.[7] Father Dunne weaves into his story an account of their controversial policies of missionary accommodation which erupted into the "Chinese Rites Controversy" later in the century.

There had been a Franciscan mission to China in the fourteenth century, but it disappeared without a trace in 1368; few Chinese were converted. The "Road to Cathay" had to be rediscovered by Portuguese navigators in the sixteenth century. Francis Xavier brought thousands in India and Japan into the Church. In Japan he realized the importance of China and set out for that unknown and mysterious land. He died, destitute, on the island of Sancian in 1552, a few miles from the Chinese coast. His tragic death helped Western Europe discover the importance of Chinese culture. For thirty years, missionaries of different religious orders tried to get a foothold in that for-bidding land, but they were turned back by the hostile rulers of China.

It was Father Alessandro Valignano, a Jesuit official visitor in the Far East, who devised a way of penetrating China. He told the missionaries to prepare themselves thoroughly by learning the language and adapting themselves to the culture and mentality of the Chinese. When Father Matteo Ricci, an-other Italian Jesuit, found a foothold in China in 1583, he was superbly prepared, for he was a brilliant mathematician who spoke Chinese well. At first he dressed like a Buddhist monk, but soon learned that the most respected class was that of the scholars. He adopted their garb and gained their respect by displaying the scientific instruments he had brought from the West and by discussing science and Christianity with them. Because of his new approach to preaching the Gospel and his adaptation, with fruitful zeal and wisdom, to the realities of the highly literate and rigidly stratified society, he planted the seeds of Faith which bloomed bountifully through the seven-teenth century. Father Ricci spent his last nine years at the Imperial Court in Peking. When he died in 1610, the two thousand five hundred Catholics in China included many of the intellectuals and nine of the eighteen Jesuits in China were natives of China. When Ricci died, he could say to his succes-sors, "I leave before you an open door… "

Two of the Jesuits who entered China through that open door were astronomers. One was Johann Adam Schall of Ger-many, who rose to the highest position a foreigner could achieve during the reign of the first Manchu emperor, who had ousted the Ming dynasty in 1643. In 1661, his younger as-sociate, Father Ferdinand Verbiest of Belgium wrote of him: "Schall has more influence on the emperor than any viceroy, or than the most respected prince." In 1650 another Jesuit wrote from Shanghai that "all of us who are in this mission bask by divine favor in the aura of Father Adam."

Astronomers Schall and Verbiest helped reform the Chi-nese calendar. At the recommendation of Hsu Kuang-ch'i, a leading Chinese Catholic, the emperor in Peking allowed the Jesuits to head the attempt at reform. When they successfully accomplished the scientific correction of the calendar and gave it to the emperor in 1634, the prestige of the missionaries increased throughout the empire.

The three Jesuit priest-scientists who were thanked in our time for their help to Chinese science were successful because they adapted their methods to the Chinese culture of the time. Father Ricci initiated the controversial policy of adaptation in what he called "accidental" features without, he claimed, compromising the "substance" of the Faith. Ultimately, the defense of their accommodations to certain Chinese religious rites led to the bitter "Chinese Rites" controversy. The Jesuit missionaries and others had permitted Chinese converts to retain various religious practices which seemed superstitious to their critics. The controversy raged later in the seventeenth century and the "Chinese Rites" were finally forbidden by an apostolic constitution of Pope Clement IX in 1715.

The religious rites which the Jesuits had permitted Chinese converts to keep were chiefly Confucianism and veneration of their ancestry. As we think of the many ways in which the Mass is adapted to native customs today, after Vatican II, we are haunted by one of the great "What if" questions in the history of the Church. *What if* there had been more understanding and less rigidity by Church authorities in China and Rome in the seventeenth century? What would be the state of the Faith if Matteo Ricci's policy of missionary accommodation had not been condemned? The position of Chinese Catholicism in a country of one billion people would, I think, be far different today.

Saint Robert Southwell

A Jesuit Poet and Martyr

In her spirited and inspiring book, *Saint-Watching*, Phyllis McGinley, a Pulitzer Prize winner for poetry, wrote several pages about St. Ignatius Loyola and the Society of Jesus which he founded. She wrote about their history:

> *Oddly enough, for all the fame of their intellectual geniuses, they produced until recently few literary geniuses. Scientists, yes, biographers, historians, and writers on every subject under the sun, but no poets of stature except Southwell in the late sixteenth century, whose "The Burning Babe" even Dr. Johnson took the trouble to praise, and in the nineteenth, Gerard Manley Hopkins.[8]*

Robert Southwell, like Edmund Campion, was one of the Jesuits canonized among the "Forty Martyrs of England and Wales" by Pope Paul VI in 1970. Like Campion also, he was savagely executed because he refused to repudiate his Catholic faith by taking the Oath of Supremacy which would mean that he acknowledged the king or queen of England as head of the English Church.

Robert Southwell was born of a well-to-do family at Horsham St. Faith (Norfolk) in 1561, the son of Sir Robert Southwell, a Catholic who later conformed to the Anglican faith. Since all institutions of learning had become Protestant, he was sent for his education to the Jesuit College at Douai in Belgium. At the age of seventeen, he asked to join the Jesuits but was refused because he was too young. He walked to Rome and was accepted into the Jesuits there. He made his religious vows in Tournai, Belgium, in 1580; after studies in philosophy and theology, he was ordained priest in 1584, then appointed prefect of the English College in Rome, a seminary that trained priests for England. He begged to be sent to minister to the English Catholics — ministry forbidden by Queen Elizabeth I under penalty of death.

With another Jesuit and later martyr, Father Henry Garnet, he secretly entered England on a secluded coast near Folkestone and made his way alone to London, where he had been assigned. He narrowly escaped capture; it was the time of the Babington Plot against the Catholic Mary Stuart, Queen of Scots, which he later exposed in an eloquent *An Humble Supplication to her Majestie.*

The young priest worked mostly around London. For most of his six years' apostolate his base of operation was Arundel House, the home of the Catholic Countess of Arundel, whose husband, Sir Philip Howard, was imprisoned for his faith. For six perilous years Southwell brought the comfort of the Catholic religion to "recusant Catholics" who refused to join the Anglican church. In June, 1592, he was trapped into coming to a Catholic home where he thought a woman wanted the Sacraments. The trap was sprung by Richard Topcliffe, a notorious priest-hunter. Topcliffe was exultant over his catch; he expected to learn, in his own private torture chamber, the names and locations of all the priests at work in England. The Jesuit priest, despite excruciating pain and seventeen torture sessions, never revealed anything about other priests; he would only say that he was a Jesuit priest who had returned to England to preach the Catholic faith and that he was ready to die for it.

It was in several prisons, including the Tower of London, that Southwell spent his last three years. Many of his poems were written then. After his execution those poems, together with others he had written while in hiding during his ministry, were published as St. *Peter's Complaint,* which became very popular among Catholics.

Robert Southwell had longed for martyrdom since the moment he had volunteered in Rome for the "English Mission." His prayer was answered on February 21, 1595, when he was dragged to Tyburn in London after a trial in which he was falsely accused of high treason. Beneath the gallows, and with the noose around his neck, he said that he prayed constantly for the Queen; then he spoke his final prayer: "Into your hands, O Lord, I commend my spirit." The cart was then drawn away from under him. He was thirty-four years old.

A critique of the Jesuit martyr as poet, in *British Authors Before 1800,* says of him that:

... his shorter poems display great lyrical power and vivid imagination, with simple but profound symbolism. Ben Jonson said he would gladly have destroyed many of his own poems if he could have written Southwell's The Burning Babe... He himself was a sweet natured man, brilliant and witty, and sincere to the point of martyrdom.[9]

At the end of his biography of Southwell in the *Dictionary of National Biography,* Sidney Lee stated that "by modern critics Southwell's poetry has rarely been underrated... A genuine poetic vein is latent beneath all the religious sentimentalism."[10] After a criticism of some of his "extravagant conceits," Lee concludes: "But many poems, like *The Burning Babe*, which won Ben Jonson's admiration, are as notable for the simplicity of their language as for the sincerity of their sentiment, and take rank with the most touching examples of sacred poetry."

Here is *The Burning Babe* as I found it in an 1856 London edition:[11]

As I in hoary winter's night
stood shivering in the snow,
Surprised was I with sudden heat
which made my heart to glow;
And lifting up a fearful eye
to view what fire was near,
A pretty babe all burning bright
did in the air appear,
Who scorch'ed with exceeding heat
such floods of tears did shed,
As though His floods
should quench His flames
with what His tears were fed;
Alas! quoth He, but newly born
in fiery heats of fry,
Yet none approach
to warm their hearts
or feel my fire but I!
My faultless breast
the furnace is,
the fuel wounding thorns;
Love is the fire

and sighs the smoke,
the ashes shame and scorns;
The fuel Justice layeth on,
and Mercy blows the coals;
The metal in this furnace wrought
are men's defiled souls,
For which, as now on fire I am,
to work them to their good,
So will I melt into a bath,
to wash them in my blood:
With this He vanish'd out of sight,
and swiftly shrunk away,
And straight I call'ed unto mind
that it was Christmas day.

(1856 London Edition)

Saint Edmund Campion

On October 25, 1970, Pope Paul VI canonized the "Forty Martyrs of England and Wales." They were selected from two hundred already beatified by previous popes. Most were savagely executed because they refused to take the Oath of Supremacy, which would mean that they recognized the king or queen of England as the head of the English Church. This oath was imposed on the people in Britain after the pope refused to give Henry VIII an annulment for his marriage to Catharine of Aragon, his first wife. Some were martyred simply because they were priests or harbored priests in their homes. Thirty-three were secular priests or members of religious orders; seven were layfolk, four men and three women. Thirteen were seminary priests, three Benedictine, and three Carthusian monks, one Brigittine, two Franciscans, and one Austin friar. Ten of the forty martyrs were Jesuits. Edmund Campion, S.J., is the best known of the forty.

I was first introduced to the Reign of Terror under Queen Elizabeth I, in which Catholics were hunted down relentlessly and executed, when I read a novel written by Robert Hugh Benson, a popular Catholic novelist in the early years of the twentieth century. The son of the Anglican archbishop of Canterbury, Benson joined the Roman Catholic Church. His popular novel *Come Rack! Come Rope!* told the story of a priest named Robin Audrey who, just before they hanged him, spoke to the mob which had come to enjoy his death. He denied that he was part of a conspiracy against Queen Elizabeth. Then he cried out:

> So you see very well for what it is that I die. It is for the Catholic Faith that I die — that which was once the faith of all England — and which, I pray, may one day be its faith again. In that have I lived, and in that I will die. And I pray God, further, that all who hear me today

may have the grace to take it as I do — as the true Christian religion (and none other) — revealed by our Saviour Christ.[12]

Those last words of Father Audrey were fiction, but they express the feelings of the Forty Martyrs as they faced death. In his homily at the Mass of their canonization, Pope Paul VI spoke fact, not fiction, as he quoted the unanimous and joyful responses the martyrs gave in the last moments of their lives on earth:

The martyrs' response was unanimous: "I can do no more than repeat for you that I died for God and the sake of my religion." St. Philip Evans said, "I consider myself so fortunate that, if I were able to live many other lives, I would be most ready to sacrifice them all for so noble a cause." St. Philip Howard, Count of Arundel, asserts, "I regret that I have only one life to offer for this noble cause." With touching simplicity, St. Margaret Clitherow concisely expressed the meaning of her life and death, "I die for the love of my Lord, Jesus." Similarly, St. Alban Roe cried out, "What a small thing this is when compared with the very cruel death that Christ suffered for us."[13]

On June 25, 1581, a merchant in jewelry named Mr. Edmunds landed at Dover after crossing the English Channel from France. The port authorities watched carefully for disguised Catholic priests entering England. Priests were forbidden to practice there and even the Mass was outlawed. Mr. Edmunds was finally passed through after long questioning. They did not know that he was the Jesuit Father Edmund Campion.

Father Campion has been described as a debonair and romantic adventurer. In her inspiring book, *Saint-Watching*, Phyllis McGinley called Campion a "cavalier ... the most dashing holy man who ever played hounds and hare with fate. He is a kind of spiritual Scarlet Pimpernel, reckless, gallant, glorying at once in his mission and in outwitting his pursuers."[14]

Edmund Campion was born in London on June 25, 1540, of Catholic parents who were later converted to the Anglican Church. He went to St. John's College at Oxford on a scholarship. A brilliant scholar with an outstanding personality, he soon became a leader of the "Campionists" who gathered around him. When Queen Elizabeth visited Oxford in 1566, the University chose Campion to give a polished Latin address to welcome her. The Queen and her advisors, Lords Cecil and Leicester, were so impressed that they invited him to join the Queen's service, with the implied promise that he would rise high in the Anglican hierarchy. Campion declined. He was ordained a deacon in the Church of England in 1569. Although he had taken the Oath of Supremacy in 1566, he began to have serious doubts about that Church. After a three-year stay in Ireland, he was convinced that the Roman Catholic Church had the true Faith. He went to the English College at Douai in Belgium, where he rejoined the Catholic Church and entered the Society of Jesus. He was ordained a priest at Prague in 1578.

Campion and Robert Persons were asked by the Jesuit superior to begin the "English Mission" to the Catholics of their homeland. To do so Campion entered the country as a jewel merchant in June of 1581.

Edmund Campion, a mobile and resourceful priest, went to dozens of homes and manors to celebrate Mass, hear confessions, and give Communion to hundreds of Catholics. He was always in peril of his life from the pursuers of priests and often went about in disguise. On July 16, 1581, the "Pursuivants" caught up with him at Lyford Granbe in Berkshire when he was betrayed by an informer who pretended to be a member of the congregation. After vain efforts to make him conform to the new faith and after repeated torture, he was condemned to death under a trumped-up charge of treason. Before they hanged him, they asked him to confess his treason. He replied: "I am a Catholic man and a priest; in that faith I have lived and in that faith I intend to die. If you esteem my religion treason, then I am guilty; as for other treason, I never committed any. God is my judge." In his final words he forgave those who condemned him, bowed his head in prayer as they dragged the cart from under him. He was left hanging. Father Joseph Tylenda, S.J., in his book, *Jesuit Saints and Martyrs* tells what happened then: "The executioner then cut him down and further desecrated his body by tearing out his intestines and heart and hacking his body to pieces."[15]

In 1935 the English Catholic novelist Evelyn Waugh wrote a biography of Edmund Campion. As an appendix he included a defense of the Jesuits in England which has come to be known as "Campions's Brag." It was printed without his knowledge and spread wide to hearten his fellow Catholics. It is one of the most stirring pieces of literature I have ever read. It was not a boast; it was a proclamation of his right to say Mass and teach the old faith. It described his mission as one of "free cost to preach the Gospel, to minister the Sacraments, to instruct the simple, to reform sinners, to confute errors; in brief, to cry alarm spiritual against foul vice and proud ignorance, wherewith many of my dear countrymen are abused."

Saint Edmund Campion the Martyr ended his "Brag" with a peroration of which Evelyn Waugh wrote, "Every sentence is aflame with his own fiery spirit." Here is part of it:

And touching our Societie, be it known to you that we have made a league — all the Jesuits in the world, whose succession and multitude must overreach all the practices of England — cheerfully to carry the cross you shall lay upon us, and never to despair your recovery, while we have a man left to enjoy your Tyburn, or to be racked with your torments, or consumed with your prisons. The expense is reckoned, the enterprise is begun; it is of God, it cannot be withstood. So the faith was planted; so it must be restored.

If these my offers be refused, and my endeavours can take no place, and I, having run thousands of miles to do you good, shall be rewarded with rigour, I have no more to say but to recommend your case and mine to Almightie God, the Searcher of Hearts, who sends us His grace, and set us at accord before the day of payment, to the end we may at last be friends in heaven, when all injuries shall be forgotten.[16]

Father Rupert Mayer

The Apostle of Munich

On May 14, 1983, Pope John Paul II watched as the Vatican Congregation for Saints' Causes promulgated the decree proclaiming the heroic virtues of Father Rupert Mayer, S.J., and four other candidates for sainthood. Heroic virtue, one of the criteria for beatification, is a preliminary step before canonization. Father Mayer was now officially "the Venerable Servant of God." He was beatified by John Paul II in Munich on May 3, 1987.

I am sure that many who read this will ask, "And who was Rupert Mayer?" I first heard of him in July, 1952, on my first visit to Munich, that great city in the heart of Catholic Bavaria in Southern West Germany. I walked into a church on the Marienplatz — St. Mary's Square — the religious and business center of the city. In the crypt of the church I found a mound of flowers before an altar with a statue of the Mother of God on it. Under the flowers was a slab of marble over a grave with an inscription carved into it: "Peter Rupert Mayer, S.J., 23.I.1876, 1 XI 1945."

Thirty-three years later I went back again to the grave in that church in Munich. Once more it was covered with a mound of fresh flowers. (I read recently that there was a shortage of hamburger buns, taco shells, shopping hours, parking spaces, and sunshine in Munich, but there does not seem to be a shortage of flowers for Father Mayer's grave.)

In 1983, the Jesuit weekly *America* printed the bare details of Rupert Mayer's life:

Father Mayer was ordained a Jesuit priest in 1899 and became a chaplain in World War I, during which he lost a leg in action while giving absolution to a German soldier. After the war he worked among the poor in Munich and, after Hitler's rise to power, was one of the first clergymen to challenge Nazism, declaring 'a true Catholic cannot be a National Socialist.' The Nazis arrested him several times and forbade him to preach: in 1939 he was arrested and placed in solitary confinement for four years and was finally released by Allied troops in 1945. He returned to Munich, renewed his apostolate and died among the poor.[17]

On All Saints' Day, 1945, Father Rupert Mayer was celebrating a morning Mass at the altar of the Church of St. Michael on the Marienplatz in Munich, a church founded four hundred years before by St. Peter Canisius. He had just begun his homily on the "Holy Eucharist, a source of sanctity," when his voice faltered and he slumped against the altar; two hours later he died of a stroke. The "Apostle of Munich," as people called him, was buried in a grave at the Jesuit University of Pullach, a suburb of Munich.

Three years later, after a request by the Catholics he had served in Munich who loved him, his body was buried in the crypt of the Burgersaal (the Church of the Congregation) on the Marienplatz. This was the center for the Men's Sodality of Our Lady, whose chaplain he had been for many years. One hundred twenty thousand people marched in a triumphal procession or lined the streets of Munich as the funeral cortege wound its way through the city.

On my first visit to that grave in 1952 I saw the throngs of people, averaging six thousand a day, who made it a flower-strewn shrine. The crowds and the visitors still come to pray to him, and as many will tell you, "to speak to him as though he were still alive."

Rupert Mayer was born of zealous Catholic parents on January 23, 1876, into a fairly affluent family in Stuttgart, Germany. The environment was hostile to Catholics and in his early years at school he learned how to defend his religious beliefs. He was an outstanding athlete in riding, fencing, swimming, and gymnastics. After his classical studies he wanted to join the Jesuits, but he obeyed the wishes of his father, who wanted him to be incardinated in the diocese of Rothenburg. Mayer studied at universities in Fribourg in Switzerland, Munich, and Tübingen. In 1898 he went to the major seminary in Rothenburg and was ordained a diocesan priest in 1899.

After a year of zealous pastoral work he went, with the approval of his parents and his bishop, to begin his Jesuit training in the novitiate in Feldkirch. In 1906 he began six years of missionary work in Switzerland, Germany, and Holland. In 1912 the archbishop called him to Munich, at a time of rapid urbanization and industrialization, when thousands of immigrant workers were crowding into the city. The archbishop of Munich asked him to become the pastor of these men and women who had come from the countryside into the dangers of life in the big city.

Soon he became known as the "Apostle of Munich." His three decades of pastoral work gave him another name — the "Apostle of Charity." He walked among the immigrant workers, shared their joys and sorrows, solved their problems, and often gave away most of his clothing to the poor and needy of the city. He became the leader of the Men's Sodality of the Blessed Virgin and traveled day after day, preaching, sometimes more than seventy sermons a month. His flock doubled, reaching seven thousand. Father Mayer knew that thousands went to the mountains each Sunday, so he celebrated masses at 3:10 and 3:45 A.M. in the main railroad station for ten years. His congregations did not know that he had heard confessions for hours before that and that he would give several addresses to men afterwards.

With the outbreak of World War I in 1914, Mayer volunteered as a chaplain in a field hospital and was on both the Eastern and Western fronts in some of the fiercest battles of the war. He was always with the soldiers, caring for them with utter fearlessness during the fighting. Once a badly wounded man groaned to the others, "Take me along." Father Mayer covered his body with his own and told him, "It's all right, comrade, if anyone is hit, it will be me first."

When the Nazis began their campaign of racism and atheism, Mayer preached boldly against them. He was imprisoned for six months in 1937, but released because the Nazis feared public opinion. With constant courage, Mayer ignored every attempt at intimidation. Cardinal Faulhaber, the Archbishop of Munich, who himself spoke openly against the Nazis, said of him, "Father Mayer has placed upon a candlestick the virile and heroic qualities of Catholicism, confounding charlatans and liars. A modern John the Baptist has spoken the truth in the faces of the mighty."

In 1939, the Nazis put him into the concentration camp at Sachsenhausen because he refused to break the seal of the confessional when the Gestapo interrogated him. From the hell of the concentration camp he wrote, "Now I have absolutely nothing and nobody but God. He is enough — more than enough. I try to pray and offer sacrifices. That is all God wants of me now."

The Nazi leaders did not want this popular priest of Munich to be a martyr; they transferred him to solitary confinement in the Benedictine monastery at Ettal, where he spent four years. When American soldiers reached Ettal and freed him, he hurried back to the streets and the pulpits of Munich, which was now a heap of rubble. Again he was "the priest who limps"; again he was the incessant apostle who was sustained in his heroic efforts and boundless zeal for souls by his deep love of Jesus and his Mother. Then came All Saints' Day in 1945 and the fatal stroke at the altar where he had spent so many hours.

Someday Father Rupert Mayer will be St. Rupert, and they will honor him at altars all over the world.

Teilhard de Chardin

Scientist, Poet, Evolutionist, Visionary

In 1981 the Catholic Institute of Paris celebrated the centenary of the birth of Teilhard de Chardin. Cardinal Agostino Casaroli, Vatican Secretary of State, wrote a letter on behalf of Pope John Paul II for the occasion.[18]

He quoted the Pope: "Do not be afraid, open wide the doors to Christ the immense fields of culture, civilization, and development." The Cardinal called Chardin "a witness seized by Christ to the very depths of his being, and concerned to honor faith and reason at the same time." He spoke of Chardin's "powerful poetic insight into the deep value of nature, a keen perception of the dynamism of creation, a wide view of becoming of the world which were combined in him with undeniable religious fervor."

Cardinal Casaroli told the celebrants at Paris that "the astonishing repercussions of his researches, together with the influence of his thought, have left a lasting mark on our age." It was an amazing document to come from the Vatican when his most important works had been forbidden publication by his Jesuit superiors until after his death in 1955 — a prohibition he had faithfully observed because of his vow of religious obedience.

Pierre Teilhard de Chardin was born May 1, 1881, in Sarcenat in France. He entered the Society of Jesus and following his studies, he was ordained a Jesuit in 1911. His doctoral thesis was in paleontology, the study of fossils and ancient life forms. From 1923-1946, he pioneered the exploration of the Gobi Desert and other areas in northern China and Asia. During those years of exile from his beloved Paris because his ideas were thought to be too disturbing and too novel for publication in Paris, he developed what Cardinal Feltin of Paris in 1961 called his marvelous and seductive "global vision of the universe wherein matter and spirit, body and soul, nature and supernature, science and faith find their unity in Christ."

On Easter afternoon, April 10, 1955, Father Teilhard died of a sudden heart attack in a hotel room in New York City. His death was peaceful — and hardly noticed. A Jesuit friend of mine told me how the Jesuit provincial in New York announced the death of their brother French Jesuit and asked for volunteers to accompany the body for burial in an obscure Jesuit cemetery sixty miles north of the city. Only a few responded. The body of the world-famed Jesuit is buried under a simple stone marker.

Today many consider him one of the greatest visionaries of our century. He was a brilliant scientist, a paleontologist who was a co-discoverer of Peking Man, an important link in the chain of evolution. He wrote two classic works, *The Phenomenon of Man,* a theoretical account of his evolutionary — and revolutionary — ideas, and *The Divine Milieu,* a practical application of those ideas to Christian spirituality.[19] Both books made him world-famous a few years after his death. They had been written years before, but Church officials and his Jesuit superiors had forbidden him to publish them after many futile efforts on his part to get permission to publish them. Their poetic vision, in which he combined science, philosophy, and theology, pushed the theory of evolution far beyond the narrow vision of traditional Catholic thinkers of his time. One does not have to accept all his interpretations of Catholic theology, which raise some difficulties about his view of the traditional teachings, to admire his profound insight into the role of the Cosmic Christ in the universe.

I first heard of Teilhard de Chardin as one of the few outstanding Catholic proponents of scientific evolutionary theories in my studies of Anthropology at the Catholic University of America in the early Forties. When we could read after World War II what Catholic theologians in Europe were saying during the War, I learned of the controversies — and mistaken appraisals — which swirled around the man who was Teilhard de Chardin. I realize why Cardinal Casaroli could remind the meeting at Paris that "the complexity of the problems tackled, as well as the variety of approaches adopted, have not failed to raise difficulties, which rightly motivate a critical and serene study — on the philosophical and theological level — of his exceptional work." I have profited greatly from reading Teilhard, and I am delighted at the change in tone with which the Vatican of John Paul II speaks of him.

My understanding of Vatican Council II, the most exciting event of my teaching career, owes much to what I have learned of his historical and evolutionary approach to development in its relation to my Catholic faith. I have admired Teilhard as, with humble obedience to his vows as a Jesuit, he strove to break through the encrusted mold of traditional thought and to speak meaningfully of God and the World to men and women of our time.

The name and the books of Father Teilhard de Chardin were not cited much at the Second Vatican Council, but his un-voiced ideas were a powerful influence on the great majority of the bishops who voted overwhelmingly at its end to accept the epoch-making *Pastoral Constitution on the Church in the Modern World*.

The Spirituality of Teilhard de Chardin

Father Teilhard de Chardin's mother taught him the fervor of her French piety centered on the Sacred Heart of Jesus. His father directed a small natural history museum and Teilhard from his earliest years was fascinated by earth sciences. Personal attachment to the Sacred Heart was the seed of his Christology, which in turn formed the most substantial part of his religious thought. In almost everything he wrote he strove for a synthesis between evolutionary theory and his ardent Catholic faith. At the end, even though his superiors forbade him to publish anything but scientific articles during his lifetime, he thought he had conquered the divisions which the scientists of his time and traditional theologians had erected between the two.

All his life was spent on the boundaries between the two worlds of science and religion. In an essay in his book, *How I Believe*, he wrote:

The originality of my life lies in its being rooted in two domains of life which are commonly regarded as antagonistic. By intellectual training I belong to the "children of heaven," but by temperament and by my professional studies, I am a "child of the earth ...." The

one has not destroyed, but has reinforced the other. Today I believe
probably more profoundly than ever in God, and certainly more
than ever in the world.[20]

Teilhard de Chardin, among many other works, wrote what
are regarded as his two classics: *The Phenomenon of Man*,
written in exile in China from 1938 to 1940, contained the ker-
nel of his scientific thought; *The Divine Milieu*, written in the
Gobi Desert and Africa in 1927, is the key to the religious meditations and profound insights which accompany all his work.
The sub-title for *The Divine Milieu* was "An Essay on the Interior Life." The dedication quoted Jesus' "For God so loved the
world," and said simply, "For those who love the world."

There are theologians of considerable stature who maintain
that *The Divine Milieu* is perhaps the finest work of the spiritual life to appear in the past hundred years. Some critics, on
the other hand, called it "the maximum of seduction with the
maximum of error." A reviewer in the *Church Times* of England called it unforgettable, a unique book in its own sphere,
an outpouring of devotion to God written in impressively
beautiful language. I think that Father Henri de Lubac, S.J.,
one of the greatest theologians of our times, a friend of Teilhard for forty years, and author of five books on his religious
thought, was right to say that the book established Teilhard as
the master of a new spiritual life, one that is still utterly traditional in the best theological sense.

One of the basic themes in *The Divine Milieu* is that, in
place of a spirituality which looks only to the future world, fo-
cuses only on prayer and spiritual exercises, and looks on the
present world as a place of spiritual danger, Teilhard believes
that we touch the divine by our activity and commitment in
and upon the world. His is a spirituality which gives meaning
to our everyday life and work.

Teilhard de Chardin can liberate us from a truncated spirituality which puts a false separation between the spiritual and
the temporal. In a well-known plaintive lament in the book, he
said:

I do not think I am exaggerating when I say that nine out of ten
Christians feel that their work is always at the level of a "spiritual en-
cumbrance".... The general run of the faithful dimly feel that time

*spent in the office or the studio, in the fields or in the factory is time
diverted from prayer and adoration. A few moments of the day can be
salvaged for God, yes, but the best hours are absorbed, or at any rate
cheapened, by material cares.*[21]

Teilhard de Chardin added a wonderful piece of advice
which, if we pray it over, could change the way we look at God
and the world and our own selves:

*Try, with God's help, to perceive the connection — even physical
and natural — which binds your labor with the building of the Kingdom of Heaven; try to realize that heaven itself smiles upon you and
through your works, draws you to itself; then, as you leave the church
for the noisy streets, you will remain with only one feeling, that of
continuing to immerse yourself in God ... Never at any time, "whether
eating or drinking," consent to do anything without first of all realizing
its significance and constructive value in* Christo Jesu *and pursuing it
with all your might. This is not a commonplace precept for salvation;
it is the very path to sanctity for all according to their states and call-
ings... Right from the hands that knead the dough to those who consecrate it, the great and universal Host should be prepared and handled
in a spirit of adoration.*

Long ago I read a sentence from Teilhard de Chardin which
has haunted me ever since. It sums it all up: "We make our way
to heaven by doing the work of the world."

Karl Rahner

He Guided the Church After Vatican II

Karl Rahner celebrated his eightieth birthday on March 4, 1984. The great German Jesuit theologian died a few weeks later on March 30. The tributes to his memory poured in from Catholic and other religious presses in all parts of the world soon after his death.

The *London Tablet* called him "the world's foremost living theologian" when he reached the age of 80. Many tributes included references to his paramount influence on the theology which developed at the Second Vatican Council. It was said of him that "Father Rahner's insight, brilliance, and pastoral concern guided the Church through the tumultuous post-Vatican II era."

Several of the great pioneers in the development of what was criticized by traditional theologians in the Forties and Fifties of this century as the "New Theology" were vindicated when their basic ideas were written into the sixteen documents issued by the Council. I think of Teilhard de Chardin, S.J., who was not allowed to publish his revolutionary ideas in his lifetime, but it has been said by those who had reasons to know that, although he was seldom quoted in the footnotes of the Vatican II documents, his theology and his philosophy of religious evolution were powerful factors in the minds of the majority of the bishops when they voted to approve those documents by large margins.

Father Yves Congar, the Dominican theologian, had published ideas on the role of the laity in the Church and on ecumenism which were highly suspect at Rome before the Council; but these ideas were incorporated into the Council documents on those topics.

I think, too, of the American Jesuit theologian, Father John Courtney Murray, who was silenced by his superiors and bitterly attacked by a few theologians at Catholic University in America in the Fifties because of his defense of religious liberty for all persons against the textbook traditions of restricted religious liberty.

Murray was not allowed to be at the first session of the Council as a theological adviser to the American bishops, but he is widely acknowledged as the "architect" of the epoch-making decree on religious liberty which the American bishops defended strongly and which embodied the American tradition of the separation of Church and State.

Karl Rahner, who had also been treated with suspicion and restraints from Rome, achieved his great moment of triumph at the Second Vatican Council. In his stimulating book, *Catholic Thinkers in the Clear*, William Herr wrote that Rahner "ran afoul" of Cardinal Ottaviani, who pleaded with Pope John XXIII — unsuccessfully — to send Rahner back to Austria.[22] But whereas Murray managed to get the Council to pass one declaration, the entire work and spirit of Vatican II was a vindication of Rahner's way of doing theology.

What some think is the ultimate accolade and guarantee of Karl Rahner's orthodoxy came in a letter which Pope John Paul II wrote to congratulate him on his eightieth birthday. The pope wrote of his esteem for Rahner's "tireless scientific activity" and with his apostolic blessing sent a "remembrance in prayer from my heart."

Karl Rahner was born in Freiburg-im-Breisgau, Germany, in 1904. In 1922 he entered the Jesuit novitiate in Feldkirch, Austria, where his brother Hugo, also a theologian, had gone three years earlier. He showed a special aptitude for philosophy and he was sent to Freiburg to study for a doctorate. The renowned Martin Heidegger, who had a great influence in contemporary philosophy, was teaching there. He attended as many of Heidegger's classes as he could, and was assigned to do research under Martin Honecker, who was an advocate of a pseudo-Thomistic philosophy. When Rahner wrote a dissertation which combined the philosophy of Thomas Aquinas with contemporary approaches to a theory of knowledge, Honecker rejected it. Rahner later published it as a book, *Spirit in the World*.[23] It won instant acclaim for him and was the foundation in some respects of his later work in theology, to which he turned when he was assigned to teach at the University of Innsbruck, where his brother Hugo also taught.

The enormous influence of Karl Rahner is in great measure due to his prodigious output of books and articles on every phase of theology. He wrote one thousand five hundred works, mostly articles, before he died, and when you count the translations into many languages, that output comes to more than three thousand five hundred works.

Many of his articles, published in twenty volumes of his *Theological Investigations*, are scientific studies in theology. (Toward the end of his life he summarized his life work as a systematic theologian in a book he called *Foundations of Christian Faith*.)[24] Some of the articles are what he called "works of piety," in which Rahner wrote a pastoral and spiritual application of his theoretical works to the everyday Christian's way of life. In 1982 many of these more practical (and much easier to read) articles about spirituality were published in his book, *The Practice of Faith: A Handbook of Contemporary Spirituality*.[25]

There have been certain peak moments in the history of Catholic thought when a theologian of towering genius extracts the meaning of a theological teaching from the particular formulation that the Catholic doctrine had received in his time and reshapes it in terms that would have more relevance for the people of his own time. Augustine was such a theologian who forged a new synthesis of Christian revelation and Platonic philosophy in the fifth century that dominated Catholic education for a thousand years. Aquinas likewise used Aristotelian philosophy to form a system in the thirteenth century which was a dominant influence in Catholic thought until quite recently.

So too was Karl Rahner in our own century. He used contemporary philosophy to renew the Catholic and Thomistic heritage in a meaningful way for the modern Church. The result was summed up by Father William Lynn, S.J., a professor of systematic theology who knew Father Rahner personally:

"There are many theologians, simple priests, and lowly folk (one can be all three at once), who are grateful to Rahner for helping them understand that the human spirit, made for Mystery, encounters that Mystery in every circumstance of daily life, in countless ways that are not always recognized for what they are — experiences of grace. God is not far off. He is much nearer than we think. He does not reveal Himself in rare moments, but at every turn. Christ can claim not only those whom the census counts as Christians, but every person who accepts the hidden light that comes without a name to every human heart. One need not worry about the future of God or the Church. One need worry only about one's own response to God's surprising word."[26]

I shall let Karl Rahner have the last word. In a Vatican Radio address on his eightieth birthday a few weeks before his death, he said: "In the first place, everyone has a responsibility to thank God each day ... since each of these days was given and represents for us the possibility of attaining eternal life with God."

Chapter 7

Saints of the Early and Medieval Church

Saint Justin the Martyr

The First Christian Philosopher

The first lines in the Opening Prayer of the Mass of Justin Martyr on June 1 are: "Father, through the folly of the cross you taught St. Justin the sublime wisdom of Jesus Christ."

The phrase, "the folly of the Cross," takes us back to the first chapter of First Corinthians, where St. Paul asks the new Christians of Corinth, "How many of you were wise that God chose what is foolish by human reckoning" (I Cor. 1:26-27). Paul had just introduced that question by saying, "The language of the cross may be illogical to those who are not on the way to salvation, but those of us who are on the way see it as God's power to save ... God's foolishness is wiser than human wisdom, and God's weakness is stronger than human strength" (I Cor. 1:18,25).

The life of Justin Martyr was a search for truth; he finally found it when he came to believe in God's wisdom rather than that of the Greek philosophers whom he studied. He came to his journey's end in his search when he found it in the folly of the cross. He became the first Christian philosopher: he was the most important of the second century Apologists in the defense of the Christian Church against its enemies among the pagan philosophers.

Justin was born of pagan parents around the year 100 A.D. in Flavia Neapolis in ancient Samaria. The city in modern Israel is called Nablus, but its original name was Schechem. Justin's family was of Greek origin and Justin was well-educated in rhetoric, poetry, and history before he turned to the search for ultimate wisdom, philosophy.

But which system of philosophy would slake his burning thirst for wisdom? For a while he studied the Stoic philosophy, but he rejected it when he found it could teach him nothing about God. He went to the school of Pythagoras but was told that he would have to know geometry, music, and astronomy. Aristotle was taught by the Peripatetic School but the teacher's greedy demand for fees turned him off. An eminent disciple of Plato did try to teach him something about God.

One day, as he walked in a field near the seashore, probably at Ephesus in Asia Minor, thinking about one of the maxims of Plato, he encountered a venerable old man who was following him. Soon he was discussing the problems that tormented him. The stranger spoke to him of a philosophy nobler than any he had studied. It was foretold by the ancient Hebrew prophets and reached its summit in the life and teachings of Jesus Christ. The old man urged Justin to pray for light so that he might achieve a knowledge of God which only God could give him.

Justin had already heard of the Christians. "Even at the time when I was content with the doctrines of Plato," he later wrote, "when I heard the Christians accused, and saw them fearlessly meet death and all that is considered terrible, I felt that such men could not possibly have been leading the life of vicious pleasure with which they were credited."[1]

Justin was about thirty when he was baptized. His search for truth had come to an end with his faith in Christ but he continued to wear the philosopher's cloak. He felt that many would welcome the Christian Way of Life if it were explained to them. He travelled across the Eastern Mediterranean world and held disputes with Jews, pagans, and heretics, especially at Rome, where he arrived about the year 135. There he lived in a house in which he preached the Good News of the death and resurrection of Jesus and the victory Christ had brought to all men and women through the cross. Remaining a layman, Justin taught and wrote for the non-Christians who knew little about that small but growing band of followers who believed that Jesus of Nazareth whom they worshipped was the Son of God. The Christians were for the most part simple, poor, and unlearned people who kept their secrets to themselves to avoid the misrepresentations and calumnies of the pagans; they did not want their beliefs profaned.

Justin, however, believed he must openly teach the enemies of the Church. He said that "it is our duty to make known our doctrine, lest we incur the guilt and punishment of those who have sinned through ignorance." One part of his apostolate was the writing of books, called *Apologies* in defense of the Church.

In *The Oxford Dictionary of Saints,* David Hugh Farmer summed up Justin's writings and their basic purpose and content:

> *His surviving writings, which comprise the two Apologies and the Dialogue with Trypho, are among the earliest products of the sub-apostolic age which reflect the outlook of a Christian intellectual. They tell of the faith of the Christians, the rite of Baptism and the Eucharist, and the distribution of alms. They refute accusations of immorality and atheism and show that loyalty to the Emperor is based on the teaching of Christ and Paul. Justin's aim was always apostolic; he thought that pagans would become Christians if they were made aware of Christian doctrine and practice through articulate, well-presented writings.[2]*

In Rome Justin argued with a Cynic philosopher called Crescens. He proved him not only ignorant about Christianity but guilty of willful misrepresentation. Through Crescens it is thought that Justin was accused before the Roman authorities during the persecution of the Emperor Marcus Aurelius.

There exists an authentic account of *The Acts of Justin and his Companions.* When Justin stood before Rusticus, the Roman Prefect, he was urged to submit to the gods and obey the Emperor. The *Acts* recount the last dialogue of Justin and Rusticus:

> *Rusticus: "Come here and sacrifice to the gods."*
> *Justin: "Nobody in his senses gives up truth for falsehood."*
> *Rusticus: "If you do not do as I tell you, you will be tortured without mercy."* To which Justin replied: *"We ask nothing better than to suffer for the sake of our Lord Jesus Christ and so be saved. If we do this, we can stand confidently and quietly before the fearful judgment seat of that same God and Savior, when in accordance with divine ordering all this world will pass away."[3]*

His six companions agreed — and St. Justin and they were beheaded and gave their final witness to Christ. It was in the year of the Lord, 165.

Saint Augustine of Hippo

In the third Eucharistic Prayer there is a prayer to the Father that Jesus "will enable us to share in the inheritance of your saints ... on whose constant intercession we rely for help." St. Athanasius writes in one of his letters that "the feasts of the saints proclaim the wonderful work of Christ in his servants and offer fitting example for the faithful to follow." The Church has always believed that its memorials of the saints proclaim and renew the Paschal Mystery of Christ and urges us to seek their help in our search for God.

Across the centuries many have found Aurelius Augustine of Hippo in his quest for divine wisdom and peace of soul. Many, too, have followed this quest through the pages of his masterful spiritual autobiography, the *Confessions;* they have found in that book "the wonderful work of Christ" in the soul of a man who lived in turmoil through his first thirty-two years until he found the peace he had searched for so ardently.

After his conversion to Christ he became one of the supreme teachers of the Church with a profound impact on the development of Christian doctrine and spirituality. A towering genius, he wrote prolifically on the mystery of Christ and his Church. Christopher Dawson said of him, "He was, to a far greater degree that any emperor or war lord, a maker of history and builder of the bridge which has led from the old world to the new."[4] Frank Sheed, who was one of many who have translated the *Confessions* into English, wrote about him, "Every man and woman in the western world would be a different man or woman if Augustine had not been, or had been different."[5]

On November 13, 354, in the busy market town of Tagaste in what is now Algeria in North Africa, a young Christian mother named Monica gave birth to a son named Aurelius Augustinus.

His father was Patricius, a pagan Roman official. The dust of more than sixteen centuries has drifted across Tagaste since the boy played in its streets and stole some pears, as he later confessed in a well-known passage, in an orchard nearby. Nobody would ever think of the town today, presently Souk Ahras, but it will always be mentioned in the history books because the boy grew up to become the bishop of Hippo (another forgotten town), a Doctor of the Church, and one of the makers of the Christian mind.

The theological genius and, more importantly, the sanctity of St. Augustine was so versatile and ranged so widely that no one book can hope to do him justice. When he died at Hippo on August 28, 430 A.D., he had produced a series of books in philosophy and theology and sacred scripture which dominated and molded the thought of Western Christianity for a thousand years. In the Christian tradition he is called the Doctor of Grace, the greatest of the Fathers of the early Church.

Augustine was brought up as a Christian but was not baptized as an infant. In 370 A.D. he went to the university of Carthage to study rhetoric, the art of persuading through speech, in order to become a lawyer, but soon turned to literature, abandoned his Christian faith, took a mistress with whom he lived fifteen years and by whom he had a son named Adeodatus. (Ironically, the name means "given by God.") He became intensively interested in philosophy and in his quest for wisdom, he embraced Manichaeism, which purported to have the answer to the question of evil in the world. The Manichaeisms solved the problem by teaching that two supreme principles ruled the world — good and evil — and that evil could be traced to a supreme evil being. Augustine began to teach rhetoric for the next decade at Tagaste and Carthage. He went to Rome in 383 A.D. and opened a school, but could not stand his students' attitudes and in 384 A.D. accepted an offer to teach rhetoric in Milan.

In Milan he was impressed by a tutor named Simplicianus and the sermons of St. Ambrose, then bishop of Milan; he returned to his faith in Christ and was baptized on the eve of Easter in 387 A.D.

Augustine's conversion to the religion of his mother, for which she had fervently prayed for many years, came only af-

ter a horrendous struggle to free himself from the powerful lure
of the sexual excesses in which he had reveled so long. In a
celebrated passage in his *Confessions* he wrote about the torment he suffered:

*"I, wretched young fellow that I was, more wretched even in the
very entrance into my youth, had even then begged chastity from
God and said: "Give me chastity and continency, but do not give it
yet." For I was afraid that thou wouldst hear me too soon, and too
soon deliver me from my disease of incontinency; which my desire
was rather to have satisfied than extinguished....*

*My lower instincts ... were stronger than the higher.... They
plucked at my garment of flesh and whispered, "Are you going to dis-
miss us? From this moment we shall never be with you again, for ever
and ever. From this moment you will never again be allowed to do
this thing or that, for evermore!" Could Augustine, he asked himself,
close your ears to the unclean whispers of your body?*[6]

On that September day Augustine was reading the epistles of
Paul, and in his *Confessions* he tells what happened. He heard
a child's voice piping some words. "Take it and read; take it
and read." In the old Loeb Classics' translation by W. Watts,
he wrote,

*Whereupon refraining the violent torrent of my tears, up I gat me;
interpreting in no other way, but that I was from God himself commanded to open the book, and to read that chapter which I would first
light upon... Hastily therefore went I again to that place where Alypius
was sitting; for there had I laid the Apostle's book when as I rose from
thence. I snatched it up, I opened it, and in silence I read that chapter
which I had first cast my eyes: "Not in rioting and drunkenness, not in
chambering and wantonness, not in strife and envying; but put ye on
the Lord Jesus Christ, and make not provision for the flesh, to fulfill
the lusts thereof." No further words would I read; not needed I. For
instantly, even with the end of this sentence, by a light as it were of
confidence now darted into my heart, all the darkness of doubting va-
nished away.*[7]

Augustine marked the place and looked at Alypius, his
friend; together they quietly re-read the passage from Paul. As
Alypius read, he "applied this to himself." They then walked
into the house to tell Monica, his mother, "who was overjoyed
... she was jubilant with triumph." It was the end of thirty-three
years of praying for her son's conversion. Augustine summed

it up as completely God's doing and told God: "You converted me to yourself, so that I no longer desired a wife or placed
any hope in this world but stood firmly upon the rule of faith,
where you had shown me to her in a dream so many years
before."

That afternoon in a villa garden near Milan those words of
St. Paul to the Romans marked the moment of St. Augustine's
conversion to Christ. It was the end of a lifetime search for
what he called "Wisdom." After indulging in gross sensuality
and trying the pagan philosophies of North Africa, he found
his "Wisdom" in the words and deeds of Jesus Christ. After the
flood of grace which God sent to him through St. Paul, he
could say with the Apostle of the Gentiles, "To me to live is
Christ."

Augustine went to St. Ambrose, the Archbishop of Milan,
who introduced him to the central mysteries of the Trinity and
Redemption and the articles of the Catholic Creed. His quest
for peace came to its ultimate end on Easter Eve in 387 A.D.,
when he was baptized by Ambrose. Afterward, he told Ambrose that he was convinced not so much by his instruction as
by "the love you showed me." It must have been the greatest
day in the life of Saint Monica, the patroness of praying and
persistent mothers.

The most quoted sentence in the *Confessions* is in the first
paragraph: "You have made us for Thyself, O Lord, and our
hearts are restless till they rest in Thee." Monica's son closed
his spiritual autobiography by confessing that the peace he
had sought outside himself had been within himself, unacknowledged. He regretted that he had not found it sooner. He
wrote an oft-quoted lament toward the end of the *Confessions*,
"Late have I loved Thee, O Beauty so ancient and so new; late
have I loved Thee. For behold, Thou wert within me and I outside.... Thou didst touch me, and I have burned for Thy
peace."[8]

One might suppose, from some of the things I have written
about Augustine, that his works are of interest to scholars only;
however, his *Confessions* are found on every list of the classics
of Christian spirituality. With many editions by a variety of
translators, the *Confessions* are still published and are available in bookstores today. As the story of his love affair with

God, the *Confessions* tells how he achieved the peace St. Paul proclaimed to be "past all understanding." Into that book, written at the end of the fourth century, he put all his sins, his vanity, his pride and lust, his search for "beauty ever ancient and ever new" down a dozen bypaths of error, his triumph over doubt, his exaltation in Christ, his hymn of praise to the Church and the faith which brought him peace at last.

There are countless men and women who in the uncertainties and confusions of our times are thrust into the same doubts and dilemmas that tormented Augustine of Hippo over sixteen centuries ago. They, too, may find their way to the happiness and peace of truth as Augustine takes them through his life. Because he was a profoundly sympathetic psychologist as well as theologian, his *Confessions* is not only the story of one person's quest for God. It stirs up universal echoes and is valid for all people and, as the Quakers say, "it speaks to my condition."

St. Augustine's analysis of time and memory and the fundamental emotions in the *Confessions* is psychologically superb; he wrote the first and probably the greatest theology of history in a long work, *The City of God;* he broke the back of some of the most dangerous heresies of the early Church; he was more profound than others in his exploration of the meaning of what St. Paul called the "New Life" in Christ Jesus, and later theologians called him the Doctor of Grace because of his speculation on the gift of grace with which God raised his human creatures to a level of participation in his own life.

St. Augustine died a great saint. With that last of his achievements I have credited to him, I have named the most important of them all. The memorial feasts of the Church proclaim and renew the Paschal Mystery of Christ. For sixteen hundred years St. Augustine, the Doctor of Grace, has been an occasion of grace to those who read his works.

Saint Augustine's Christmas Paradox

In the Mediterranean world into which Augustine — and Jesus — were born, the almost constant brilliance of the sun was frequently used by poets, philosophers, prophets, and theologians as a metaphor for the God who said, "Let there be light." In one of the Hebrew psalms there is a prayer to God in which Augustine, among others, used to speak of God as the source of divine wisdom. "In your light," the psalmist prayed, "we see light." Isaiah the poet of Advent, speaks of the coming Messiah, "The people who walked in darkness have seen a great light." In John's prologue about Jesus, the Word of God, he says that Jesus is "the true light which enlightens everyone who comes into the world." Jesus called himself the Light of the World.

St. Augustine of Hippo based his whole theory of knowledge on the human mind's illumination by God. In his Christmas sermons at the cathedral of Hippo in the first years of the fifth century, Augustine as bishop meditated profoundly on the mystery of the birth of the baby in Bethlehem, the Light of the World. He ran through a long series of changes on the central and stupendous Christmas paradox — God become human, the Word made Flesh, a baby who was the Son of God and Son of Mary.

A paradox may be defined as an assertion that seems to contradict common sense at first but on reflection turns out to be true.

Gilbert Keith Chesterton, a master of paradox in the first half of the twentieth century, often wrote about the paradox of the Incarnation:

> *Upon this paradox, we might almost say, upon this jest, all the literature of our faith is founded ... The scientific critic laboriously explains the difficulty which we have always defiantly and almost derisively exaggerated and mildly condemns as improbable something we have almost madly exalted as incredible, as something which would be much too good to be true, except that it is true.*[9]

Not even Chesterton, the master of paradox, can match the many passages in his Christmas sermons where Augustine forces us to think out the meaning of the truth that the Creator who filled the world was found enclosed in a creature's womb:

> *Maker of the sun, he is made under the sun. Disposer of all ages in the bosom of the Father, he consecrates this day in the womb of his mother; in him he remains, from him he goes forth. Creator of heaven and earth, he was born on earth under heaven. Unspeakably wise, he is wisely speechless, filling the world. He lies in a manger; ruler of the stars, he nurses at his mother's bosom. He is both great in the nature of God and small in the form of a servant.*[10]

The idea of a speechless infant who was the Eternal Word slips often into the sermons of Augustine:

He who made man was made man; he was given existence by a mother whom he brought into existence ... He nursed at breasts which he filled; he cried like a babe in the manger in speechless infancy — this Word without which human eloquence is speechless... Take to heart the lesson of this great humility, though the Teacher of it is still without speech ... your Creator, because of you, lay speechless, and did not call even his mother by her name.[11]

St. Augustine preached those Christmas homilies in a church and city which have long since been covered over by the dust of centuries, but he can bring us to the heart of our Christmas celebration with stirring words of hope which still come to us across the centuries: "Rejoice, you who are free! It is the birthday of him who makes us free. Rejoice, you Christians all! It is Christ's birthday!"

Saint David of Wales

A good friend of mine asked me recently, "Why don't you write a column about Saint David?" (By no coincidence, his name was David.) When I heard the name, my memory recalled a scene at the beginning of the fourth act of Shakespeare's "King Henry V." The scene was set in the English camp in France before the battle of Agincourt. Shakespeare brings two soldiers before the King; they were Pistol, an Englishman, and Fluellen, a Welshman. Pistol asks the King, "What is thy name?" Here are the next few lines:

King Henry. *Harry le Roy*
Pistol. *LeRoy! a Cornish name: art thou of Cornish crew?*
King Henry. *No, I am a Welshman.*
Pistol. *Knows't thou Fluellen?*
King Henry. *Yes.*
Pistol. *Tell him I'll knock his leek about his pate*
      Upon Saint Davey's Day.[12]

In *A Dictionary of Saints* Donald Attwater refers to the scene and says that the association of leeks with St. David's Day (March 1) has not been satisfactorily explained: his emblem is a dove.[13] Hugh Farmer in his *Oxford Dictionary of Saints* says that the custom of Welshmen wearing leeks or daffodils on St. David's Day is described by Shakespeare as 'an ancient tradition begun upon an honourable request,' but no satisfactory explanation of it has yet been made."[14] One explanation was hazarded: St. David was leading his people against the Saxons and ordered them to wear a leek, a type of onion, in their hats to distinguish them from the enemy. There is no mention of leeks in St. David's life.

St. David (in Welsh, Dewi) was the bishop of Menevia in Wales; his name was later changed to a Welsh word which meant "David's House." St. David, the patron saint of Wales, is said to have been canonized by Pope Callistus II in 1120.

It is unfortunate that we have no early account of the life of David, who was perhaps the most celebrated of early English saints. All the accounts preserved to us are based on a biography written about 1090 by Rhygyfarch, anglicized as Ricemarch. He was a learned man and his claim to have drawn on written sources is probably justified, but he was also concerned to uphold the fabulous primacy of the diocese of St. Davids in Wales and the pre-eminence of David against the pretensions of the newly arrived Normans. Ricemarch, Butler tells us, was incapable of distinguishing historical fact from the wildest fables.

In its article on St. David of Wales, the *New Catholic Encyclopedia* says he was probably born about 520 A.D. and died about 589 A.D. in an area known as Pembrokeshire (in Welsh, Dyfed).[15]

He was the son of a *Sant* or a Welsh prince. It was a golden age in the history of Welsh Christianity, when many sons of high birth found that their Faith led them to the life of a monk. One was Illtyd, who left his career as a soldier to lead the celibate life as a soldier for Christ. (Some think he was the model from whom the story of Sir Galahad at King Arthur's Court was taken.) Illtyd founded a monastery at Llantwit. David was ordained a priest.

David became abbot of Menevia; his rule of life was very strict. David's monks lived in extreme hardship, imitating the early monks of Egypt in their regime of heavy manual labor and eating only bread and vegetables. They drank water only — unusual in those days — and the fact that his monks drank no alcoholic beverages gave the abbot the nickname *Aquaticus* — the "Waterman." For their work in the field David allowed no oxen, declaring that every monk was his own ox. They followed a rigid rule of attendance at services and spent most of the day in strict silence. David devoted himself to works of mercy and practiced frequent genuflections and total immersion in cold water as his favorite austerities.

David was called to the synod of Brevi and preached to such effect that, as David Farmer in his Oxford Dictionary of Saints reports, he was made abbot and his monastery declared the metropolitan see of the country, so that whoever ruled it should be accounted archbishop. One author said that, despite the severe life at the monastery, St. David was no killjoy; wherever he went, "he spread good humour and fun."

In Victor J. Green's book, *Saints for All Seasons,* we find that

> *The Bishop of Llandaf became Archbishop of Caerleon and, when he died, David succeeded him. He could not leave the monastery at Menevia, so a new cathedral was built there. Today that site is known as St. David's great cathedral with its Norman nave, set among ruins dating back to the sixth century, with the remains of little chapels dotted about. When the news that David was dying went out, crowds came from all over Wales to be near. His last message was, "Brothers and sisters, be joyful and keep your faith and do the little things that you have seen and heard with me." He was buried in the cathedral-abbey church, probably on March 1,589.[16]*

St. David is one of the most popular saints of Wales — and even of England. The oldest written evidence about him, however, comes from Ireland, where the Catalogue of Saints (about 730) says that "they received the Mass from Bishop David and Britons Gillas (Gildas) and Teilo," and the earliest martyrologies (about 800) place his feast on March 1 and locate his monastery at "Menevia," i.e. St. David's.

There are few hard facts about St. David and it is difficult to separate them from the legends surrounding the lives of many early and medieval saints. Some of those myths would make him the eighteenth lineal descendant of the Virgin Mary. Another would claim that his birth was forecast by an angel thirty years before, that at his approach waters were made warm and salubrious, that he healed the sick and revived the dead, that hills rose up from level ground to form a pulpit for his speeches, and that when he preached a white dove sat on his shoulder.

The truth remains, however, that St. David was a most important influence in the development of Welsh and Celtic Catholicism in the sixth century and that he still remains one of the most popular saints of Great Britain and the pride of the Welsh people, who revere him as the patron saint of their country and still celebrate March 1 as "St. Davey's Day."

Saint Emeric

The Saint Who Named America

A few years ago I was skimming through one of those booklets written to help liturgy committees prepare for the Sunday celebrations, and was stopped short by a note under the suggestions for the First Sunday of Lent: "Tuesday (March 10) is the 530th anniversary of Amerigo Vespucci's birth, the voyager after whom our country is named. In turn, his name derives from that of St. Emeric, who thus becomes a secondary patron of our nation."

Intrigued by that last sentence, I did some research. Long ago, a teacher told us how by some mistake America came to have the name of Amerigo Vespucci (Latin, *Americus Vespucius*) instead of being called Columbia, after the great navigator who made the first landfall in 1492.

My research led me to Martin Waldseemueller (1475-1522?), a Swiss map-maker or cartographer, who published a book in 1507 to accompany a great wall map and small globe in which the name America first appears to designate this part of the world. In an appendix he published a Latin translation of four letters written by Vespucci to describe his four voyages, beginning in 1499, to the New World. One of the letters, published in Latin in 1507, was reprinted by Waldseemueller the same year. (The Latin translation of a letter of Christopher Columbus describing his voyage in 1498 was not available until the following year.) The Swiss cartographer put Vespucci's Christian name in its Latin form on his 1507 map. On a later map in 1530 he dropped the "America" name and gave credit to Columbus by using his name for the New World. By that time Amerigo, who was something of a publicity hound, had his first name established on the many maps which followed that of Waldseemueller.

Now we sing "Columbia, the Gem of the Ocean," but not in

the same way we sing "America the Beautiful." It is fixed in the minds of the people that Amerigo discovered the lands which bear his name — and the name of Saint Emeric, for whom he himself was named: Emeric was the name with which he was baptized.

Saint Emeric was the only son of St. Stephen I, the King of Hungary. He was born in 1007 at the time when his father was bringing political order into Hungary by uniting various tribes of the land and zealously promoting the spread of Christianity in his kingdom. In the Hungarian language, Emeric's name was Imre, which became Americus in Latin, Amerigo in Italian, and Emeric in English.

The young prince Imre was the son of Stephen and his wife, Blessed Gisela; he was educated by Saint Gerard Sagredo. We know very little about Imre beyond the fact that he seems to have made a vow of virginity, but married about 1026 for reasons of state. His father, planning to have Imre succeed him as King, took great pains to educate him, but Imre was killed prematurely in a hunting accident at the age of twenty-four. King Stephen said of him, "God loved him, and so He took him away very soon." Many miracles were reported at his tomb at Szekesfehervar, and Imre was canonized, with his father, in 1083. In our own century his cult was revived in the years between the two great wars as the patron of Hungarian youth. His feast day is November 4.

In my research for traces of the life of St. Emeric of Hungary, I was surprised to discover how his brief life crossed the paths of quite a few other men and women who have been beatified or canonized as Saints of the Church.

His father was St. Stephen (973-1038), who was crowned the first king of Hungary by Pope Sylvester II on Christmas Day in the year 1000 A.D. Stephen was a staunch supporter of the Church, zealous in evangelizing the Hungarian tribes, founder of ten episcopal sees and many monasteries. Emeric's mother was not canonized but is revered as Blessed Gisela (973 A.D.–1061 A.D.). His uncle, the brother of Gisela, was St. Henry II, born in 937 A.D. and Holy Roman Emperor from 1002 A.D. to 1014 A.D. He and his wife, St. Kunegunde, the aunt of St. Emeric, are buried in two tombs in the cathedral of Bamberg, Germany.

Catholics in this country know that St. Mary, the Mother of God, was officially proclaimed the heavenly patroness of the United States in 1846 under the title of the Immaculate Conception. Few of them, I surmise, know that they can also pray to St. Emeric of Hungary as a secondary patron of our country because a cartographer made a mistake some five centuries ago.

Saint Francis of Assisi

In 1982 the Catholic world celebrated the eight hundredth anniversary of the birth of St. Francis of Assisi. Indeed, in some ways, the whole world celebrated it to some extent because the Poor Man of Assisi appeals to millions outside the Church also.

A Franciscan friend of mine back in 1982 said, "Surely you will write something to celebrate that!" The difficulty in responding to that request is that one has to begin with a question: "Which St. Francis are you talking about?" In the minds of many, Francis is the saint who most closely imitated the life of Jesus, and like Jesus, he can ask the question, "Who do people say I am?"

The American Franciscans designated an official poster for the anniversary. Under a picture of the saint was a summation of his life: "Friend of God, Brother of Creation." Too many would think only of the second part of that statement (Francis is the Church's official patron of ecology) when they write — or make movies about — the saint who has become so popular in our own century. There is a romanticized picture of him in which he often comes across, as the Franciscan Father Leonard Foley put it, "as a slightly balmy romantic cavorting amid amber waves of grain with no visible means of support (a blond and lovely Clare, equally unemployed, hovering in the background)." Someone wrote a book about him a few years ago and called it "The Hippie Saint."[17]

The caricature of St. Francis as a sentimental lover of nature, or as a hippie dropout from society, omits the real sternness of his character and neglects his all-pervasive love of and identification with Christ's sufferings. It is this that makes sense of his life. It is true that John Paul II named him patron of ecology, but that is one of the lesser aspects of the profound spirituality of this saint whose statue, with flowers or animals, stands in the background gardens of so many homes. It is easy to dwell on the sunny side of Francis, but many prefer not to think of the penitent who scourged himself until the blood ran down and who was not ashamed to go weeping through the hills of Umbria for the Passion of Christ.

Most Christians are familiar with the life of St. Francis of Assisi. A rich merchant's son, he was steeped in romantic dreams of a career as a soldier; he was a leader of the carefree society of youths and also prisoner of war at Perugia for a year. When he returned to Assisi, he experienced a complete personal conversion to the practice of prayer and penance and absolute poverty. At the age of twenty-five he heard from the crucifix at the chapel of San Damiano the commission of Christ: "Francis, repair my house which, as you see, is falling into ruin." He came to understand "my house" as the Church. In 1209 A.D. he heard some verses of Matthew, (chapter 10), and was given to understand that the program of his life should be to follow the Way that Jesus taught in the Gospel. This mystical experience became the essence of his spirituality: to be united to Christ with God in prayer, to be an apostle of the Church, and to imitate literally the life of Christ.

Later in life, after thousands had flocked to join the three Franciscan orders he founded — for religious men, for women under the leadership of St. Clare of Assisi, and for a "third order" for laypeople — he wrote a document he called his Testament:

> *While I was in sin, the sight of lepers nauseated me beyond measure; and the Lord himself led me among them, and I had pity on them. And when I went away, what had seemed bitter to me was burned into sweetness of soul and body. After that I waited a while, and then I left the world.*[18]

One day Francis got off his horse and embraced a leper on a side road near Assisi. Gilbert K. Chesterton in his beautiful book, *St. Francis of Assisi,* wrote a sentence I remember vividly; he wrote that "the history of Europe changed when St. Francis embraced the leper on the road." One thing Chesterton meant, I think, was that the thousands of Franciscan men and women who flocked to the order Francis founded fanned out across Western Europe and preached to all the people, not only the rich, and put their preaching into practice by lives of poverty, the imitation of Christ, and a burning love for Christ and all men and women. The Franciscan spirit, like the Dominican spirit born about the same time, inaugurated a new era in the history of the Church.

Somewhere in the thick file I have accumulated about St. Francis I found this paragraph telling us the ways in which he can help us all to get the priorities straight in our lives:

He is a reminder to young and old of the value of penance in a world seeking to have its sins explained away rather than forgiven; of simplicity in a world of complexity; of meditation in a world of action; and of tranquillity in an age of anxiety, of inner peace... Francis reminds us, of course, that spiritual values can easily be lost if we are slaves to the material possessions which can so easily choke the spirit with their demands of attention.

The "Preface for Holy Men and Women" gives the reasons God has for sending saints like Francis into his world:

> You renew the Church in every age
> by raising up men and women outstanding in
>   holiness,
> living witness of your unceasing love.
> They inspire us by their heroic lives,
> and help us by their constant prayers
> to be the living sign of their saving power.

I know of few saints to whom those words may be applied with greater justification than St. Francis of Assisi.

The Song of St. Francis

The reverence which St. Francis of Assisi paid to all creation inspired him to compose his *Canticle of Creatures* just before he died.

Brother Francis died in 1226. Two years later, after insistent clamor by the people, Pope Gregory IX solemnly canonized him. In 1980, Pope John Paul II named him the Church's official patron of ecology and environmentalism, the science of the relationship between living creatures and their environment. And St. Francis would add — their relationship to God.

On that day of the canonization of Francis of Assisi in 1228, the pope asked Thomas of Celano, a Franciscan priest whom Francis himself had received into his order some twelve years before, to write what is known as the "first" life of St. Francis. Here is what Thomas writes about how Francis preached to the birds and loved all creatures, admonishing them to love and praise their Creator:

The most blessed Father Francis was making a trip through the Spoleto valley. He came to a certain place near Bevagna where a very great number of birds of various kinds had congregated, namely, doves, crows, and some others popularly called daws. When the most blessed servant of God, Francis, saw them, he left his companions in the road and ran eagerly toward the birds. Not a little surprised that the birds did not rise in flight, as they usually do, he was filled with great joy and humbly asked them to listen to the word of God:

"My brother birds, you should praise your Creator very much and always love him; he gave you feathers to clothe you, wings so that can fly, and whatever else was necessary for you. God made you noble among his creatures, and he gave you a home in the purity of the air; though you neither sow nor reap, he nevertheless protects you without any solicitude on your part."

And Francis, passing through their midst, touched their heads and bodies with his tunic. Finally he blessed them, and gave them permission to fly away to some other place. From that day on, he solicitously admonished all birds, all animals and reptiles, and even creatures that have no feeling, to praise and love their Creator....[19]

I have celebrated Mass in a small chapel on one of the hills surrounding Assisi, where, it is said, that Francis composed his poem-prayer called *The Canticle of the Creatures* — in 1225 when he was blind and already dying of intestinal cancer. It cannot help but gladden the hearts of gardeners everywhere as he sings in it: "Praise to thee, my Lord, for our sister, Mother Earth, who sustains and directs us, and brings forth varied fruits, and colored flowers and plants." A friend of mine plants a beautiful flower garden each spring and puts a statue of St. Francis amid the blooms he raises.

Early in this century, before he became a convert to Catholicism in 1911, Gilbert K. Chesterton wrote a small masterpiece recording his wonder and his admiration for the paradoxes in the life of the Poverello, the "Poor Man," as he called himself. He began it by saying that there were three ways to treat the life of St. Francis:

> *First, he may deal with this great and good man as a figure in secular history and a model of social virtues ... The writer might describe in a purely historical spirit of that great Franciscan inspiration ... He may try to do it, as others have done, almost without raising any religious questions at all. In short he may try to tell the story of the saint without God; which is like being told to write the life of Nansen and forbidden to mention the North Pole. Secondly, he may go to the opposite extreme and decide, as it were, to be defiantly devotional ... He can stamp the whole history with the Stigmata, record facts like fights against a dragon ... Such a study of St. Francis would be unintelligible to any one who does not share his religion, perhaps only partly intelligible to one who does not share his vocation ... The only difficulty about doing it this way is that it cannot be done. It would really require a saint to write the life of a saint ... Third, he might try to do it as I have done here ... He may say to the modern English reader: "Here is an historical character which is admittedly attractive to many of us already, by its gaiety, its romantic imagination, its spiritual courtesy, and camaraderie, but which also contains certain elements (evidently equally sincere and emphatic) which seem to you quite remote and repulsive.*[20]

Then Chesterton, in describing his own approach tries to leave both the Catholic reader, "who may not see any inconsistencies to reconcile," and those who may be materialists, who do not care about it, and the sympathetically skeptical with

> *... at least a glimmering of the way the poet who praised his lord the sun, often hid himself in a dark cavern, of why the saint who was so gentle with his Brother the Wolf was so harsh to his Brother the Ass (as he nicknamed his own body), of why the troubadour who said that love set his heart on fire separated himself from women, of why the singer who rejoiced in the strength and gaiety of the fire rolled himself in the snow, of why the very song which cries with all the passion of a pagan, "Praised be God for our Sister, Mother Earth, which brings forth varied fruits and grass and growing flowers." ends almost with the words, 'Praised be God for our Sister, the death of the body."*[21]

Those last sentences of Chesterton evoke the spirit of St. Francis' *Canticle of the Creatures.* In 1977, Father Nicholas van Doornik published a biography, *Francis of Assisi: A*

Prophet for our Time,[22] which gives the context in which
Francis composed his canticle. He knew that he was suffering
from an incurable disease and asked to be brought to the convent of San Damiano in Assisi to take leave of St. Clare, who,
inspired by him, had founded the Franciscan Sisters.

They put him in a hovel next to the convent, where he suffered a terrible depression, a crisis of loneliness from God,
torn by doubt whether he would ever win back the love of his
Master. The crisis lasted two months and then there came to
him the overwhelming certainty that he was in God's love and
would remain there. He was inspired to sing in the dialect of
Umbria, *"Altissimu, omnipotente, Bonsignore ...* Most High
and Omnipotent Lord..." And thus he began the *Canticle of
the Creatures*.

In the Middle Ages the four essential elements of the universe were thought to be earth, water, air, and fire. Someone
commented that, because Jesus walked the earth, earth is holy;
because he drank water, water is holy; because he breathed
the air, air is holy; because he said he came to cast fire on the
earth, fire is holy. The four elements were his brothers and sisters and Francis enters into them and praises God through
them.

I once visited the great basilica of St. Francis in Assisi, one
of several churches in Assisi recalling the life of its most mem-
orable citizen. In a bookstore I bought some postcards there
which reproduced, in several languages, the *Canticle of the
Creatures*. Here is the English translation of the Canticle I
found on one of them:

> Most high omnipotent good Lord, to Thee
> Praise, glory, honor, and every benediction.
> To Thee alone Most High do they belong,
> And no man is worthy to pronounce Thy Name.
> Praise be to Thee my Lord with all Thy creatures,
> Especially for Master Brother Sun
> Who illuminates the day for us,
> And Thee Most High he manifests.
> Praise be to Thee my Lord for Sister Moon and for the stars.
> In heaven thou hast formed them, shining, precious, fair.
> Praise be to Thee my Lord for Brother Wind

For air and clouds, clear sky and all thy weathers
Through which Thou sustainest all Thy creatures.
Praise be to Thee my Lord for Sister Water.
She is useful and humble, precious and pure.
Praise be to Thee my Lord for Brother Fire.
Through him our night Thou dost enlighten,
And he is fair and merry, boisterous and strong.
Praise be to Thee my Lord for our sister Mother Earth,
Who nourishes and sustains us all,
Bringing forth diverse fruits
And many-colored flowers and herbs.
Praise be to Thee my Lord
For those who pardon grant for love of Thee,
And bear infirmity and tribulation.
Blessed be those who live in peace,
For by Thee Most High they shall be crowned.
Praise be to Thee my Lord for our Sister Bodily Death,
From whom no living man can flee;
Woe to them who die in mortal sin
But blessed they who shall be found in Thy most holy Will
To them the second death can do no harm.
O bless and praise my Lord all creatures,
And thank and serve Him in deep humility.

The Six Saints of 1248

Five Touched the Life of St. Thomas Aquinas

At the World's Fair in Brussels in 1958 there was a primitive type of computer which could answer in five languages a question about the most important event in every period since the birth of Christ. Since I was teaching a course in medieval philosophy in those days, I asked it about the year 1248 A.D. The answer disappointed me: it was something about a king in southern Italy.

I had hoped for some item about the intellectual renaissance of the thirteenth century, or some mention of the saints who were helping shape a new world in 1248 A.D.

Six saints were living in 1248 A.D. whose careers intertwined. Each left his mark on history, especially intellectual history. The six saints living in 1248 were: St. Thomas Aquinas, a Dominican theologian; St. Albert the Great, Dominican scientist and theologian; St. Bonaventure of Bagnorea; St. Louis IX, king of France; St. Raymond of Penyafort, a Dominican canon lawyer; Blessed Pope Gregory X.

The young Thomas Aquinas was twenty-four years old in 1248 A.D., a student in Cologne, Germany. His teacher was Albert the Great, a fellow Dominican. Thomas was a quiet unassuming scholar, and some classmates even thought him a dunce, for they called him the "Dumb Ox." But Albert sensed his genius and made a famous prophecy: "You call him a dumb ox: But I tell you this dumb ox will bellow so loudly that his bellowings will fill the world."[23] The philosophy of Thomas Aquinas inspired whole centuries of Catholic teaching. Millions have looked to him for guidance and an explanation of their Faith. He has been the "Common Doctor" of the Church.

The teacher of Thomas, St. Albert, may be called the founder of the teachings of Thomas Aquinas; he also warned us not to neglect St. Bonaventure, who wrote so beautifully of the "Journey of the Mind to God."

In 1248, St. Raymond of Penyafort was born in 1180 in Catalonia in Spain; he was educated at Barcelona and later at Bologna in Italy, where he took doctorates in civil and canon law. In 1222 he joined the Dominican order. He is best known for his compilation of the Decretals of canon law, which was commissioned by Pope Gregory IX. It remained the standard collection for nearly 700 years. In 1238 he was elected Master General of the Dominicans. Two years later he resigned and returned to Spain from Rome. He encouraged St. Thomas Aquinas to write his *Summa Contra Gentiles* for the use of Catholic scholars who were debating the Moslems in Spain. He died in 1275.

Blessed Pope Gregory X (Pope Benedict XIV added his name to the Roman Martyrology) ruled the Church from 1271 to 1276. His name was Tedaldo Visconti, born c. 1210 at Piacenza,and was a layman on a Crusade in Palestine when he heard of his election. After being ordained priest, he was consecrated in 1272. Between 1248 and 1252 he studied in Paris and met St. Thomas Aquinas there. In 1274 he asked Aquinas to write a "Compendium of Theology" to be used at the Council of Lyons in 1274, but Thomas died on the way to the Council. (St. Bonaventure died at the Council.)

The six saints of 1248 — a Dominican scientist-theologian, a French king, an Italian bishop and cardinal, a pope, a canon lawyer, and a philosopher-theologian from an Italian castle called Aquino — were co-workers or friends whose lives touched; they give the lie to the ignorant assumption that the Middle Ages contributed nothing to the making of the modern mind.

Saint Thomas Aquinas

Toward the beginning of the twentieth century Dr. James Walsh wrote a book he called *The Thirteenth: Greatest of Centuries.*[24] Most historians, I think, would dispute that claim, but it is true that in the thirteenth century there lived a cluster of poets, philosophers, theologians, and scientists who made that century a peak era in the intellectual history of the Catholic Church.

The Franciscans, St. Bonaventure, Alexander of Hales, Roger Bacon, William of Ockham, and Duns Scotus introduced a variety of philosophical systems which still have influence today. Dante Alighieri wrote *The Divine Comedy*, which, someone said, put the *Summa Theologica* of St. Thomas Aquinas into musical poetry. St. Francis of Assisi, it is often said, lived a life closer to the Christian ideal than any other saint in history. The Franciscan spirit infuses the lives of hundreds of thousands of people in our own time.

Then there were the great Dominican scholars— St. Dominic himself, the founder; St. Albert the Great, in some ways the founder of modern science; St. Raymond of Penyafort, and, of course, St. Thomas Aquinas, the greatest philosopher and theologian in the Church of the thirteenth century.

Thomas Aquinas was born in 1225 of a royal family at Rocca Secca near Aquino in Italy. He was educated from the age of five to thirteen at the monastery of Monte Cassino founded by St. Benedict. He then went to the University of Naples for five years.

There he met some Dominican friars and decided to join the Order. His family objected strongly because the Dominicans were mendicants, but Thomas was attracted to the intellectual apostolate of the friars. He was traveling toward

Paris with one of them when some of the family captured
him and imprisoned him for a year at Rocca Secca, which
he spent reading.

The family then relented, and Thomas joined the Dominicans in 1244. From 1245 to 1252 he studied under St. Albert
the Great at Paris and Cologne.

Albert's philosophy included a dependence on the Greek
philosopher Aristotle, which inspired Thomas to an intellectual mission that would be based primarily on Aristotle rather
than the other great Greek philosopher, Plato, although he
used Plato also. His introduction of Aristotelian philosophy to
undergird his theology met with stiff resistance from the followers of St. Augustine, but in the end Aristotle helped Thomas as the foundation for his vast theological synthesis.

Thomas spent the rest of his life writing, preaching, lectur-
ing, and praying incessantly. A contemporary described
Thomas as "tall erect, large and well-built, with a complexion
like ripe wheat and whose head early grew bald." In his *The
Oxford Dictionary of Saints*, David Hugh Farmer writes about
Thomas, "His deep contemplative devotion at prayer, which
was sometimes ecstatic, was matched by an intense power of
concentration and an ability to dictate to four secretaries at
once."[25]

Thomas spent a period of preparation for his life work in
Paris from 1252 to 1260. He taught first at the Dominican
house of studies at Paris, where he began to outline a new approach to philosophy. His public lectures brought him
recognition as a master teacher. He studied for his degree in
theology at the University of Paris. When the secular priests
who taught there attacked the mendicant orders, Dominicans
and Franciscans, Thomas wrote a strong defense. At the early
age of thirty-one he became a Master of Arts, the equivalent of
a doctoral degree at that time.

By 1259 he had begun his *Summa Contra Gentiles,* a theological statement of the Christian faith in which he partly used
pure reason, not faith, to argue against Moslem, Jewish, and
pagan philosophers. Some Moslem philosophers, from
whom Thomas borrowed some of his ideas, were famous interpreters of Aristotle; Thomas proposed to argue against
them from Aristotle himself.

Thomas spent most of the next decade (from 1259-1268) at the papal court. He moved with it, teaching at Anagni, Orvieto, Rome, and Viterbo in Italy. He also organized Dominican houses of study at various places. For Pope Urban IV (1261-1264) he wrote the liturgy of Corpus Christi with its well-known hymns (though this is disputed by some scholars). Pope Urban asked Thomas to "baptize" Aristotle. At the pontifical courts he wrote commentaries on seven works of Aristotle which were a great improvement over those of his teacher, Albert the Great.

In 1265 Aquinas began to write his greatest work, the *Summa Theologica.* In *The Oxford Dictionary of Saints,* David Hugh Farmer summarized its five substantial volumes as

> ... *a comprehensive treatise of his mature thought on all the Christian mysteries; it proceeds through objections and authoritative replies in each article to a concise summary of his view on the matter under discussion, after which the various objections are answered. Although in his own day his work was seen as one among several* summae *(others were composed by Franciscans such as Bonaventure), and in the later Middle Ages many of his positions were attacked, the emergence of a series of gifted Dominican commentators and the explicit approval of Pius V and later of Leo XIII powerfully assisted its adoption as the standard theological text in many schools and universities.*[26]

In 1269 Thomas was recalled to Paris. There he was consulted by the King, St. Louis IX, and by the University of Paris. Three years later he was recalled to Naples as regent of studies for the Dominicans. On December 6, 1272, he experienced a revelation of God and said that in comparison to that experience he saw his works "as so much straw." Thomas wrote no more, leaving the *Summa Theologica* unfinished.

At the request of Blessed Pope Gregory X he set out for the Council of Lyons in 1274, but on his return journey he suffered a breakdown and died at the Cistercian monastery of Fossa Nuova on March 7, 1274. He was canonized in 1323; his body was buried eventually at the basilica of Saint-Sernin in Toulouse in 1368.

At the Council of Trent his *Summa Theologica* was placed next to the Holy Scriptures as an honor to an extraordinarily prolific and cherished theologian. In Thomas, however, his frequent contemplative prayer and holiness of life would be more important. He was truly worthy of the title given him — the "Angelic Doctor." He was also called the "Common Doctor," the universal Teacher of the Church.

Jacques Maritain, a French follower of Thomas Aquinas and one of his most eminent interpreters, writing about him in his volume, *The Angelic Doctor,* quotes popes from John XXII in the thirteenth century to the twentieth who commended Thomas Aquinas to everyone — seventy popes in all.[27] The late Pope Paul VI said that "his teaching constitutes a treasure of inestimable value ... for this reason ... in the works of Thomas can be found a compendium of the universal and fundamental truths, expressed in the clearest and most persuasive form."[28]

Some of the encomiums heaped on Aquinas are, shall we say, somewhat exaggerated. There is a story that when a few of Thomas' propositions were condemned by the archbishop of Paris after his death, St. Albert made the long journey from Cologne to Paris to defend the memory of Thomas, his student ... It is reported, too, that when the aged St. Albert returned to Cologne, he asked that all the works of Brother Thomas should be read to him in a set order, then concluded with a statement that no theologian today, I am sure, would dare to make: "The same Brother Thomas had in his writings put an end to everybody's labor right up to the end of the world, and that from now on all further work be without purpose."

For centuries in many seminaries and colleges Thomas Aquinas dominated the curriculum. That is not true today. There is a great pluralism in theological approaches today. The modern Catholic theologians will respect the great advance made by Thomas in the development of Catholic thought, but will not teach him as *the* theologian of the Church, as many used to treat him. When the Dominican Archbishop Dino Staffa intervened at the Vatican Council twenty-five years ago in a debate over the role of Aquinas in modern seminary studies, he demanded that Thomas should retain his exclusive place; Cardinal Paul-Emile Leger of Montreal rose to cry out against him, "We are not a church of one book," he said. As a matter of fact, the works of Aquinas were not as influential at the Council as those of Cardinal John Henry Newman or Teilhard de Chardin, S.J. Teilhard de Chardin was not quoted directly very much, but his evolutionary ideas on the relation of the Church to the modern world helped many of the Council fathers to understand why the Council document on *The Church in the Modern World* found its basic theme in words they overwhelming approved at the beginning of that Constitution:

> *At all times the Church carries the responsibility of reading the signs of the times and of interpreting them in the light of the Gospel ... Ours is a new age of history with critical and swift upheavals spreading rapidly to all corners of the earth ... The accelerated pace of history is such that one can scarcely keep abreast of it ...* And so the human race substitutes a dynamic and more evolutionary concept for a static one, *and the result is an immense series of new problems calling for a new endeavor of analysis and synthesis.*[29] *(emphasis added)*

The Thomistic vision has often been dismissed in recent years as too static, too little conscious of development, but Thomas himself, in modern research, is seen to be much more dynamic than those of his interpreters at the start of our century. They tried to mix his own thought with that of other authors of the past, only to freeze his more dynamic approach into the static system called "scholasticism," which was the standard fare of most American seminarians not too long ago. In his philosophy he emphasized the actual existence of things and not the abstract essences which some scholastics, influenced by Plato and Aristotle, made the chief objects of knowledge.

The famous Dominican friar lived only forty-nine years, but he traveled much, from his birthplace near Aquino in central Italy to Paris, Cologne, Rome, Avignon, Naples, and to a Cistercian monastery where he died.

Thomas Aquinas wrote two masterpieces which were summaries of his theology, using some key principles of Aristotle to impose order all through it. One is the *Summa Contra Gentiles*, which is still published in English, a summary of the Catholic Faith in which he used his philosophical insights to counter the arguments of the non-Christian Moslem philosophers (he called them "gentiles"). The other is his most studied and celebrated work, his *Summa Theologica*, which is also available in English today. He intended this "Summary of Theology" to be an introduction for beginning students, like "milk for the mouth of babes," he called it, but it is far more than that.

Thomas wrote much. His two Summas should not obscure his other biblical, theological, and philosophical writings. Thomas prayed much — and dedicated his enormous talents to the investigation of the sublime truth of God in the light of faith and human intellect. A fresco on the ceiling of a corridor in the Vatican Library at Rome pictures Thomas Aquinas holding two books. One was inscribed, *"In principio Deus creait ..."* ("In the beginning God created heaven and earth,") the other, *"Jesus Christus natus est"* ("Jesus Christ is the incarnate Son of God"). The first book is a symbol of his search through human reason, unaided by faith in revelation, for the relations between God, World, Man, and Woman. The second book symbolizes the revelation which God gave us through Jesus, our Savior and Redeemer. There is a picture of a dove, the Holy Spirit, hovering over the painting of Thomas. It is Thomas' integration of faith and reason which makes him one of the greatest teachers the Church has produced.

On a whole wall of the "Raphael Rooms" of the Vatican Art Gallery, Raphael painted a fresco called "The School of Athens" and opposite another of the famed frescoes, which Raphael Sanzio painted for Pope Julius II on the third floor of the Vatican Palace, is called "The Disputation on the Eucharist," which features St. Augustine and St. Thomas and other Catholic theologians standing beneath a large monstrance enshrining the Blessed Sacrament.

In his "School of Athens" painting, among early Greek philosophers, Raphael has Plato pointing his finger at the heavens to symbolize his idealistic philosophy in which he taught that the source of true and absolute knowledge is found in a world of Ideas which a person on earth comes to know by remembering them from a previous existence, for Plato believed in reincarnation. Beautiful objects on earth, for example, lead the philosopher to the knowledge of the nature of beauty after a process which Plato called Dialectic or Eros (love). Our knowledge of the things of earth is limited and uncertain; Plato likens it to opinion only.

In the fourth century St. Augustine of Hippo was deeply influenced by Plotinus, who taught a version of Platonic philosophy at the beginning of the second century A.D. Plotinus' version is called Neoplatonism. Augustine placed Plato's world of Ideas in the mind of God, not in a separate Platonic world, and he held that our knowledge of things below is effected by a special illumination from God through the Divine Ideas and through them the nature of things experienced in the world.

The Augustinian "Illumination Theory" powerfully affected the thinking of Christian theologians, philosophers, and spiritual writers and mystics for a thousand years. It led them, for the most part, to disparage the world about them and introduced a sharp distinction between body and soul, matter and spirit. Augustine had defined the human person as "a soul inhabiting a body," a somewhat similar idea to Plato's definition of the body as a "prisoner of the soul" waiting to be released.

That divorce between matter and spirit has haunted writers on spirituality and taught them to look down on "the World" as an obstacle to real spiritual progress — even to our own century.

The "contempt of the world," as it was often advocated, undervalued the worth of the world God created and found good. Teilhard de Chardin altered the view of the relationship by saying, "We make our way to heaven by doing the work of the world." Vatican Council II rejected such an overspiritualized vision of the human person. So did Pope John Paul II in his encyclical on "Human Work."

It was Thomas Aquinas in the thirteenth century who did the most to heal the breach which the "Augustinians," influenced by the great Doctor of Grace, had made between matter and spirit. Thomas defined a person as a composite of body and soul which formed one substance: for him the soul was the "form" which united it to the body, which gave the person life and rationality, the ability to sense objects outside in the world, to know their natures intellectually, and to make them the objects of their will and desires — to know, to love, to feel emotions — and to rise to a knowledge of the existence of God, to know something of God's nature and activities, to experience God's love and purpose for human beings and the world.

Such a philosophy was a daring one to propose in the thirteenth century when education in the West was dominated by Augustine, whose followers felt that when Aquinas adopted the Aristotelian philosophy which he had learned from his master, Albert, as the sub-structure of his philosophy, he had almost preached heresy. The transformation wrought by Thomas was indeed an innovative and dangerous thing to do, but it changed the way Christians thought for the last centuries.

In his fresco of the "School of Athens" Raphael painted Aristotle with his finger pointing to the ground, not to heaven, to symbolize the fact that he rejected the Idealism of his teacher, Plato, and firmly grounded his conviction that our knowledge of the natures of things comes not from an illumination from above but through our ability to abstract them through a process which begins with our sensations of the objects around us. Thomas refined this theory of knowledge considerably, but he holds firmly to the principle that all our rational knowledge begins in the senses. The knowledge process first begins with the experience of objects in this world, not in a Platonic World of Ideas above us. The philosophy of Aquinas is true Realism.

I have written an oversimplified version of the history of the influence of Plato and Aristotle on Augustine and Thomas. To give a complete picture, I would have to make more distinctions and indicate many nuances of their thought. I conclude by stating my conviction that Aristotle was a better guide than Plato, and that Thomas is a better guide than the "Augustinians" who still teach in the modern world.

Some of the most eminent theologians of the last fifty years have been, to use a phrase of James Joyce, the novelist, "steeled in the school of old Aquinas" — Karl Rahner, Yves Congar, Bernard Lonergan, Edward Schillebeeckx, and others. Amid the pluralistic approach to theology today, they developed their own variations on the tradition, but they were originally formed in the School of Aquinas.

St. Thomas lived seven hundred fifty years ago, and his

writings do not reflect the tremendous advances made in the study of history, Scripture, the sciences, contemporary philosophy and theology, sociology and psychology, and a host of other subjects. But Thomas is still a powerful voice in places. It is not yet time to say Yes to the waggish question someone asked a few decades ago, "Should Auld Aquinas be forgot, and never brought to mind?"

Aquinas Found an Island of Order

In his time, Reinhold Niebuhr was called "America's foremost Protestant theologian," even though he modestly referred to himself as a "Lutheran preacher." He once summed up the disease of disorder in modern society in words that had a touch of despair in them. "There is so little health," he said, "in the whole of our modern civilization that one cannot find the island of order from which to proceed against disorder."

Niebuhr wondered how we can find Cosmos in the Chaos of modern life. The ancient Greeks defined *chaos* as any condition or place of total disorder or confusion. When we write it with a capital C, it means, as one dictionary defines it, "the disordered state of unformed matter and infinite space supposed by some religious cosmological views to have existed prior to the ordered universe."

The Greek word, "ordered universe," is *Cosmos*, which the same dictionary defines as "the universe regarded as an orderly universe." The "religious cosmological view" comes from the first chapter of Genesis at the beginning of the Bible: "In the beginning, when God created the heavens and the earth, the earth was a formless void, while a mighty wind swept over the waters. (*The Jerusalem Bible* translates that last clause, "and God's spirit hovered over the water.") It was God the Creator who brought cosmos out of chaos — order out of disorder. That Judaeo-Christian belief is the foundation of any quest for order in the universe.

In the Book of Consolation of Israel by Isaiah, the Prophet speaks for God to the people (in the *Jerusalem Bible* translation):

> *Yes, thus says Yahweh,*
> *Creator of the heavens,*
> *who is God,*

> *who formed the earth and made it,*
> *who set it firm,*
> *created no chaos,*
> *but a place to be lived in.*

Will Durant, who with his wife wrote nine books on the history of civilization says that "order is civilization's first law, and the mother of freedom, as chaos is civilization's last travail, and the mother of dictatorship." In a famous paragraph in *The City of God,* Saint Augustine defined peace as "the tranquillity of order."

St. Thomas Aquinas, that other giant of Catholic thought, wrote that "it is the function of wise men and women to find order and to put order into the universe." I submit that Dr. Niesbuhr can find his island of order in the philosophy of Thomas Aquinas.

In the fourth century before Christ, the Greek philosopher Aristotle, who was one of the most influential teachers of Aquinas, began his philosophy with the statement that by nature everyone desires to know — to understand. The history of Western philosophy is one long search for an understanding of the One in the Many, unity in diversity, order in disorder. The human intellect can study the created world around it and find its own place in everything. Once a person has come to the knowledge that will put everything one knows into its proper place and perspective, that person has achieved wisdom.

Seven hundred years ago, Thomas Aquinas gave the best explanation, I think, of the order God put into the universe. He would tell Reinhold Niebuhr that he could find his island of order in that which was most human in him, his own human mind and will. It was Thomas' whole life task to explain the order in the universe outside us, which makes it possible for a scientist to predict what will happen in an eclipse of the sun or a chain reaction in a bomb or when to send space probes to photograph Halley's comet when it is close to the sun. The scientist calls it "uniformity of nature." Aquinas calls it the order God put into his Cosmos: "There is a twofold order in things. One is the order which our reason does not bring about, but which it discovers. The other is the order which our reasoning power will bring about."

The first kind of order, that which we find and do not make, is the subject matter of Thomistic metaphysics (we can also call it "natural theology"), which is the highest achievement of his philosophy. In his famous answer in the *Summa Theologica* to the question "Does God exist?", he writes of the five "ways" that can lead us to God. He concludes, inevitably, that order was put into the Cosmos by God, the First Cause, the Final End, the Supreme Goodness and Intelligence, the Prime mover, and the Supreme Purpose of all things.

About the second kind of order, that which we do not find but make ourselves, Thomas would say that it is order which our reason imposes upon our minds; this is the art and science of logic, which gives us the rule for correct and true thinking. It may be the order which reason puts into the actions which flow from the human will; this is the science of morality or ethics, which tells us what we do to achieve the final destiny that God has willed for us. Finally, reason can impose order on objects outside a person — external things like words or blocks of marble or blobs of paint which artists use when they give us their visions of the beautiful, which we call art.

It is easy to understand, then, why Aquinas could define the wise person as one whose task it is to bring about order. He himself was among the wisest of men. His books give the explanation of and purpose behind our Cosmos for which so many men and women are groping now in the terrors of the last quarter of the twentieth century.

St. Thomas found an island of order and can help everyone discover it. He found it in the wisdom of his own mind and in his faith in Christ and his Church. But Dr. Niebuhr might well ask, "If the human mind is our island of order, why are we lost in chaos and disorder?" The answer to that question can come from Etienne Gilson, one of the best interpreters of Aquinas in our century, when he wrote, "There is an ethical problem at the root of our philosophical difficulties; for men are most eager to find the truth but most reluctant to accept it ... finding the truth is not hard; what is hard is not to run away from the truth once we have found it."

Blessed Fra Angelico

On April 18, 1984, Pope John Paul II joined the Dominican friars at the basilica of Santa Maria sopra Minerva in Rome in the first celebration of the new liturgical feast of Blessed Fra Angelico of the Dominican order.

On October 5, 1983, the Pope had signed the *motu proprio* permitting the liturgical cult for the Dominicans in honor of their brother, Fra Angelico, who may now be officially called Blessed. At the end of his apostolic letter John Paul commented: "Certainly, Fra Giovanni, an exceptional man for spirituality and art, has always attracted our sympathy. We believe, then, that the hour has come to place him in a special place in the Church of God, to which he does not cease even today to speak with his heavenly art."[30]

Fra Angelico, born Guido di Pietro, was born in Viccio in Mugello (Florence), Italy, in 1400 A.D. He was baptized Guido; his Dominican name was Giovanni, but he is always "Fra Angelico" to those who admire him because of the deep spirituality of his life, which he transferred to his paintings.

About 1420 A.D., after working as a painter and a miniaturist in Florence, he entered the Dominican order in the new convent of San Domenico in Fiesole (Florence), taking the name Giovanni. His Prior and student master was Saint Antoninus of Florence, who is famous in the history of canon law and moral theology. With his brother, Benedetto, he was ordained a priest and they lived in the same convent. As a Dominican friar, he continued his career as a painter until his death on February 18, 1455 A.D.

Art historians divide Fra Angelico's career into two phases. In the first (from 1418 to the mid-1430's), he represents an artist in transition from a Gothic style to the style of the Renaissance. His early work betrays a close relationship to what is called International Gothic, i.e., the unified style and subject matter found primarily in painting throughout Western Europe in the late Gothic period, which began at the end of the fourteenth century. Fra Angelico used its techniques of gold backgrounds, elegant delicate figures, and its rhythmically swinging drapery. It shows the influence of Neoplatonic mysticism.

The *New Catholic Encyclopedia* explains:

> *The soul, by contemplation and intense concentration sloughs off all material experience in its attempt to return to paradise, the great source of Light from which it originally emanated; hence the striated gold backgrounds, sunbursts, and the childlike, naive figures that fill Angelico's paintings at that time. "Except ye ... become as little children ye shall not enter the Kingdom of Heaven."*[31]

Great examples from his more mature period are the "Deposition from the Cross" and the marvelous frescoes in the convent of San Marco in Florence; these figures in flowery Tuscan meadows evince a new *positive* mysticism. For a positive mystic, salvation and paradise are attained by contemplating and imitating the life of Christ on this earth according to the Lord's words; "I am the Way..." One critic says that his most famous work is a series of thirty-five paintings for the doors of a silver chest in the church of St. Annunziata in Florence.

Angelico was much in demand during his last ten years. He began a "Last Judgment" fresco in the cathedral of Orvieto, but almost immediately Pope Nicholas V called him to Rome to decorate the "Nicholas Chapel" in the Vatican. There he showed his mastery of Renaissance techniques in form and perspective as he painted scenes from the lives of St. Stephen and St. Lawrence. Pope Nicholas wanted to make him bishop of Florence, but he asked to be excused and his brother Dominican, St. Antoninus, was named instead.

In 1450 A.D. Fra Angelico was elected prior of the convent of San Domenico in Fiesole near Florence, succeeding his brother, Benedetto, who had died. He was prior for three years and then finished work he already had under commission.

From 1453 until his death in 1455 Fra Angelico lived in the

Dominican convent next to Santa Maria sopra Minerva in Rome, a basilica built in 1250 among the ruins of the Temple of the Roman goddess Minerva. The body of Saint Catherine is buried there. So, too, is Fra Angelico, an unusual honor because Dominicans are not usually buried in churches. During the seven centuries of its existence, the Minerva has become a veritable museum of art treasures. One of them is the tomb of Angelico in a chapel near the back entrance.

In 1550, Giorgio Vasari, an uninspired painter but an inspired art historian, published his *Lives of the Most Eminent Painters, Sculptors, and Architects.* He begins his chapter on the friar: "Fra Giovanni Angelico da Fiesole, who was known in the world as Guido, was no less excellent as painter and illuminator than he was upright as churchman." Vasari intimates that the best clue to his paintings is to be found in his character, which Vasari described with simple eloquence:

> *Fra Giovanni was a man of simple and blameless life ... He was such a friend to the poor that I think his soul must now be in heaven ... He might have been placed in a position of power and authority, but he declined on the ground that it was easier to obey than to command; that the temptation was less ... He painted incessantly, but would never represent anything but a sacred subject ... Some go so far as to say that Fra Giovanni never touched a brush without first humbling himself in prayer. He never painted the crucified savior without having his cheeks bathed in tears.*[32]

Most of those who analyze the painting of the Dominican master include the sentiment expressed by Michelangelo in one of his sonnets: "Any beautiful thing must raise the pure and just desire of man to God, the fount of all."

In the seventh chapter of the *Constitution on the Sacred Liturgy* the bishops at Vatican II wrote about sacred art:

> *The fine arts are rightly classified among the noblest activities of a person's genius; this is especially true of religious art and its highest manifestation, sacred art. Of their nature the arts are directed toward expressing in some way the infinite beauty of God in works made by human hands. Their dedication to the increase of God's praise and of his glory is more complete, the more exclusively they are devoted to turning minds devoutly to God.*[33]

Fra Angelico could have been in the minds of the authors who wrote that paragraph. He himself summed up the powerful impact of his painting with a sentence which Pope John Paul II quoted when he raised him to the honors of the altar: "He whose work is connected with Christ must ever live with Christ."

Chapter 8
A Woman for Our Time

Venerable Mary Katharine Drexel

(1858-1955)

Foundress of the Sisters of the Blessed Sacrament for Indians and Colored People

In its issue of November, 1956, a Paulist magazine called *Information* reprinted an article by the late Archbishop Fulton J. Sheen with the title, "America Needs a Saint." This was its first paragraph: "America needs a saint, an American saint. After three hundred years of Catholic life, we can point to no saint who was born in this great land, who was educated in our schools and showed in crisis how an American Catholic can relive the life of Christ crucified. We have the greatest Catholic school system in the world, the widest forms of charity work, the most compact army of teachers and religious, but the niches of our churches are empty."

Archbishop Sheen would write a bit differently today than he did in the pre-Vatican years. For one thing, there are not too many niches for saints in many of our newly designed churches. And seven years after Sheen wrote, Pope Paul VI beatified John Neumann, the fourth bishop of Philadelphia, in 1963 and said in his homily: "This beatification is an excellent document which dispells the erroneous belief that American Catholicism is not oriented to a singular and sublime expression of sanctity but rather toward the ordinary Christian life, nor dissimilar from the environment of modern life. Behold," the Pope said, "America, too, has its saints."[1]

Archbishop Sheen lived to know that the first saint born in America was canonized by Pope Paul VI during the Holy Year of 1975. She was St. Elizabeth Seton, foundress of the first American religious women's order, the Sisters of Charity.

Now another American-born religious foundress is closer to canonization. In January, 1987, eight cardinals, members of the Vatican Congregation of the Saints, agreed that Mother

Katharine Drexel should be called "Venerable," which is the first official step toward eventual canonization. The London Catholic, *The Tablet,* noted it in its January 31, 1987, issue. The notice summarized her life: "Mother Drexel, born in 1858, was the daughter of a rich American family. She gave up a considerable fortune to enter a contemplative religious order, and in 1891 founded the Sisters of the Blessed Sacrament for Indians and Colored People. Cardinal Krol of Philadelphia said, '... although her apostolate to the blacks and Indians was unpopular, misunderstood, and resented, she never swerved from her dedication.' There are now 375 members of her order working in 16 dioceses."

Katharine Drexel retired from her heroic service to blacks and Native Americans in 1937 because of illness and died in 1955 at the age of 97. She will now be known as Venerable Katharine Drexel, and further advancement of her cause — beatification and canonization — will await the checking of miracles judged to have been performed through her intercession.

One of the reasons given by the Congregation of Saints was Mother Katharine's "heroic service" to blacks and Indians. Her background was such that this would seem an unlikely development. She was born on November 26, 1858, the daughter of a wealthy Philadelphia banker Francis Drexel, and Hannah Jane Langstroth, who died when Katharine was an infant. Two years later her father married Emma Bouvier, who proved to be a devoted mother to Katharine and her sister Elizabeth. She was educated privately at home and traveled extensively in Europe and the United States and was prominent in the social life of Philadelphia. Her stepmother died in 1883 and her father in 1855. From both she inherited a considerable fortune, which she decided to donate to religious works.

From November 9 to December 7, 1884, seventy-two bishops of the United States met at Baltimore for the Third Plenary Council of Baltimore, at which Archbishop James Gibbson of that city presided. By that year the Church in the United States was increasing by about two million members every decade, largely as a result of immigration. One of the decisions of the Council was to commission a committee to care for the missions among the black and Indian citizens of the United

States. That committee appealed to the Drexel sisters for help. Katharine resolved to use her considerable inheritance for the spread of the Church among the blacks and Indians.

During a visit to Rome she met Pope Leo XIII and asked him to recommend a religious order to which she could give her fortune with the condition that it be used only for the Indian and the Negro. She decided her vocation for the rest of her life when the Pope challenged her to be their missionary. She wholeheartedly gave herself and her money to the cause. Under the direction of Bishop James O'Connor of Omaha and later under Archbishop James Ryan of Philadelphia, she began a two-year novitiate with the Sisters of Mercy in Pittsburgh. She was 31 years old at the time.

The next year Pope Leo XIII sent his apostolic blessing to Sister Mary Katharine Drexel and her companions, who were to be the nucleus of a new congregation of religious women. The foundress was Mother Katharine, who established the order temporarily in the old Drexel summer mansion at Torresdale, near Philadelphia, on February 12, 1891. They took the name, "Sisters of the Blessed Sacrament for Indians and Colored People." The foundress stated the special purpose of her Sisters as "the total gift of self for the souls of Indian and colored people."

The article on the Blessed Sacrament Sisters in the *New Catholic Encyclopedia* traces the development of the congregation as it was given various degrees of approval from Rome. In 1961 the Congregation for Religious approved a general revision of the constitutions. In 1963 the Sisters' 545 members served Indians and blacks in colleges, secondary and elementary schools, clinics, catechetical centers, retreat houses, centers of social service, and one university (Xavier, New Orleans) in ten archdioceses and nineteen dioceses in the United States.[2]

In 1935 Mother Katharine Drexel suffered a heart attack, but she continued her grueling schedule, including long day train trips to her forty-nine foundations in the Northeast, Middle West, and Deep South. For her golden jubilee in 1941 Pope Pius XII sent her a letter which described her life work as a "glorious page in the history of the Church."

During the last years of her long life she was an invalid; she spent those last years in a wheelchair and in prayer. She and her family had given more than twelve million dollars to the apostolate of the Sisters of the Blessed Sacrament for the Indians and Colored People.

The Official Catholic Directory for 1986 reports that there are 372 Professed Sisters and 5 Novices in the Blessed Sacrament. They exercise their special ministry to Indians and blacks at Xavier University in New Orleans, three Day High Schools, sixteen Day Elementary Schools, one Day Catechetical School, eight Houses for Catechetical, eight Adult Education and Social Service Centers, one Communication Center, one House of Prayer, and one Spiritual Center. The daughters of the Venerable Katharine Drexel serve in eight archdioceses and eight dioceses in the United States. They and the rest of the American Catholic Church look forward eagerly to the eventual canonization of another American-born saint.

Notes

Preface

[1] Vatican II, *Dogmatic Constitution on the Church,* #49. Austin Flannery, O.P., General Editor, *Vatican Council II: The Conciliar and Post Conciliar Documents.* (Northport, N.Y.: Costello Publ. Co., 1975) pp. 409-10.

Introduction

[1] Joseph N. Tylenda, S.J., *Jesuit Saints and Martyrs.* (Chicago: Loyola University Press, 1984) p. 241.

[2] Romano Guardini, *The Saints in Daily Christian Life.* (New York: Dimension Books, 1966) p. 31.

[3] *Ibid.,* p. 29.

[4] Ronald Knox, *University Sermons of Ronald Knox.* Ed. Philip Caraman, S.J. (Montreal: Palm Publishers, 1963) pp. 70-1.

[5] *The Oxford Dictionary of the Christian Church.* F.L. Cross and E.A. Livingstone (Ed.) (New York: Oxford University Press, 1983). The article "Saints, Devotion to," is on pp. 1227-8.

[6] Thomas Aquinas, *Summa Theologiae,* II-II, q.121, art. 2. (English translation by T.C. O'Brien in Vol. 41, 287 of the *Summa: Virtues of Justice in the Human Community* Blackfriars, 1972). Printed in England by Eyre and Spottiswoode Ltd.

[7] Donald Attwater, Ed., *The Catholic Dictionary.* (New York: Macmillan, 1949). The article "Communion of Saints, The" is on p. 110.

[8] Albino Luciano, *Illustrissimi-Letters from Pope John Paul I* (Boston: Little Brown, 1978) pp. 151-2.

[9] *The Roman Martyrology,* translated by Raphael Collins, O.P. (Westminster, Md.: The Newman Bookshop, 1946) pp. 253-4.

[10] *Theological Dictionary*, ed. by Karl Rahner, S.J. and

Herbert Vorgrimler, S.J., Translated by Richard Strachan (New York: Herder and Herder, 1965) p. 391.

11 "Decree of the Sacred Congregation for Divine Worship," in *Rite of Funerals.* (New York: Catholic Book Publ. Co., 1971) pp. 7-8.

12 *Code of Canon Law Latin-English Edition.* Translation published by The Canon Law Society of America (Washington: 1983).

13 Flannery, *Documents,* p. 41

14 James I. Tucek, "Saints are Patrons of Every Lawful Labor," *National Catholic Register* (March 3, 1957) p. 1.

15 Leonard J. Fick, "The 'Who's Who of Heaven," *The Josephinum Review,* (published by the Pontifical College Josephinum, Worthington, Ohio: November 4, 1953) p. 1.

16 Quoted from the *National Catholic Register.*

17 Mary O'Connell, "Why Catholics Keep Bugging the Saints," *U.S. Catholic* (May, 1986) pp. 6-14.

18 Robert Burns, "If you got 'em, flaunt 'em," *U.S. Catholic,* (Jan. 84), Inside front cover.

19 Lawrence S. Cunningham, *The Catholic Heritage* (New York: Crossroad, 1983). See Chapter 11 on "Saints," pp. 206-25.

20 Thomas Aquinas, *Summa Theologiae,* III, q.25, art. 6. Edited and translated by Colman E. O'Neill, O.P., in Vol. 50, 203 of the *Summa, The One Mediator* (London: Blackfriars/Eyre and Spottiswoode, 1965) p. 103.

21 Cyril Martindale, *The Vocation of Aloysius Gonzaga,* cited in Calvert Alexander, S.J., *Catholic Literary Revival* (Milwaukee: Bruce Publ. Co., 1935) p. 328.

22 D. H. Farmer, review of David Sox, *Relics and Shrines, The Tablet* (London: March 29, 1986) p. 345.

Chapter 1
Mother of God — Mother of the Faithful

1 Pope John Paul II, *Pilgrim of Peace: The Homilies and Addresses of Pope John Paul II on the occasion of his visit to the United States,* (Washington: Publications Office USCC, 1979) p. 155.

2 Robert McAfee Brown, "American Catholicism Now: a Protestant View" in Michael Glazier (Ed.). *Where We Are: American Catholics in the 1980's* (Wilmington: Michael Glazier, 1985) pp. 22-3.

[3] Xavier Rynne, *Vatican Council II* (New York, Farrar, Straus and Giroux, 1968) pp. 75-6.

[4] Pope Leo XIII, *Quamquam Pluries* in Claudia Carlen, I.H.M., *The Papal Encyclicals,* II (McGrath Publishing Co. 1981) p. 208.

[5] Vatican II, *Pastoral Constitution on the Church in The Modern World,* #34. Flannery, *Documents,* pp. 933-34.

[6] Frances Parkinson Keyes, *St. Anne: Grandmother of Our Savior* (London: Allen Wingate, 1956) p. 18.

[7] *Ibid.,* p. 19

[8] J. P. Asselin "Anne and Joachim" *New Catholic Encyclopedia* (New York, 1967) I, 559-60.

[9] Vatican II, *Dogmatic Constitution on the Church,* Ch. 8, pp. 52-69. Flannery, *Documents,* pp. 413-23.

[10] Pope Paul VI, *Marialis Cultus:* On Devotion to the Blessed Virgin Mary, Feb. 2, 1974, printed in *Osservatore Romano* (April 4, 1974).

[11] National Conference of Catholic Bishops, *Behold Your Mother: Woman of Faith,* a Pastoral Letter on the Blessed Virgin Mary. Nov. 21, 1973 (Washington: Publications Office NCCB, 1973).

[12] John Henry Newman, *Fifteen Sermons Preached Before the University of Oxford* (London: Longmans, Green and Co., 1892).

[13] *Dogmatic Constitution on the Church,* #54 Flannery, *Documents,* p. 414.

[14] H.H. Manteau-Bonamy, "Vatican II and Mary," *Dictionary of Mary* (New York: Catholic Book Publishing Co., 1985) pp. 361-68.

[15] Flannery, *Documents,* p. 418.

[16] *Ibid.,* p. 423.

[17] This homily of St. Cyril of Alexandria at the Council of Ephesus is printed as Reading II in the *Liturgy of the Hours* on the feast of the Dedication of St. Mary Major. August 5 (New York: Catholic Book Publishing Co., 1975) pp. 1271-2.

[18] Flannery, *Documents,* p. 414.

[19] John Jay Hughes, Homily for feast of the Assumption, *The Priest* (July-August, 1982) p. 23.

[20] See, for example, the commentary by Agnes Cunningham, S.S.C.M., on Vatican II's "Decree on Ecumenism," in Timothy E. O'Connell (Ed), *Vatican II and Its Documents*

(Wilmington, DE: Michael Glazier, 1986) pp. 62-78; See also Robert McAfee Brown, note 2, above.

21 The hymn, by an anonymous poet and altered by the Dominican Sisters of Summit in 1972, can be found in *The Liturgy of the Hours* (New York: Catholic Book Publishing Co., 1975), II, 1627.

22 Pope Pius XII had just published an encyclical on the Queenship of Mary, *Ad Caeli Reginam,* and instituted the feast (*The Pope Speaks* v. 1 no. 4, 1954), 325 ff.

23 Hilaire Belloc, *Sonnets and Verse* (New York: Sheed and Ward, 1944) p. 51.

24 Bernard of Clairvaux, The text of the homily is found in Cistercian Publications, series 28, of *Magnificat Homilies in Praise of the Blessed Virgin Mary* (Kalamazoo, MI, 1979) pp. 15-31. See # 17.

25 Gilbert Keith Chesterton, *The Collected Poems of G.K. Chesterton* (New York: Dodd, Mead and Co., 1949). The poem "Lepanto" is on pp. 106-11.

26 For this treatment of the *Sub Tuum Praesidium,* I am much indebted to an unpublished manuscript by Father Arthur Lenti, SDB, which I have used with his permission. Father Lenti wrote it in 1967.

27 Herbert Thurston, S.J., "Hail Mary," *The Catholic Encyclopedia,* Vol. 7 (New York: Appleton, 1910) p. 111.

28 *Ibid.,* p. 101.

29 Thomas Aquinas, *The Three Greatest Prayers: Commentaries on the Our Father, the Hail Mary and the Apostles' Creed,* translated by Laurence Shapcote, O.P. (Westminster, MD: The Newman Press, 1956). This commentary is limited to the first section of the prayer; the second section with its "pray for us sinners" was added in a later century. See the English translation, pp. 30-2.

30 A.A. DeMarco, "Angelus," in *The New Catholic Encyclopedia* Vol. I (New York: McGraw-Hill Book Co., 1966.) p. 521.

31 Vatican II, *Constitution on the Liturgy, #12* (Flannery, Documents, p. 7).

32 *Ibid.,* p.422.

33 Avery Dulles, S.J., in his introduction to Vatican II's document on the Church. Walter Abbot, *The Documents of Vatican II* (New York: 1966) pp. 9-13.

34 Frederick M. Jelly, O.P., "Prayer Beads in World Religions: The Rosary," *Worldmission* (Spring, 1980) pp. 20-25.

35 See note above.

36 Gilbert Keith Chesterton, "Lepanto." See note 25 above.

37 Pope Leo XIII, *Rerum Novarum: On the Rights and Duties of Capital and Labor*. One text is found in Etienne Gilson, *The Church Speaks to the Modern World: The Social Teachings of Leo XIII* (Garden City, NY: Doubleday & Co., 1954). See the last few pages, 236-39, for the importance of the spiritual solution to the Social Question.

38 Pope Leo XIII, *The Rosary and the Social Question* in Joseph Husslein, S.J., "Social Wellsprings — Fourteen Epochal Documents of Pope Leo XIII" (Milwaukee: Bruce, 1940) pp. 208-14.

39 Pope Pius XII, "The Lourdes Pilgrimage" #57 *The Pope Speaks* v.4 (Autumn, 1957), 107-17.

40 Pope John Paul II, Broadcast, May 17, 1981. *Origins* (May 28, 1981) vol. 11, No. 2, 17.

41 Marguerite Hamilton, *Red Shoes for Nancy* (Garden City NY: Catholic Family Book Club, 1956)

42 Patricia Lefevere. "Templeton Prize Awarded to Priest-Scientist," *National Catholic Reporter* (May 8, 1987) pp. 6-7.

43 Emile Zola, *Lourdes* (London: Chatto and Windus, 1894).

44 Franz Werfel, *The Song of Bernadette* (New York: The Viking Press, 1942) p. 6.

45 Henry Adams, *Mont-Saint-Michel and Chartres* (Boston and New York: Houghton Mifflin Co., 1905) p. 92.

46 *Encyclopedia of World Art* (New York: McGraw-Hill Book Co., 1959). See the term *Chartres* in the Index (Vol. 17, 109).

47 Whitney Stoddard, *Monastery and Cathedral in France* (Middletown, CT: Wesleyan Univ. Press, 1966) p. 173.

48 *Ibid.,* p. 174.

49 Alfred McBride, *The Story of the Church* (Cincinnati: St. Anthony Messenger Press, 1983) p. 58.

50 Pope John Paul II, *Pilgrim of Peace,* p. 161 (Cf. note 1 above).

51 Gilbert Keith Chesterton, *Christendom in Dublin* (London: Sheed and Ward, 1933) p. 1.

52 Daniel Sargent, *Our Land and Our Lady* (Notre Dame: University of Notre Dame Press, 1931) p. 1.

53 Anna Wirtz Domas, *Mary USA* (Huntington, IN: Our Sunday Visitor Press, 1978) p. 5.

54 Samuel Eliot Morrison, *The European Discovery of Ameri-*

ca: *The Southern Voyages A.D. 1492-1616* (New York, Oxford Univ. Press, 1974) (Cited by Domas, p. 5).

55 Willa Cather, *Death Comes for the Archbishop* (New York: Vantage Books, 1979).

56 Paul Horgan, *Lamy of Santa Fe: His Life and Times* (New York: Farrar Straus and Giroux, 1975) pp. 415-6.

57 Chesterton's "Ballad of the White Horse" may be found in *The Collected Poems of G. K. Chesterton* (New York: Dodd, Mead and Co., 1911) pp. 203-99.

58 See also L. Garnet Thomas, "Mysticism in *The Ballad of the White Horse," The Chesterton Review,* (Vol. VI, No. 2), 205-11.

Chapter Two
Eight Role Models for Priests

1 *Origins* (July 14, 1984) p. 124.

2 St. Francis De Sales, *Introduction to the Devout Life,* translated and edited by John K. Ryan (New York: Harpers 1949) p. 6.

3 Butler's *Lives of the Saints,* Complete Edition, Revised and Supplemented by Herbert Thurston, S. J. and Donald Attwater. Reprinted in four volumes (Westminster, MD: Christian Classics, Inc., 1980) III, 141.

4 The summary was printed in a brochure published by the national headquarters of the St. Vincent de Paul Society to commemorate the 150th anniversary of the founding of the Society by Frederic Ozanam in 1983.

5 "John Bosco" in Donald Attwater, *A Dictionary of Saints* (Baltimore, MD: Penguin Books Inc., 1965) p. 197.

6 The letter of Don Bosco is quoted in the second reading for his feast day, January 31, in *The Liturgy of the Hours* (New York: Catholic Book Publ. Co., 1975) II, 1338.

7 *The Liturgy of the Hours* IV, 1269.

8 The three talks John Paul II gave at Ars in a retreat for priests, deacons, and seminarians may be found in *L'Osservatore Romano* (English weekly edition of Nov. 10, 1986) p. 5ff. John Paul's 1986 letter to priests is in *Origins* (April 3, 1986).

9 *The Tablet,* London (March 22, 1986) p. 324.

10 Attwater, p. 285.

11 *Ibid.,* pp. 83-4.

12 John J. Delaney, *Pocket Dictionary of Saints* (Garden City, NY: Image Books, Doubleday & Co., 1983) p. 87.

13 Phyllis McGinley, *Saint-Watching* (Garden City, NY: Image Books, Doubleday & Co., 1974) p. 118.

Chapter Three
Missionary Martyrs

1 Vatican II, "Constitution on the Sacred Liturgy," #102, ed. by Walter M. Abbott, S.J., *The Documents of Vatican II,* p. 168.

2 *Ibid.,* #103-4.

3 Pope Paul VI, "Apostolic Letter," Feb. 14, 1969, in *Roman Calendar: Text and Commentary* (Washington: Publications Office, USCC, 1975) p. 2.

4 *Saint Andrew Bible Missal* (New York: DDB Publishers, Inc., 1962). See the Index to the Proper of the Saints pp. 1520-6.

5 Farmer, *The Oxford Dictionary of Saints,* p. xix.

6 *Roman Calendar,* p. 2.

7 *Ibid.,* p. 36.

8 Pope Paul VI, *The Liturgy of the Hours.* Second Reading for the feast of Charles Lwanga and Companions, June 3, vol 3, pp. 1453-4.

9 John Mbiti, "The Future of Christianity in Africa," *Cross Currents* vol. 28, (Winter, 1978-9), 387-394, David B. Barrett, Editor, *World Christian Encyclopedia* (New York: Oxford University Press, 1982).

10 Pope Pius XII, *The Gift of Faith,* Claudia Carlen, I.H.M., *The Papal Encyclicals from 1939-1958* (Wilmington, NC: McGrath 1981) 321-33, p. 151.

11 *The Catholic Mind* (February, 1955) p. 102.

12 The Liturgy of the Hours, Second Reading for feast of St. Peter Chanel, April 28, Vol 2, 1791-2.

13 The Liturgy of the Hours, Second Reading for feast of St. Paul Miki and Companions of February 6, Vol. 3, 1368.

14 Nicholas Maestrini, P.I.M.E., *Mazzucconi of Woodlark* (Hong Kong: Catholic Truth Society, 1983) p. 205.

Chapter Four
Missionaries to the Americas

1 *Pastoral Letters of the United States Catholic Bishops, vol 4, 1975-1983* (Washington: USCC-NCCB, 1984) p. 344.

2 Farmer, *Oxford Dictionary of Saints,* p. 384.

3 C.C. Martindale, S.J., *What are Saints? Fifteen Studies in Sanctity,* revised edition (Wilmington, DE: Michael Glazier, 1982) pp. 95-101.

4 Arnold Lunn, *Saint in the Slave Trade* (New York: Sheed and Ward, 1935).

5 *The Tablet* (London) (May, 1985) , p. 545.

6 Robert J. Curran, *Homiletic and Pastoral Review* (June 1980) p. 25.

7 For Stevenson's classic letter in rebuttal to Rev. C. M. Hyde, see chapter XVIII of John Farrow, *Damien the Leper* (New York: Sheed and Ward, 1937) pp. 203-20.

8 Sr. Mary Laurence Hanley, O.S.F. and O.A. Bushnell, *A Song of Pilgrimage and Exile: The Life and Spirit of Mother Marianne of Molokai* (Chicago: Franciscan Herald Press, 1980) Dedication Page.

9 Amleto Giovanni Cicognani, *Sanctity in America* (Paterson, N.J.: St. Anthony Guild Press, 1941) p. 54.

10 John J. Delaney, *Dictionary of American Catholic Biography* (Garden City, NY: 1984) p. 31.

11 James Plough, "The Forgotten Martyr: The Story of a Jesuit Priest and a Sioux Tomahawk," *The Josephinum Review* (April 25, 1951) p. 6.

12 Emmett A. Shanahan, *Minnesota's Forgotten Martyr* (Crookston, MN: 1949) p. 21.

13 Plough, *ibid.*

14 "De Smet, Pierre-Jean," *Dictionary of American Biography* (New York: Charles Scribner's Sons, 1930) Vol. V., p. 256.

15 Delaney, *Dictionary,* p. 141.

16 Pope Paul VI, "The Canonization of St. John Neumann," *Origins* Vol. 7, n. 6 (Washington: NCCB Publications Office, 1977) 81.

17 *Time* "The Saint They Almost Overlooked" (June 20, 1977) p. 70.

18 *Ibid.*

19 *Origins,* 84.

Chapter Five
Nine Foundresses

1 Winthrop Hudson, *Religion in America: An Historical Account of the Development of American Religious Life,* third edition (New York: Charles Scribner's Sons, 1981) p. 249.

[2] James Hennesey, S.J., *American Catholics: A History of the Roman Catholic Community in the United States* (New York: Oxford University Press, 1981) p. 173.

[3] *The New Catholic Encyclopedia,* vol. 1, 1.

[4] *Das Grosse Brockhaus,* "Hensel, Luisa" (Wiesbaden: F.A. Brockhaus, 1954) Vol. 5, 387.

[5] Sisters of the Poor Child Jesus, *Manete in Me, Rule of Life* (undated.) p. 2.

[6] John T. McNicholas, O.P. *Mother Frances Schervier,* pamphlet (Mount Alverno Convent, Warwick, NY, undated) p. 6.

[7] Donald M. Schlegel, "The Early Days of St. Francis Hospital in Columbus," *Bulletin of the Catholic Record Society, Diocese of Columbus, Ohio* (vol. IX, 8, 9 July/August 1983), 242.

[8] McNicholas, pp. 7-8.

[9] Amleto Giovanni Cicognani, Introduction to Sister Pauline, *Frances Schervier Mother of the Poor* (Cincinnati: Sisters of the Poor of St. Francis, 1946) p.10.

[10] Sacred Congregation for the Causes of Saints, protocol no. 286, Paderborn, *Beatification and Canonization of the Venerable Pauline von Mallinckrodt Report and Votes of the Special Meeting on her Virtues,* January 26, 1982 Translated by Sr. M Julitta Gaul, S.C.C. (Wilmette, IL, Sisters of Christian Charity, 1983) p. 50.

[11] Vatican Council: *Perfectae Caritatis "Decree for the Appropriate Renewal of the Religious Life,"* Abbott, *The Documents of Vatican II* #2, p. 468.

[12] *Ibid.,* pp. 468 ff.

[13] Sister Mary Evelyn Hannan, C.S.J., *The Concept of Ministry in the Sisters of Saint Joseph of Baden, Pennsylvania* (The School of Religious Studies, Gonzaga University, 1980).

[14] *Ibid.,* p. 30.

[15] *Ibid.*

[16] James J. Hartley, *Diocese of Columbus: The History of Fifty Years, 1868-1918* (Diocese of Columbus, 1918) p. 572.

[17] Code, Joseph Bernard, *Great American Foundresses* (New York: Macmillan, 1929) p. 253.

[18] Katherine Burton, *Make the Way Known* (New York: Farrar, Straus and Cudahy, 1959).

[19] Gertrude von Le Fort, *The Song at the Scaffold* (New York: Sheed and Ward, 1933).

[20] Georges Bernanos, *The Fearless Heart* (Westminster, MD: The Newman Press, 1952) p. 128.

[21] Pope John XXIII, "Discourse at a Formal Veneration of Blessed Elizabeth Ann Seton on the Day of Her Beatification," March 17, 1963 (*The Pope Speaks,* Vol. 8, No. 4, 1963) 339.

[22] Joan Barthel, "A Saint for All Reasons" *The New York Times Magazine* (September 14, 1975) p. 80.

[23] *The Liturgy of the Hours,* Vol. I (New York: Catholic Book Publishing Co., 1975) 1668-88.

Chapter Six
Eight Jesuits

[1] Edward Wakin, "Paris Anniversary," *Company: a magazine of the American Jesuits,* Vol.2, No.1 (October, 1984) pp. 22-7 (published by the Jesuit Conference of the ten Jesuit provinces of the United States in Chicago, IL). This section about the seven students owes much to Edward Wakin's article.

[2] Bernard Bassett, S.J., Introduction to Joseph N. Tylenda, S.J., *Jesuit Saints and Martyrs* (Chicago: Loyola University Press, 1983) p. XIX.

[3] Ignatius Loyola, S.J., *The Spiritual Exercises of St. Ignatius.* One translation is by Louis Puhl, S.J. (Westminster, MD: Newman Press, 1954).

[4] Alfred McBride, *Saints are People: Church History through the Saints* (Dubuque, IA: Religious Education Division, Wm. C. Brown Co., 1981) p. 109.

[5] Phyllis McGinley, *Saint-Watching,* p. 179.

[6] Farmer, *Oxford Dictionary of Saints,* p. 416.

[7] George H. Dunne, S.J., *A Generation of Giants: the Story of the Jesuits in China in the last decades of the Ming Dynasty.* (Notre Dame: University of Notre Dame Press, 1962).

[8] Phyllis McGinley, *Saint-Watching,* p. 183.

[9] "Robert Southwell," Stanley J. Kunitz and Howard Haycraft, Editors, *British Authors Before 1800* (New York: H.W. Wilson, 1952) p. 485.

[10] "Southwell, Robert," *The Dictionary of National Biography* (Oxford University Press, 1917, reprinted 1973). Edited by Leslie Stephen and Sidney Lee. The Southwell article is by Sidney Lee, vol. 18, 702-07.

[11] Robert Southwell, *The Poetical Works of the Rev. Robert Southwell*, now completely edited by William B. Turnbull (London: John Russell Smith, 1856).

[12] Robert Hugh Benson, *Come Rack! Come Rope!* (New York: Dodd, Mead and Co., 1913) p. 467.

[13] Pope Paul VI, "Homily for the Canonization of the Forty Martyrs of England and Wales," October 25, 1970 (Rome: *Acta Apostolicae Sedis,* vol. 62, No. 7, 1970) 750.

[14] Phyllis McGinley, *Saint-Watching,* p. 151.

[15] Joseph N. Tylanda, S.J., *Jesuit Priests and Martyrs,* p. 445.

[16] Evelyn Waugh, *Edmund Campion* (New York: Sheed and Ward, 1935) p. 249.

[17] *America* (June 4, 1983: Vol. 148) 431.

[18] Cardinal Agostino Casaroli, "A Letter on the Centenary of Pierre Teilhard's Birth," *Catholic Mind* (January, 1982, Vol. 80, No. 1359), 9-10.

[19] Teilhard de Chardin, S.J., *The Phenomenon of Man* (New York, Harper and Row, 1965).

[20] Teilhard de Chardin, *How I Believe* (New York: Harper and Row, 1969).

[21] Teilhard de Chardin, *The Divine Milieu,* quoted by George G. Higgins, "Economic and Social Life" in John H. Miller, C.S.C., *Vatican II: An Interfaith Appraisal* (Notre Dame: University of Notre Dame Press, 1966) p. 497.

[22] William Herr, *Catholic Thinkers in the Clear* (Chicago: The Thomas More Press, 1985) p. 262.

[23] Karl Rahner, S.J., *Spirit in the World* (London: Sheed and Ward, 1968).

[24] Karl Rahner, S.J., *The Foundations of Christian Faith* (New York: A Crossroad Book, The Seabury Press, 1978).

[25] Karl Rahner, S.J., *The Practice of Faith: A Handbook of Contemporary Spirituality* (New York: Crossroad Publ. Co., 1983).

[26] William D. Lynn, S.J., "Karl Rahner: In Memoriam 1904-1984," *The Josephinum Journal of Theology* (Vol III, No.1 Spring/Summer, 1984) 5.

Chapter Seven
Saints of the Early and Medieval Church

[1] Justin Martyr, *The First Apology,* quoted in Butler *Lives of the Saints,* II, 89.

[2] Farmer, *The Oxford Dictionary of Saints,* p. 228.

3 *The Acts of Justin and his Companions,* quoted in Butler, *Lives of the Saints,* II, 90.

4 Christopher Dawson, quoted in F. J. Sheed in the introduction to his translation of *The Confessions of St. Augustine Book I-X* (New York: Sheed and Ward, 1942) p. v.

5 *Ibid.*

6 Augustine, *Confessions* VIII, 7. See Sheed translation, p. 139.

7 Confessions, *St. Augustine's Confessions,* with an English translation by William Watts (Cambridge, MA.: Harvard University Press, 1978) VIII, 12, 465.

8 Augustine, *Confessions.* For the "Late have I loved thee" passage see *The Liturgy of the Hours,* second reading, Vol. III, 273.

10 Augustine, *Sermons for Christmas and Epiphany,* translated by Thomas Comerford Lawler (Westminster, MD: Newman Press, 1952) p. 85.

11 *Ibid.,* p. 93

12 William Shakespeare, *King Henry V,* Act IV, Scene 1.

13 Donald Attwater, *Dictionary,* p. 208.

14 David Hugh Farmer, *Oxford Dictionary,* p. 104.

15 I. Evans, "David of Wales, St.," *New Catholic Encyclopedia,* Vol. 4, 660.

16 Victor J. Greene, *Saints for all Seasons* (New York: Avenel Press, 1982) p. 24.

17 Leonard Foley, O.F.M. and Norman Perry, O.F.M., "The Real Francis," *St. Anthony's Messenger* (Vol. 84) p. 28.

18 *The Testament of St. Francis,* quoted in Sr. Margaret Carney, O.S.F., "Francis of Assisi: Poetry or Praxis" (*Charities USA,* February, 1983) p. 4.

19 Thomas of Celano, O.F.M., *The First Life of St. Francis,* quoted in Barbara Beckwith, "Beyond the Birdbath," in a special isssue, "Francis of Assisi-His Spirit Lives On" in *St. Anthony Messenger* (Vol. 90: October, 1982) p. 29.

20 G. K. Chesterton, *St. Francis of Assisi* (Garden City, NY: Doubleday and Co. 1950) pp. 11-7.

21 *Ibid.*

22 Fr. N.G. van Doornik, *Francis of Assisi: A Prophet for Our Time,* translated by Barbara Potter Fasting (Chicago: Franciscan Herald Press, 1979) ch. 18 pp. 185-200.

23 G. K. Chesterton, "The Dumb Ox," *Saint Thomas Aquinas* (New York: Sheed and Ward, 1933).

24 James J. Walsh, *The Thirteenth Greatest of Centuries* (New

York: Catholic Summer School Press, 1907).

25 Farmer, *Oxford Dictionary*, p. 375.

26 *Ibid.*

27 Jacques Maritain, *The Angelic Doctor* (New York: Sheed and Ward, 1931).

28 See Pope Paul VI "Letter to the Dominican Master General on the 700th anniversary of Aquinas," *The Pope Speaks*, v. 19 (1974) Dec. 5, 1974, p. 288.

29 Vatican II, *The Church in the Modern World*, #4-5. Flannery, *Documents*, pp. 905-07.

30 *Acta Apostolicae Sedis*, Vol. 75, p. 799 (Oct. 1, 1983).

31 E.T. DeWald, "Angelico, Fra" (Giovanni de Fiesole) *The New Catholic Encyclopedia*, vol. I, 504.

32 Giorgio Vasari, *Lives of the Most Eminent Painters, Sculptors, and Architects* (New York: Modern Library, Random House, 1959) p. 109.

33 Flannery, *Documents*, p. 34.

Chapter Eight
A Woman for Our Times

1 See *Origins*, Vol. 7, No. 6 (June 30, 1977) p. 84 for the quotation by Pope Paul VI of his homily at the time he beatified St. John Neumann on October 13, 1963.

2 H.J. Sievers, "Blessed Sacrament Sisters for the Indians and Colored People," *New Catholic Encyclopedia*, vol. 2, p. 612.

Bibliography

Abbott, Walter, S.J., General Editor, *The Documents of Vatican II* (New York: America Press, 1966)

Adams, Henry, *Mont-Saint Michel and Chartres* (Boston: Houghton Mifflin Co., 1905)

Alexander, Calvert, S.J., *Catholic Literary Revival* (Milwaukee: Bruce Publishing Co., 1935)

Attwater, Donald, *A Dictionary of Saints* (Baltimore: Penguin Books, 1965)

Attwater, Donald (Ed.), *The Catholic Dictionary* (New York: Macmillan, 1949)

Augustine, Saint, *Confessions,* translated by F.J. Sheed (New York: Sheed and Ward, 1942)

Augustine, Saint, *St. Augustine's Confessions,* with an English translation by William Watts (Cambridge, MA: Harvard University Press, 1978)

Augustine, Saint, *Sermons for Christmas and Epiphany,* translated by Thomas Comerford Lawler (Westminster, MD: Newman Press, 1952)

Belloc, Hilaire, *Sonnets and Verse* (New York: Sheed and Ward, 1944)

Benson, Robert Hugh, *Come Rack! Come Rope!* (New York: Dodd, Mead & Co., 1913)

Bernanos, Georges, *The Fearless Heart* (Westminster MD: Newman Press, 1952)

Bernard of Clairvaux, *Magnificat Homilies in Praise of the Blessed Virgin Mary* (Kalamazoo, MI: Cistercian Publications, Series 28, 1979)

Burton, Katharine, *Make the Way Known* (New York: Farrar, Straus and Cudahy, 1959)

Butler, Alban, *Lives of the Saints* Complete Edition, revised and supplemented by Herbert Thurston, S.J. and Donald Attwater (Westminster, MD: Christian Classics, Inc., 1980)

Carlen, Claudia, I.H.M. (Ed.), *The Papal Encyclicals* (Wilmington, NC: McGrath Publishing Co., 1981)

Cather, Willa, *Death Comes for the Archbishop* (New York: Vantage Books, 1979)

Chesterton, Gilbert Keith, *Christendom in Dublin* (New York: Sheed and Ward, 1933)

Chesterton, Gilbert Keith, *The Collected Poems of G.K. Chesterton* (New York: Dodd, Mead and Co., 1911)

Chesterton, Gilbert Keith, *St. Francis of Assisi* (Garden City, NY: Doubleday & Co., 1950)

Chesterton, Gilbert Keith, *Saint Thomas Aquinas* (New York: Sheed and Ward, 1933)

Cicognani, Amleto G., *Sanctity in America* (Patterson, NJ: St. Anthony Guild Press, 1941)

Ciriden, James A., Green, Thomas J., Heintschel, Donald E., *The Code of Canon Law — A Text and Commentary,* commissioned by The Canon Law Society of America (New York/Mahwah, NJ: Paulist Press, 1985)

Code, Joseph Bernard, *Great American Foundresses* (New York: Macmillan, 1929)

Collins, Raphael, translator, *Roman Martyrology* (Westminster, MD: The Newman Press, 1946)

Cross, F.L. and Livingstone, E.A. (Editors) *The Oxford Dictionary of the Christian Church,* Second Edition (Oxford: 1983)

Cunningham, Lawrence S., *The Catholic Heritage* (New York: Crossroad, 1983)

Delaney, John J., *Dictionary of American Catholic Biography* (Garden City, NY: Doubleday & Co., 1984)

Delaney, John J., *Pocket Dictionary of Saints,* Abridged Edition (Garden City, NY: Image Books, Doubleday & Co., 1983)

Domas, Anna Wirtz, *Mary USA* (Huntington, IN: Our Sunday Visitor Press, 1978)

Dunne, George H., S.J., *A Generation of Giants* (Notre Dame IN: University of Notre Dame Press, 1962)

Farmer, David Hugh, *The Oxford Dictionary of Saints* (Oxford: Clarendon Press, 1978)

Farrow, John, *Damien the Leper* (New York: Sheed and Ward, 1937)

Flannery, Austin, O.P. (General Editor), *Vatican Council II: The Conciliar and Post Conciliar Documents* (Northport, NY: Costello Publ. Co., 1975)

Francis de Sales, St., *Introduction to the Devout Life,* translated and edited by John K. Ryan (New York: Harpers, 1949)

Gilson, Etienne (Ed.), *The Church Speaks to the Modern World: The Social Teachings of Leo XIII* (Garden City, NY: Image Books, Doubleday & Co., 1954)

Glazier, Michael, (Ed.), *Where We Are: American Catholics in the 1980's* (Wilmington, DE: Michael Glazier, 1985)

Greene, Victor, *Saints for All Seasons* (New York: Avenel Press, 1982)

Guardini, Romano, *The Saints in Daily Christian Life* (New York: Dimension Books, 1966)

Hamilton, Marguerite, *Red Shoes for Nancy* (Garden City, NY: Catholic Family Book Club, 1956)

Hanley, Sr. Mary Laurence, O.S.F., *A Song of Pilgrimage and Exile: The Life and Spirit of Mother Marianne of Molokai* (Chicago: Franciscan Herald Press, 1980)

Hannan, Sr. Mary Evelyn, *The Concept of Ministry in the Sisters of Saint Joseph of Baden* (Gonzaga, WA: The School of Religious Studies, Gonzaga University, 1980)

Hartley, Bishop James J., *Diocese of Columbus: The History of Fifty Years* (Columbus, OH: Diocese of Columbus, 1918)

Hennessy, James, S.J., *American Catholics: A History of the Roman Catholic Community in the United States* (New York: Oxford University Press, 1981)

Herr, William, *Catholic Thinkers in the Clear* (Chicago: The Thomas More Press, 1985)

Horgan, Paul, *Lamy of Santa Fe* (New York: Farrar, Straus and Giroux, 1975)

Hudson, Winthrop, *Religion in America — An Historical Account of the Development of American Religious Life,* third edition (New York: Charles Scribner and Sons, 1981)

Husslein, Joseph, S.J., *Social Wellsprings, Vol I: "Fourteen Epochal Documents of Pope Leo XIII"* (Milwaukee: Bruce Publishing Co., 1940)

Keyes, Frances Parkinson, *St. Anne: Grandmother of Our Saviour* (London: Allen Wingate, 1956)

Knox, Ronald, *University Sermons of Ronald Knox,* Ed. Philip Caraman, S.J. (Montreal: Palm Publishers, 1963)

Lenti, Arthur, S.D.B., *Sub Tumm Praesidium* (Unpublished manuscript)

The Liturgy of the Hours According to the Roman Rite, Four Volumes (New York: Catholic Book Publishing Co., 1976)

Luciano, Albino (Pope John Paul I), *Illustrissimi — Letters from Pope John Paul I* (Boston: Little Brown, 1978)

Lunn Arthur, *Saint in the Slave Trade* (New York: Sheed and Ward, 1935)

Maestrini, Nicholas, P.I.M.E., *Mazzucconi of Woodlark* (Hong Kong: Catholic Truth Society, 1983)

Manteau-Bonamy, H.H., "Vatican II and Mary," *Dictionary of Mary* (New York: Catholic Book Publishing Co., 1985)

Maritain, Jacques, *The Angelic Doctor* (New York: Sheed and Ward, 1931)

Martindale, Cyril, S.J., *What Are Saints? Fifteen Studies in Sanctity* (Wilmington, DE: Michael Glazier, 1982)

McBride, Alfred, *Saints are People: Church History Through the Saints* (Dubuque: Wm. C. Brown Co., 1981)

McBride, Alfred, *The Story of the Church* (Cincinnati: St. Anthony Messenger Press, 1983)

McGinley, Phyllis, *Saint-Watching* (Garden City, NY: Image Books, Doubleday & Co., 1974)

McNicholas, John T., O.P., *Mother Frances Schervier* (Warwick, NY: Mount Alverno Convent, undated)

Miller John H, C.S.C., *Vatican II: An Interfaith Appraisal* (Notre Dame, IN: University of Notre Dame Press, 1966)

Morrison, Samuel Eliot, *The European Discovery of America: The Southern Voyages A.D. 1491-1616* (New York: Oxford University Press, 1974)

Newman, Cardinal John Henry, *Fifteen Sermons Preached Before The University of Oxford* (London: Longmans Green & Co., 1982)

O'Connell, Timothy E. (Ed.), *Vatican II and Its Documents* (Wilmington, DE: Michael Glazier, 1986)

Puhl, Louis, S.J., (Translator), *The Spiritual Exercises of St. Ignatius* (Westminster MD: Newman Press, 1954)

Rahner, Karl, S.J., *The Foundations of Christian Faith* (New York: The Seabury Press, 1978)

Rahner, Karl, S.J., *The Practice of Faith: A Handbook of Contemporary Spirituality* (New York: Crossroad Publ. Co., 1985)

Rahner, Karl, S.J., *Spirit in the World* (London: Sheed and Ward, 1968)

Rahner Karl, S.J. and Vorgrimler, Herbert, S.J. (Eds.), *Theological Dictionary* (New York: Herder and Herder, 1965)

Rynne, Xavier, *Vatican Council II* (New York: Farrar, Straus and Giroux, 1968)

Sacred Congregation for the Causes of Saints, protocol no. 286, Paderborn, *Beatification and Canonization of the Venerable Pauline von Mallinckrodt: Report and Votes of the Special Meeting on Her Virtues,* translated by Sr. M. Julita Gaul, S.C.C. (Wilmette, IL: Sisters of Christian Charity, 1983)

Sargent, Daniel, *Our Land and Our Lady* (Notre Dame, IN: Universtiy of Notre Dame Press, 1931)

Shakespeare, William, *The Annotated Shakespeare,* Vol II edited by A.L. Rowse (New York: Clarkston N. Potter, Publ., 1978)

Shanahan, Emmett A., *Minnesota's Forgotten Martyr* (Crookston, MN: Diocese of Crookston, 1949)

Sisters of the Poor Child Jesus, *Manete in Me — Rule of Life* (undated)

Southwell, Robert, S.J., *The Poetical Works of the Rev. Robert Southwell,* William B. Turnbull, Ed. (London: John Russell Smith, 1856)

Stoddard, Whitney, *Monastery and Cathedral in France* (Middletown, CT: Wesleyan University Press, 1966)

Teilhard de Chardin, S.J., *The Phenomenon of Man* (New York: Harper and Row, 1965)

Teilhard de Chardin, S.J., *How I Believe* (New York: Harper and Row, 1969)

Thomas Aquinas, *The Three Greatest Prayers,* translated by Laurence Shapcote, O.P. (Westminster MD: The Newman Press, 1956)

Thomas Aquinas, *The One Mediator,* Vol. 50 of the *Summa Theològiae,* edited and translated by Colman E. O'Neill, O.P. (London: Blackfriars/Eyre and Spottiswoode, 1965)

Thomas Aquinas, *Virtues of Justice in the Human Community* Vol. 41 of the *Summa Theologiae,* edited and translated by T.C. O'Brien (London: Blackfriars/Eyre and Spottiswoode, 1972)

Tylenda, Joseph N., S.J., *Jesuit Saints and Martyrs* (Chicago: Loyola University Press, 1984)

United States Catholic Conference, "Decree of the Sacred Congregation for Divine Worship," *Rite of Burials* (New York: Catholic Book Publ. Co., 1971)

USCC, *Pilgrim of Peace,* The Homilies and Addresses of His Holiness Pope John Paul II on the Occasion of His Visit to the United States of America, October 1979 (Washington, DC: Publications Office, USCC, 1979)

USCC, *Roman Calendar: Text and Commentary* (Washington, DC: Publications Office, USCC, 1976)

USCC, *Pastoral Letters of the United States Catholic Bishops,* Vol. 4 (Washington, DC: Publications Office, USCC, 1984)

Von Le Fort, Gertrude, *The Song at the Scaffold* (New York: Sheed and Ward, 1933)

Van Doornik, N.G. *Francis of Assisi: A Prophet for our Time* (Chicago: Franciscan Herald Press, 1979)

Vasari, Giorgio, *Lives of the Most Eminent Painters, Sculptors, and Architects* (New York: Modern Library, Random House, 1959)

Walsh, James J., *The Thirteenth: Greatest of Centuries* (New York: Catholic Summer School Press, 1907)

Waugh, Evelyn, *Edmund Campion* (New York: Sheed and Ward, 1935)

Werfel, Franz, *The Song of Bernadette* (New York: The Viking Press, 1942)

Zola, Emile, *Lourdes* (London: Chatto and Windus, 1894)